Judaism and Christianity
in the
Age of Constantine

Chicago Studies in the History of Judaism

EDITED BY

Jacob Neusner, William Scott Green, and Calvin Goldscheider

Judaism and Christianity in the Age of Constantine
History, Messiah, Israel, and the Initial Confrontation

Jacob Neusner

The University of Chicago Press

Chicago and London

The University of Chicago Press, Chicago 60637
The University of Chicago Press, Ltd., London

© 1987 by The University of Chicago
All rights reserved. Published 1987
Printed in the United States of America

96 95 94 93 92 91 90 89 88 87   5 4 3 2 1

Library of Congress Cataloging-in-Publication Data

Judaism and Christianity in the age of Constantine.

(Chicago studies in the history of Judaism)
Bibliography: p.
Includes index.
1. Judaism—relations—Christianity.   2. Christianity
and other religions—Judaism.   3. Judaism—History—
Talmudic period, 10–425.   4. Christianity—Early church,
ca. 30–600.   5. Midrash—History and criticism.
I. Neusner, Jacob, 1932–   . II. Series.
BM535.J822   1987   292.3'872   87–5952
ISBN 0–226–57652–3

JACOB NEUSNER is University Professor and the Unger-
leider Distinguished Scholar of Judaic Studies at Brown
University. He is the author of many scholarly works including *Judaism and Scripture: The Evidence of the Leviticus
Rabbah* and *Judaism: The Classical Statement: The Evidence of the Bavli,* both published by the University of Chicago Press.

For my nearest and dearest colleagues

WENDELL S. DIETRICH
ERNEST S. FRERICHS
CALVIN GOLDSCHEIDER
ALAN ZUCKERMAN

My teachers, my companions

Better the honor of enjoying the friendship
of these aristocrats of intellect and of heart
than any honors the world has in its power
to confer.

I glory in these colleagues,
I take pride that mine is the merit
of sharing career, profession, life itself
with such as these.

. . . *einen besseren findst du nicht* . . .

Contents

Preface

Judaism and Christianity as they would live together in the West met for the first time in the fourth century. It was then that Judaism addressed the historical triumph of Christianity in a political form that would persist, and that Christianity met the Israel defined by the sages of the dual Torah, the Israel that would enjoy enduring life in the Jewish people from then until now. Beginning with the conversion of Constantine in 312 and ending with the recognition of Christianity as the religion of the Roman Empire in the Theodosian Code of 387, Christianity reached that position of political and cultural dominance that it would enjoy until the twentieth century. In our own day Christianity has entered an age no longer responsive to its politics. This book is about the first meeting, a confrontation that, for Judaism, defined three important terms of the Judaic system from that time onward. Specifically, in the fourth century, in response to the triumph of Christianity in the Roman Empire, Judaism as shaped by sages in the Land of Israel defined its doctrines of history, Messiah, and the identity of Israel. Those doctrines successfully countered the challenge of Christianity from then to the point at which Christianity lost its status as self-evident truth in the West. It follows that Judaism as we have known it was born in the matrix of triumphant Christianity as the West would define that faith.[1]

The age of Constantine was marked by the interplay of issues that were defined in the same way by Judaism and Christianity. In the context of triumphant Christianity, Judaic thinkers represented in the important documents of the late fourth or early fifth century, the Talmud of the Land of Israel of the Land of Israel, Genesis Rabbah, and Leviticus Rabbah, sorted out those three central questions that had long presented points on which each party framed its own ideas. But, transformed by the events of the age from merely chronic

---

1. In my *Death and Birth of Judaism* (1987a) I argue that the success of Judaism in the West derives from its response (a self-evidently valid one, to Jews) to the urgent and paramount question presented by triumphant Christianity. This is a point I further work out in my *Self-Fulfilling Prophecy* (1987b).

to urgent and acute issues, these matters demanded the attention of the Judaic sages. A debate unfolded in which the issues were framed so that a confrontation of an intellectual character took place: people arguing about the same things, drawing upon the same logic, appealing to essentially the same facts. I claim that the issues as framed by the Judaic sages and Christian theologians encompassed precisely the same questions, that the modes of argument on these issues followed the same rules of reason and discourse, and that the facts adduced in evidence by the two parties derived from a shared core of texts available, in essentially the same wording, to both parties; that there was, in short, an argument, a dialogue, a true debate.

The two groups—one represented by the authorship behind the sages' documents, the other by three important theologians, Eusebius, in the beginning of the century, Aphrahat, in the middle and in the Iranian empire, and Chrysostom, at the end—resorted to the same corpus of Scripture, framed the issues in nearly identical terms, and drew from Scripture answers and implications that exhibit a remarkable congruence. This is the first—and last— moment in the history of Judaism in the context of Christianity when both sides asked and answered the same questions, framed the same way, in response to the same circumstances. Because for once both parties asked the same questions and answered them in parallel ways, the shape of the dialogue between Judaism and Christianity was set for the rest of their shared history in the West.

In many ways, therefore, the fourth century marks the point of intersection between the histories of the two religious, Judaism and Christianity. Before that time there was no confrontation. For Judaism and Christianity in late antiquity present histories that mirror each other. When Christianity began, Judaism was the dominant tradition in the Holy Land and expressed its ideas within a political framework until the early fifth century. Christianity was subordinate and had to operate against the background of a politically definitive Judaism. From the time of Constantine onward, matters reversed themselves. Now Christianity predominated, expressing its ideas in political and institutional terms. Judaism, by contrast, had lost its political foundations and faced the task of working out its self-understanding in terms of a world defined by Christianity, now everywhere triumphant and in charge of politics. As Rosemary Radford Ruether first pointed out, the important shift came in the early fourth century, the West's first century.[2] That was when the West began, in the union of Christian religion and Roman rule. It also was when the Judaism that thrived in the West reached the definition it was to exhibit for the next fifteen centuries.

The thesis argued here contradicts the theory that Judaism ignored its competition and went its way in splendid isolation. Historians of Judaism take as

2. The conception of the fourth century as the first century of Christianity and Judaism originates with Rosemary Radford Ruether, "Judaism and Christianity: Two Fourth-Century Religions" (1972).

dogma the view that Christianity never made any difference to Judaism. Faith of a "people that dwells apart," Judaism explored paths untouched by Christians. Christianity—people hold—was born in the matrix of Judaism, but Judaism, from the beginning until now, ignored the new "daughter" religion and followed its majestic course in lonely dignity. Since (the argument is implicitly made) Judaism is supposed always to have ignored, and never to have been affected by, Christianity in any form, the future security of the faith of Judaism requires the continuation of this same policy, pretending that Christianity simply never made, and now does not make, any difference at all to Israel, the Jewish people. This dogma of scholarship carries with it an imperative for contemporary policy. Without intending to comment on how to shape Judaic policy for the future, I argue here that quite to the contrary, the Judaism expressed by the writings of the sages of the Land of Israel in the fourth century—the age of Constantine—not only responded to issues raised for Israel by the political triumph of Christianity but did so in a way that, intellectually at least, made possible the entire future history of Judaism in Europe and beyond.

Let me now place this book into its larger context in my own work. It forms the middle component of a trilogy, in which I present a general theory of the history of Judaism, beginning, middle, and, in its received form for most of the Jews of the West, end. The work begins with *Judaism in the Matrix of Christianity* (1986a), continues with the present work, and concludes with *The Death and Birth of Judaism* (1987a). In the first work I set forth the thesis that Judaism in its received and classical form took shape in the fourth century. That thesis, further, is argued on the strength of the results of my Foundations of Judaism series: vol. 1, *Midrash in Context* (1983a); vol. 2, *Messiah in Context* (1984a); vol. 3, *Torah* (1984b). In those exercises I repeatedly came to a single result, which is that, when we come upon the first expression or, at least, adumbration, of what becomes the definitive statement of a matter, we find ourselves time and again in the pages of the Talmud of the Land of Israel. That led me to the thesis that it was in the fourth or early fifth century that Judaism took shape in the form that became normative.

To extend and test that thesis, this second book of the trilogy compares the treatment of three important topics confronting the two fourth-century heirs of ancient Israel's heritage, asking how each dealt with an issue that both had to consider. In this way I wish to compare and contrast the one with the other and so to place into a larger context the initial results of the Foundations of Judaism series and *Judaism in the Matrix of Christianity.* In The *Death and Birth of Judaism* I place the issue in the context of the Christian West. My view is that, when Christianity lost its status as self-evident truth to Christians, the Judaism framed in the encounter with that claim likewise lost its self-evidence to Jews. After the end of self-evidence—looking back, we call it innocence—came self-consciousness. For Jews, that is when the modern age in the history of Judaism began. The trilogy proposes a general theory on why Judaism worked—that is, enjoyed self-evidence for Israel, the Jewish people—when it worked, and therefore, also, why it did not work when it did not work. Perhaps, in time to come, I may make some suggestions on how it may be made to work again. That theological interest formed part of my original intent, but I hear no compelling call to realize that intent very soon. But the initial probing led me to *Self-Fulfilling Prophecy: Exile and Return in the History of Judaism* (1987b), a historical study pointing in theological directions.

It remains to point to a feature of this book. I have quoted in the chapters of the book only a small sample of important passages on the themes at hand of the Talmud of the Land of Israel, Genesis Rabbah, and Leviticus Rabbah. Too many sources given verbatim present formidable obstacles to the reader and render the book tedious. On the other hand, I wanted readers to have access to a rich repertoire of pertinent sources. The documents at hand, which I have translated, do not rest on every reader's bookshelf.[3] So to provide readers with a broad selection of relevant statements, I have added in appendixes extensive citations of materials, which, in the body of the book, I cite only in abbreviated versions. What I do, then, is present *in toto* materials given in brief abstract in the pertinent chapters. This leads to a slight measure of repetition, but I think it improves the book.

Let me close on a personal note. I place myself in the tradition of those who, by rereading the past, imagine that they can find a direction for the future. This project does not pretend to deserve the exalted status of theology. It is, rather, a humble and pedestrian sort of description, a mere collection of facts; that is, the history of *a* religion, one among many, perhaps intending also to contribute, by way of supplying an example of a general theory, to the history of *religion*. But that intent does not bring us upward to theology. Still, my original motive in turning toward these sources rather than others, or to another way of life rather than the scholarly one altogether, was theological. I revere these sources, which is why I lovingly collect and present so many of them in the appendices. I began, thirty years ago, to study the Judaic sources because I wanted to make myself, then merely a believing and religious Jew, into a knowledgeable one as well. For the ignorant person cannot attain true piety. I wished, on my own and for myself, to see the whole, altogether, in its entirety, and all at once. I further determined that I should read the sources myself, and so, on my own, I would form a vision of my own. I wanted to take it all apart and put it back together, to possess what was mine by making it totally and completely my own.

In all this I find myself a disciple of Goethe, who, at what for Judaism was the beginning of the modern age, said what it meant to be "modern":

3. *The Talmud of the Land of Israel: A Preliminary Translation and Explanation* (1982–); *Judaism and Scripture: The Evidence of Leviticus Rabbah* (a fresh translation of Margulies' text and a systematic analysis of problems of composition and redaction) (1985b); *Genesis Rabbah: The Judaic Commentary on the Book of Genesis* (1985a); *Aphrahat and Judaism: The Christian-Jewish Argument in Fourth-Century Iran* (1971).

> *Was du ererbt von deinen Vaetern hast,*
> *Erwirb es um es zu besitzen.*
> Whatever you have as a heritage from your fathers
> You must earn it if you would possess it.[4]

What comes as heritage has yet to be possessed in full consciousness and therefore, of necessity, in prickly self-consciousness. By citing Goethe through the medium of a later writer, I move squarely into the modern situation of Judaism: making one's own what in times past came as a heritage unearned and possessing, rather than possessed. That is to say, I move from self-evidence to self-consciousness.

But that, after all, is what we do when we sign our own names to our books, rather than speaking in the name of inherited Scripture and tradition, as did the Christian theologians whom we shall take up, and rather than speaking anonymously, collectively, as did the sages of Judaism in the age of Constantine. We who understand that we have to earn, possess, and so make our own what reaches us as heritage stand for what it means to live in our own day and not in any other. We affirm where we are and what we are: to be ourselves, unashamedly, unregretfully, children of a wretched but challenging century. Our time of radical turning is more like the fourth century than, I think, any time in between. That is my message in this book.

That, and one more: Judaism and Christianity in the age of holocaust come together as they have not since the beginning, and as they have not been able to since the fourth century. The relationship of subordinated, patient Judaism and world-possessing Christianity—a relationship which began in the age of Constantine—has ended, to be sure not in ways either had anticipated. The confrontation has ceased. In their contemporary encounter Judaism and Christianity have entered a new epoch of relationship—not yet dialogue, but no longer confrontation. For that, at least, we have, all of us, to give thanks. Why at just this time, in just this dreadful way, God has brought us to the threshold of mature reconciliation, no one knows. Perhaps it is for a blessing, held back until, mourning unspeakable tragedy, we rejoined ranks, not before "Auschwitz" or Golgotha but before Sinai. There, in a cleft in the rock, we shall shelter before the Presence. There we shall hear, after the mighty noise, a voice of silence. And that is all.

Jacob Neusner

Erev Rosh Hashshanah 5747

Program in Judaic Studies
Brown University
Providence, Rhode Island 02912

---

4. *Faust,* 682–83, quoted by Jaroslav Pelikan in his introduction to the Torchbook edition of Adolf Harnack, *The Mission and Expansion of Christianity in the First Three Centuries* (1972).

Acknowledgments

Since for this work I have had to read a great many books outside of my ordinary area of learning, I have relied more heavily than usual on the advice of colleagues. Here it is important to absolve them of responsibility for errors of misunderstanding or misjudgment that may have crept into my account. But I owe them much for sharing their learning and experienced judgment with me.

I made heavier use of Brown University's Rockefeller Library than I have before, and once more came to appreciate the professionalism and the courtesy of its most gracious staff. It gave me special pleasure to make extensive use of the Ernest S. Frerichs Collection of Biblical and Judaic Studies at the Rockefeller Library. So my dear colleague and friend gains a measure of the enjoyment of the world to come while he is still here—to 120 years!—to enjoy it.

I also found much help in getting important books on patristics and church history at Phillips Memorial Library of Providence College. The staff gave assistance with the courtesy and goodwill I find typical of Rhode Islanders. My thanks to both libraries.

For professionalism expressed in unyielding commitment to free inquiry and the broad and free dissemination of the results, the staff of the University of Chicago Press, top to bottom, will be remembered long after all of us lie in the dirt. Each book of mine is a tribute to all of them. Let it be said that the academy in the West has never been better served by media of academic communication than is this generation by these remarkable people. The flame of free discourse yet glows, in our time, because of them.

Introduction

Religion and Political Change

This book proposes to contribute to the study of religion a theory for the impact of political change on theological confrontation between two religious groups. At issue is how theological ideas relate to political circumstances. Religion as a fact of politics constitutes a principal force in the shaping of society and imagination alike. I want to know how, in a particular case, a stunning shift in the political circumstances of a religion affected that religion's thought about the outsider, the other, the brother, and the enemy. The particular case involves Judaism at the moment at which Christianity became first licit, then favored, then for a brief interval persecuted, and finally, at the end of the fourth century, the official religion of the Roman Empire. The age of Constantine, the fourth century (roughtly, from 312, when Constantine extended toleration to Christianity, to 429, when the Jewish government of the Land of Israel ceased to enjoy the recognition of the state), marks the period in which Christianity joined the political world of the Roman Empire. In that century Christianity gained power, briefly lost it, and, finally, regained the pover that assured its permanent domination of the state. Christians saw Israel as God's people, rejected by God for rejecting the Christ. Israel saw Christians, now embodied in Rome, as Ishmael, Esau, Edom: the brother and the enemy. The political revolution marked by Constantine's conversion forced the two parties to discuss a single agendum and defined the terms in which each would take up that agendum.

The politics of Rome in the fourth century, therefore, produced the first true confrontation between Judaic and Christian intellectuals. By confrontation I mean not actual face-to-face discourse but substantive debate, each party speaking to its own group in its own idiom, to be sure, on issues defined in the same terms, through the medium of the same modes of argument, with appeal to the same facts. This had not happened before and it never happened again, until our own time. In the fourth century, the age of Constantine, Judaic sages and Christian theologians met in a head-on argument with a shared agendum and confronted the fundamental issues for the historical existence of politics and society in the West: doctrine, specifically, the meaning of history; teleology, specifically, the eschatological teleology formed by the messianic doctrine identifying Jesus as Christ; and the symbolism of the godly society, specifically, the identity of God's social medium—Israel—in the making of the world. Here I wish to prove that, for the first and probably the last time in the history of Judaism and Christianity in the West, differing people argued about the same things, sharing common premises and a single core of probative facts.

My thesis evokes the centrality of political change in shaping theological discourse. The reason that the two parties addressed issues defined in the same way, I maintain, derives from the political challenge facing them both. Each party, in its own setting, had to take up that challenge in terms essentially identical to those that confronted the other. When emperors convert and governments shift allegiance, the world shakes under everyone's feet. There was an argument on these issues, but no argument on any other issues, for a simple reason. The issues under debate bore political consequences; the others did not. True, both sides shared an interest in the issues of the scriptural canon and the exegesis of Scripture. But I cannot find points in these other issues on which they argued on the same topic in the same terms invoking the same corpus of evidence. That is why I say that the reason both parties could share a single program of debate is political.

Enormous shifts in the political facts of the world, represented by the growing control of Christianity over the institutions of state and government, raised for both Judaic sages and Christian theologians issues that, to begin with, the Scriptures of ancient Israel ("the Written Torah," "the Old Testament") had defined. These issues focused on the meaning of history, viewed by epochs, each with its message; the identity of the Messiah; and the definition of Israel, God's people, with special reference to the social metaphor and theological value imputed to that "Israel after the flesh" constituted by the Jews of the day. These three issues proved paramount, I claim, specifically because the political revolution effected in the course of the fourth century by the Christianization of the Roman Empire made them urgent and transformed them into matters of public policy. Prior to that political change, Judaic and Christian thinkers had no common argument.

No form of Christianity made an impact upon the systematic thought of any of the Judaic authorships known to us. That fact will become clear in the next section, in which we consider a Judaic system formed without any relationship to the interests of Christianity, e.g., the Messiah, the meaning of history, and similar eschatological questions. And the contrary also is the case. The formulation by Judaic thinkers of important theological categories, and the doctrines that imparted to those categories the meaning that they would have, never made an impact on the thought of the Church. What the Church knew was simply that the Jews did not believe in Jesus Christ. Before that time, the Christian theologians and Judaic sages had not accomplished the feat of framing a single program for debate. Judaic sages had earlier talked about their issues to their audience, Christian theologians had for three centuries pursued the arguments of their distinctive agenda. The former pretended the latter did not exist. The latter framed doctrines concerning the former solely within the logical requirements of the internal arguments of Christianity. There had been no confrontation of an intellectual character, since neither party had addressed the issues important to the other in such a way that the issues found a mutually agreeable definition, and that the premises of argument, the core of shared facts and shared reason, likewise formed a mutually acceptable protocol of discourse. Later on, as we shall see in the epilogue, the confrontation would shift, so that no real debate on a shared set of issues, defined in the same way by both parties, unfolded. The politics did not require it, and the circumstances prevented it.

In the fourth century, by contrast, issues urgent for Christian thinkers proved of acute, not merely chronic, concern for Judaic ones as well. In my view, this came about not because differences on Scriptures and its meaning produced, by themselves, debate. Those differences became urgent only when matters of public policy, specifically, the ideology of state (empire, for the Christians; supernatural nation or, as we shall see, family, for the Jews) demanded a clear statement on the questions at hand. When the Roman Empire and Israelite nation had to assess the meaning of epochal change, when each had to reconsider the teleology of society and system as the identity of the Messiah defined that teleology, when each had to reconsider the appropriate metaphor for the political unit, namely, people, nation, extended family, only then did chronic disagreement become acute difference. It was the progressive but remarkable change in the character of the Roman government—at the beginning of the century pagan and hostile to Christianity, at the end of the century Christian and hostile to paganism—that was decisive. In the age of Constantine the terms of the fifteen-hundred-year confrontation between Judaism and Christianity reached conclusive formulation.

Thus far I have spoken of "Judaism" and "Christianity," as though each formed an undifferentiated system. In fact I refer only to specific, but I believe exemplary, books of the former and figures in the latter, all from th : fourth and early fifth centuries. When I speak of "Christianity," I mean three fourth-century theologians; and when I speak of Judaism, I refer to three fourth- (or early fifth-) century documents. In the writings of the one and the pages of the other, I claim to find a single, sustained, and systematic argument in which important intellectuals (individual authors on the one side, a collective authorship on the other) address in common three fundamental issues.

To state matters in a simple way, before the fourth century Judaism and Christianity (as defined by their intellectuals) comprised different people talking about different things to different people. In the fourth century the shape of discourse shifted. Because of a political event that Israel could not ignore and the Church deemed probative, discourse between Judaism and Christianity would find different people talking to different people about some of the same things. The reason for the shift and for the particular topics at hand is a common politics. There is a second factor, namely, common premises, deriving from common Scriptures, about the importance of politics, that is, history. Both parties to the common argument shared a single canon—the Hebrew Scriptures ("Old Testament," "Written Torah") and, more important, both parties confronted the same political facts and had to deal with them. The common argument proved possible, therefore, because the intellectuals of the two parties shared a single intellectual and social world.

My argument in favor of the reason I propose pursues a positive course in chapters 2, 3, and 4, and a negative one in chapter 5. In the book I review what Christianity (as defined in three significant figures) and Judaism (in three critical documents) in the fourth century said about a given topic and demonstrate that both sides agreed on the definition of the issue. At the end, in chapter 5, I turn to a test of falsification. I take up two points on which both parties worked, and for which each party had its own definition and program of thought. There we do not have the case of different people arguing about the same thing for different people. We have different people talking about different things to different people: there is no point of intersection. The reason is that politics in common did not generate discourse on the same things.

Judaism without Christianity

Christians and Jews in the first century did not argue with one another. Each— the family of Christianities, the family of Judaisms—went its way. When Christianity came into being, in the first century, one important strand of the Christian movement laid stress on issues of salvation, maintaining in the Gospels that Jesus was, and is, Christ, come to save the world and impose a radical change on history. At that same time, an important group within the diverse Judaic systems of the age, the Pharisees, emphasized issues of sanctification, maintaining that the task of Israel is to attain that holiness of which the Temple was a singular embodiment. When, in the Gospels, we find the record of the Church placing Jesus into opposition with the Pharisees, we witness the confrontation of different people talking about different things to different people. The issues presented to Jews by the triumph of Christianity, which do inform the documents shaped in the Land of Israel in the period of that triumph, do not play an important role in prior components of the unfolding canon of Judaism, in particular, in the Mishnah and closely allied documents which reached closure before the fourth century. These present a Judaism, not despite Christianity, but in utter indifference to Christianity. The contrast between the Mishnah and the Judaic system emerging in the fourth-century documents tells the tale.

The two events that defined that setting of the Mishnah, a late second-century document, were, first, the destruction of the Temple in 70, and second, the defeat of Bar Kokhba in 135. The former put in motion expectations of redemption three generations later, just as had happened in the time of the destruction of the first Temple in 586 B.C.E. and the return, after three generations, to Zion. But the catastrophe of Bar Kokhba's war discredited a picture of the salvation of Israel that had enjoyed prominence for nearly seven hundred years. For it was clear that, whatever would happen, it would not be what had occurred before.

The Judaism without Christianity portrayed in the Mishnah did not present a richly developed doctrine of the Messiah. It worked out issues of sanctification rather than those of salvation. The reason is that the Mishnah laid its emphasis upon issues of the destruction of the Temple and the subsequent defeat in the failed war for the restoration. These issues, the framers of the Mishnah maintained, raised the question of Israel's sanctity: is Israel still a holy people, even without the holy Temple, and if so, what are the enduring instrumentalities of sanctification? When sages worked out a Judaism after the destruction of the Temple and cult, they produced in the Mishnah a system of sanctification focused on the holiness of the priesthood, the cultic festivals, the Temple and its sacrifices, as well as on the rules for protecting that holiness from levitical uncleanness—four of the six divisions of the Mishnah on a single theme. In the aftermath of the conversion of the Roman Empire to Christianity and the triumph of Christianity in the generation beyond Julian, "the apostate," sages worked out in the pages of the Talmud of the Land of Israel and in the exegetical compilations of the age a Judaism intersecting with the Mishnah but essentially asymmetrical with it. That Talmud presented a system of salvation, but one focused on the salvific power of the sanctification of the holy people. The first of the two Talmuds, the one closed at the end of the fourth century, set the compass and locked it into place. The Judaism that was portrayed by the final document of late antiquity, the Talmud of Babylonia, at the end, laid equal emphasis on sanctification in the here and now and salvation at the end of time.

If Christianity presented an urgent problem to the sages behind the Mishnah, for example, giving systemic prominence to a given category rather than some other, we cannot point to a single line of the document that says so. The figure of the Messiah in no way provided the sages of the Mishnah with an appropriate way of explaining the purpose and goal of their system, its teleology. A teleology appealing to the end of history, with the coming of the Messiah, came to predominate only in the Talmud of the land of Israel and in sages' documents beyond. What issues then proved paramount in a Judaism utterly out of relationship to Christianity in any form? We turn back to the Mishnah to find out.

The Mishnah presents a Judaism that answered a single encompassing question concerning the enduring sanctification of Israel—the people, the land, the way of life. What, in the aftermath of the destruction of the holy place and holy cult, remained of the sanctity of the holy caste, the priesthood, the holy land, and, above all, the holy people and its holy way of life? The answer is that: sanctity persists, indelibly, in *Israel, the people,* in its way of life, in its land, in its priesthood, in its food, in its mode of sustaining life, in its manner of procreating and so sustaining the nation. That holiness would endure. And the Mishnah then laid out the structures of sanctification: what it means to live a holy life. But that answer found itself absorbed, in time to come, within a successor system, with its own points of stress and emphasis. That successor system, both continuous and asymmetrical with the Mishnah, would take over the Mishnah and turn it into the one whole Torah of Moses, our rabbi, that became Judaism. The indicative marks are, first, the central symbol of Torah as sages' teaching; second, the figure of Messiah as sage; and third, the doctrine that Israel today is the family of Abraham, Isaac, and Jacob, heirs to the legacy and heritage of merit that, in the beginning, the progenitors earned and handed on to their children.

The system portrayed in the Mishnah emerged in a world in which there was no Christianity. What points do we not find? First, we find in the Mishnah no explicit and systematic theory of scriptural authority. We now know how much stress the Judaism in confrontation with Christianity laid on Scripture, with important commentaries produced in the age of Constantine. What the framers of the Mishnah did not find necessary was a doctrine of the authority of Scripture. Nor did they undertake a systematic exegetical effort to link the principal document, the Mishnah, to Scripture. Why not? Because the authors saw no need. Christianity made pressing the question of the standing and status of the Mishnah in relationship to Scripture, claiming that the Mishnah was man-made and a forgery of God's will, which was contained only in Scripture. Then the doctrine of the dual Torah, explaining the origin and authority of the Mishnah, came to full expression. The sages had produced a document, the Mishnah, so independent of Scripture that, when the authors wished to say what Scripture said, they chose to do so in their own words and in their own way. Whatever the intent of the Mishnah's authors, therefore, it clearly did not encompass explaining to a competing Israel, heirs of the same Scriptures of Sinai, just what authority validated the document, and how the document related to Scripture. Second, we look in vain for a teleology focused on the coming of the Messiah as the end and purpose of the system as a whole. The Mishnah's teleology in no way invokes an eschatological dimension. This Judaism for a world in which Christianity played no considerable role took slight interest in the Messiah and presented a teleology lacking all eschatological, therefore messianic, focus. Third, the same Judaism laid no considerable stress on the symbol of the Torah, though, of course, the Torah as a scroll, as a matter of status, and as revolution of God's will at Sinai, enjoyed prominence.

It follows that the position outlined in the fourth-century documents represents the first reading of Christianity on the part of Israel's sages. Prior to that time they did not take to heart the existence of the competition. Afterward, of course, they would draw on the position outlined here to sort out the issues made urgent by the success of Christianity throughout the Roman world. Prior to the time of Constantine, the documents of Judaism that evidently reached closure—the Mishnah, Pirqé Abot, the Tosefta—scarcely took cognizance of Christianity and did not deem the new faith to be much of a challenge. If the unsystematic and scattered allusions are meant to refer to Christianity at all, then the sages regarded Christianity as an irritant, an exasperating heresy among Jews who should have known better. But, then, neither Jews nor pagans took much interest in Christianity in the new faith's first century and a half. The authors of the Mishnah framed a system to which Christianity bore no relevance whatsoever; theirs were problems presented in an altogether different context. For their part, pagan writers were indifferent to Christianity, not mentioning it until about 160 (Palanque et al. 1953). Only when Christian evangelism enjoyed some solid success, toward the latter part of that century, did pagans compose apologetic works attacking Christianity. Celsus stands at the start, followed by Porphyry in the third century. But by the fourth century, pagans and Jews alike knew that they faced a formidable, powerful enemy. Pagan writings speak explicitly and accessibly.

The Judaic Sages' Canon in the Context of the Fourth Century

The premise of all that has been said is that the documents redacted at the end of the fourth century or the beginning of the fifth, the Talmud of the Land of Israel, Genesis Rabbah, and Leviticus Rabbah, testify to ideas held at that time. I have therefore to explain the basis on which I maintain that this is the case. The answer is that I work with what I know, not with what I do not know. I know—because the consensus of all scholarship concurs—that the three documents at hand reached closure at the end of the fourth century or shortly thereafter, between ca. A.D. 400 and 450. So I hold that the documents represent opinion held at that point and, I assume, prior to that point by something on the order of fifty years.

One may well wonder, however, why I do not take account of the claim that sayings in the documents derive from a period prior to the period of redaction. For the sages' documents contain numerous sayings attributed to authorities who flourished long before the half-century prior to the redaction of those documents. If I could demonstrate that those sayings really were said by the authorities to whom they were attributed, I should treat them as evidence of opinions held before the point at which the documents themselves were closed. But what I cannot show, I do not know—nor does anyone else. Accordingly, I work with the simple fact that writings closed at the end of the fourth century tell us views deemed authoritative by the framers and redactors of those writings. Those same views may well have circulated prior to the point of redaction, for the Talmud of the Land of Israel of the Land of Israel at ca. A.D. 400, for Genesis Rabbah and Leviticus Rabbah within the following half-century. If they did, then we know opinions held earlier than ca. A.D. 400. But, as I said, in this book I work with the established fact that the documents were closed at a given point, and with the equally reasonable surmise that the framers included opinions they regarded as worth preserving—hence, for whatever purpose we do not know, authoritative. I report, then, on views held by a small circle of editors, compilers, arrangers, and redactors of a college of sayings and stories, toward the end of the age of Constantine. True, the documents may well portray opinions formed before that age. No one maintains that the sages of the Talmud of the Land of Israel, Genesis Rabbah, and Leviticus Rabbah made up everything in those books—from Scripture and the Mishnah onward. But it is in this time, and not earlier, that those opinions came forth as the doctrine of the collegium of sages, in documents deemed to enjoy authority as the position of the Judaism expressed by the sages. And, when I speak of a confrontation between Judaism and Christianity, it is the sages who stand behind the documents of the day that represent Judaism.

Let me expand with special reference to the Talmud of the Land of Israel on the matter of reading a document as the voice of its framers and organizers—and as theirs alone. For we may adduce striking evidence that the Talmud of the Land Israel does speak in particular for the age in which its units of discourse took shape, and that the work was done toward the end of that long period that began at the end of the second century with the Mishnah's reception (ca. A.D. 200) and came to an end at the conclusion of the fourth century.

The Talmud of the Land of Israel speaks about the Mishnah in an essentially cogent way. Its mode of speech, as much as of thought, is uniform throughout. We know that is the fact because diverse topics produce slight differentiation in modes of analysis. The same sorts of questions phrased in the same rhetoric—a moving, or dialectical, argument, composed of questions and answers—turn out to pertain equally well to every subject and problem. The Talmud of the Land of Israel's discourse therefore forms a closed system in which people say the same thing about everything. That is a stunning fact, for it clearly defines the choice at hand. The Talmud of the Land of Israel speaks in a single voice. That voice by definition is collective, not greatly differentiated by traits of individuals.[1] The Talmud of the Land of Israel identifies no author or collegium of authors. When I say that the Talmud of the Land of Israel speaks in a single voice, I mean to say it everywhere speaks uniformly, consistently, and predictably. The voice is the voice of a book. The message is one deriving from a community, the collectivity of sages for whom and to whom the book speaks. The document seems, in the main, to intend to provide notes, an abbreviated script which anyone may use to reconstruct and

---

1. Individuals in the Talmud, unlike in the Mishnah, do not speak uniformly, but the differences are not marked.

reenact formal discussions of problems: ". . . about this, one says that. . . ."
Curt and often arcane, these notes can be translated only with immense bodies
of inserted explanation. All of this information is public and undifferentiated,
not individual and idiosyncratic. We must assume people took for granted
that, out of the signs of speech, it would be possible for anyone to reconstruct
speech, doing so in accurate and fully conventional ways. So the literary traits
of the document presuppose a uniform code of communication: a single
voice.

I cannot find among the units of discourse on the Mishnah evidence of differentiation among the generations of names or of schools. There is no interest, for instance, in the chronological sequence in which sayings took shape
and in which discussions may be supposed to have been carried on. That is to
say, the Talmud of the Land of Israel's unit of discourse approaches the explanation of a passage of the Mishnah without systematic attention to the layers
in which ideas were set forth, the schools among which discussion must have
been divided, the sequence in which statements about a Mishnah law were
made. That fact points to formation at the end, not agglutination in successive
layers of intellectual sediment. Let me spell this out. In a given unit of discourse, the focus, the organizing principle, the generative interest—these are
defined solely by the issue at hand. The argument moves from point to point,
directed by the inner logic of argument itself. A single plane of discourse is
established. All things are leveled out, so that the line of logic runs straight
and true. Accordingly, a single conception of the framing and formation of the
unit of discourse stands prior to the spelling out of issues. More fundamental
still, what people in general wanted was not to create topical anthologies—to
put together instances of what this one said about that issue—but to exhibit
the logic of that issue, viewed under the aspect of eternity. Under sustained
inquiry we always find a theoretical issue, freed of all temporal considerations
and the contingencies of politics and circumstance.

Arguments did not unfold over a long period of time, as one generation
made its points, to be followed by the additions and revisions of another generation, in a process of gradual increment and agglutination running on for
two hundred years. That theory of the formation of literature cannot account
for the unity, stunning force, and dynamism of the Talmud of the Land of
Israel's dialectical arguments.[2] To the contrary, someone (or a small group) at
the end determined to reconstruct, so as to expose, the naked logic of a problem. For this purpose, oftentimes, it was found useful to cite sayings or positions in hand from earlier times. But these inherited materials underwent
a process of reshaping, and, more aptly, refocusing. Whatever the original
words—and we need not doubt that at times we have them—the point of

---

2. The same is to be said in different terms of Leviticus Rabbah, with its remarkable syllogistic program, worked out through cogent lists of facts. But we do well to concentrate on only
a single document, allowing it to suggest the state of affairs pertaining to the others.

everything in hand was defined and determined by the people who made it all up at the end. The whole shows a plan and program. Theirs are the minds behind the whole. In the nature of things, they did their work at the end, not at the outset. Principles of chronology were not wholly ignored. Rather, they were not determinative of the structure of argument. Everything is worked together into a single, temporally seamless discourse.

It follows that the document is the work of the one who decided to make up the discussion on the atemporal logic of the point at issue. Otherwise the discussion would be not continuous but disjointed, full of seams and margins, marks of the existence of prior conglomerations of materials that have not been sewn together. What we have are not patchwork quilts, but woven fabric. Considerations of the origin of a saying play no role whatsoever in the rhetoric, or literary forms of argument. There will be no possibility of differentiation among opinions on the basis of where, when, by whom, or how they are formulated, only on the basis of what, in fact, is said. So the whole—the unit of discourse as we know it—was put together at the end. At that point everything was in hand, available for arrangement in accordance with a principle other than chronology, and in a rhetoric common to all sayings. That other principle will then have determined the arrangement, drawing in its wake resort to a single monotonous voice: the Talmud of the Land of Israel. The principle is logical exposition, that is, the analysis and dissection of a problem into its conceptual components. The dialectic of argument is framed not by considerations of the chronological sequence in which sayings were said but by attention to the requirements of reasonable exposition of the problem. That is what governs.

So, as I see it, the Talmud of the Land of Israel testifies to the opinions held by authorities during the penultimate and ultimate stages of its redaction.[3] The Talmud of the Land of Israel evidently underwent a process of redaction, in which fixed and final units of discourse (whether as I have delineated them or in some other division) were organized and put together. The probably antecedent work of framing and formulating these units of discourse appears to have gone on during a single period. By this I mean that the work went on among a relatively small number of sages working within a uniform set of literary conventions, at roughly the same time, and in approximately the same way. These framers of the various units of tradition may or may not have par-

---

3. Similar arguments can be constructed for Genesis Rabbah and Leviticus Rabbah, but the upshot is the same. We know with reasonable certainty that the documents tell us views accepted and held authoritative by the consensus of sages who stand behind them. That justifies our treating all materials in those documents as testimonies to views held in the fourth century and given recognition as authoritative at that time. That view does not deny the possibility that others held the same opinions prior to the point of redaction, but that possibility has no bearing on our problem. We focus on views people held and expressed at a given time, not on the origins of those views, or, as I have stressed, on the reasons that, at diverse times, people may have reached the same conclusions. Those reasons may prove diverse, but we do not know the reasons people in the age under discussion said the things they said. So we deal only with what we know.

ticipated in the work of closure and redaction of the whole. We do not know the answer. But among themselves they cannot have differed very much about the way in which the work was to be carried on. For the end product, the Talmud of the Land of Israel, like the Mishnah, is uniform and stylistically coherent, generally consistent in modes of thought and speech, wherever we turn. That accounts for the single voice that leads us through the dialectical and argumentative analysis of the Talmud of the Land of Israel. What follows for this book is simple. We are justified in citing the documents at hand as evidence of the views of their framers. And that is why I maintain we do have ample evidence on the state of sages' views, in the writings closed at the end of the fourth century, on the issues important in the age at hand.[4]

Their Intent, Our Interpretation

One final but unrelated point demands attention: Do I think that the Christian theologians and Judaic sages intentionally undertook the confrontation that I impute to them? I have no opinion about matters of intention. We cannot show, and therefore do not know, that the sages who framed the Judaism expressed in the fourth-century documents determined as a matter of articulated intent to define a Judaism that would confront the issues made urgent and critical by the triumph of Christianity. So we do not know that sages in full consciousness decided to reply to the Christian program on the important topics at hand.

Without access to letters, diaries, reports of conversations that actually took place, not to mention reflections and autobiographies, of the kind we

4. Whether or not these documents testify to views held before ca. A.D. 400, I do not know, but that has no bearing on the argument of this book. My point, repeated many times, is simply that the views of the Talmud of the Land of Israel, Genesis Rabbah, and Leviticus Rabbah exhibit remarkable cogency with the issues important to Israel in that age. All else follows from that fact, which, through chapters 2, 3, and 4, should prove incontrovertible.

A further point demands consideration. The documents as we have them derive from a long period of copying, during which they received materials borrowed or made up by later copyists. Accordingly, diverse manuscripts of Genesis Rabbah and Leviticus Rabbah will contain different versions of those documents. The materials cited in this book occur in most, or all, manuscripts. That is why I cite them. Still more important, my argument rests on no single item but on the repertoire of numerous and diverse materials, all well attested in manuscript evidence, and all assigned by scholarly opinion at the present to documents placed in fifth century. On that basis I believe we have a fair sample of sages' views in the fifth century, deriving from the writings that reached closure, it is unanimously held, at that time. But I emphasize that the varying representations of what is, or is not, in Genesis Rabbah or Leviticus Rabbah or the Talmud of the Land of Israel, not to mention the wording of various passages, do require attention, and have received attention in two ways. The first is my careful effort to place on display materials well attested by manuscript evidence (even though wordings may vary among the manuscripts). The second is my insistence on seeing documents as a whole and in the aggregate: What, all together, does a document tell us? The appearance or wording of a given passage in diverse manuscript representations never plays a role in my argument, because it does not have to, and because it should not.

have for such contemporaries as Augustine, for example, we have no way of settling questions of intentionality, therefore of self-conscious thought. We know only what the sages said, not why they said it. I therefore do not claim to account in other than extrinsic ways for the confluence of discourse: contemporaries talking about the same issues, defined in the same terms, drawing upon the same facts. I think the Judaic sages talked about the topics at hand because the topics gained importance in the light of political change. That is my judgment, not their articulated statement. But what the framers of the Judaic documents said did supply powerful answers to the critical challenge of the day, and that fact does speak for itself. What that fact says to me is that the issues that mattered to the one group demanded attention from the other. More than that descriptive statement, I do not offer.

Questions concerning the meaning of history, the coming of the Messiah, and the identification of Israel, God's people, certainly bore profound consequences for the politics of Israel, the Jewish people. For how the Jews interpreted history, the teleology they assigned to their life together and the definition they worked out for their own group, dictated the character of their social group viewed as a collective and therefore a political entity. The issues that confronted the fourth-century sages raised political, not solely religious, questions: whither we go, why we go, and (given the character of Scripture) whence, and therefore what, we are.

1

Judaism and Christianity in the Age of Constantine

Christianity and the Roman Empire in the Age of Constantine

In the age of Constantine important Judaic documents undertook to deal with agenda defined, for both Judaism and Christianity, by the political triumph of Christianity. Christian thinkers, represented here by Eusebius and Chrysostom on the Roman side, and Aphrahat on the Iranian,[1] reflected on issues presented by the fourth-century revolution in the political status of Christianity. Issues of the interpretation of history, the restatement of the challenge and claim of Christ as Messiah against the continuing expectation of Israel that the Messiah is yet to come, and the definition of who is Israel made their appearance in Christian writings of the day as well as in documents of Judaism brought to closure at the end of the century. We should not exaggerate the centrality of these issues. The Judaic writings dealt with a broader program, and the Christians too had a great deal on their minds, much of which had no bearing at all on theories of history, Messiah, and Israel. The quest for a unifying creed, for example, absorbed the best efforts of generations of Christian theologians[2] (Frend 1984, 473–650). To take another example, the development of Christian monasticism in the fourth century has no counterpart in Judaism (Brown, 1971, 96–112). Nevertheless, questions of history, Messiah, and Israel did demand attention and did receive it. Moreover, when Judaic sages and Christian theologians did address these questions, they defined the issues in much the same terms. This point is critical to my argument, and I

1. For Aphrahat the political problem of course was the reverse. With Christianity seen by the Iranian government as the religion of the Roman Empire, the situation of Christians became difficult, so Aphrahat had to sort out the issues of the persecution of Christians and the political prosperity of the Jews.

2. My analysis of Judaic systems in modern and contemporary times underlines the distinctive character of the crisis of the fourth century: essentially intellectual, not political, let alone economic. The response to the crisis, then, proves congruent with its character. I develop this point in my *Death and Birth of Judaism* (1987).

shall address the definition of the common issue in the opening sections of chapters 2, 3, and 4.

We shall find in the Judaism of the sages who redacted the principal documents both a doctrine and an apologetic remarkably relevant to the issues presented to Christianity and Judaism by the crisis of Christianity's worldly triumph. A shared program brought the two religions into protracted confrontation on an intersecting set of questions, a struggle that has continued until our own time. This confrontation originated in the fact that, to begin with, both religions agreed on almost everything that mattered; they differed on little, so made much of that little. Scripture taught them both that vast changes in the affairs of empires came about because of God's will. History proved principles of theology. In that same Torah prophets promised the coming of the Messiah, who would bring salvation. Who was, and is, that Messiah, and how shall we know? And that same Torah addressed a particular people, Israel, promising that people the expression of God's favor and love. But who is Israel, and who is not Israel? In this way Scripture defined the categories shared in common, enabling Judaism and Christianity to engage, if not in dialogue, then in two monologues on the same topics. The terms of this confrontation continued for centuries because the conditions that precipitated it—the rise to political dominance of Christianity and the subordination of Judaism—remained constant for fifteen hundred years.

Let us turn to the events of the age itself. Rosemary Radford Ruether, when announcing her thesis, affirmed that both Judaism and Christianity took shape in the fourth, not the first, century: "The classical form of both Judaism and Christianity was shaped by sages and theologians whose systems of thought found their fullest ripening in the fourth century after Christ" (Ruether 1972, 1). What, exactly, happened in that century, and why did it matter to the two great religious traditions of the West? Christianity became the religion of the Roman Empire—and, in due course, therefore, of the West. But this did not happen all of a sudden (Ruether 1972, 86–87). The process was slow and extended, moving in fits and starts through the fourth century, and that is why the period presents many points of interest. After a spell of ferocious persecution of Christians under Diocletian, the succeeding emperor, Constantine, converted to Christianity. What that meant, to begin with, was that Christianity attained the status of a licit religion. Constantine did not convert the army, let alone the Empire (MacMullen, 1984, 456). During the following century, however, from 312 onward, the Roman empire, its government and institutions, came under Christian domination. Writing nearly a century later, for example, Jerome captures the astonishment that Christians felt:

> . . . every island, prison, and salt-mine was crowded with Christian captives in chains . . . with the present era when (such are the seemingly impossible transformations worked by God in his goodness) the selfsame imperial government which used to make a bonfire of Christian sacred books had them adorned sumptuously

with gold, purple, and precious stones, and, instead of razing church buildings to the ground, pays for the construction of magnificent basilicas with gilded ceilings and marble-encrusted walls. (in Kelly 1975, 295)

Kelly states the simple fact: "At the beginning of the century [the Church] had been reeling under a violent persecution. . . . Now it found itself showered with benefactions and privileges, invited to undertake responsibilities, and progressively given a directive role in society" (1975, 1–2). So the age of Constantine presented even to contemporaries an era of dramatic change.

We should not exaggerate the importance of the period from Constantine's conversion in 312 to the end of the Jewish patriarchate in the Land of Israel in 429 (to take as termini two vastly disproportionate events!). The process of Christianization of the empire, the tempo of change—these are obscure matters. About a tenth of the population of the Empire was Christian as the start of the period (Goodenough 1970, 41). As Hussey writes, "In many respects the Empire in the fourth century shows no abrupt break with the earlier period; it might just as well be called late Roman as early Byzantine. It showed its close cultural affinities with the Hellenistic world, and the adoption of Christianity did not mean the rejection of pagan civilization: the learning, art, philosophy of Greece remained the prize possessions of a Christian Byzantium. Its government was in essence that of the Graeco-Roman empire. It continued to be ruled by a single absolute monarch, whose authority was enhanced by his special position as the chosen representative of the Christian God. Its administration and civil service were the fruit of long experience . . ." (1961, 12). These continuities notwithstanding, the contrast between the world at the start and at the end of the age makes the point. Constantine was the first Christian emperor and, but for a brief spell under Julian a generation later, Diocletian was the last pagan one. The West, from then to early modern times, was governed by Christians. The fourth century assuredly marks the transition from the pagan and classical age to the Christian and medieval one, hence from the ancient and the Near Eastern to the medieval and the European epoch in the formative history of the West.

Nor should the Christian commitment of Constantine come under doubt: he cared about the controversies of the Church, Donatist and Arian alike, and finally called the Council of Nicaea in 325 to solve the problem of Arianism. Whether for reasons of state or out of sincere concern for doctrine, Constantine ruled as the first Christian emperor. He did all that he could to hold the Church together. He accorded privileges to the clergy (which the Jews' clergy enjoyed as well) and made the priests state officials. He recognized the bishops' courts (and the courts of the Jews, too). The state now enforced Church discipline, treated heresy as a political crime, enforced decrees of Church councils through the state courts and administration. His sons and successors continued after him to favor the establishment of Christianity and, within a century, had firmly and finally rooted Christianity in the empire in Europe, the

Middle East, and North Africa. True, it was only later in the fourth century, after the near-catastrophe of Julian's reversion to paganism, that the Christian emperors systematically legislated against paganism so as to destroy it. Further, antipagan legislation did not necessarily cohere or follow a single line of development. But Christianity as the religion of the state did take root in this period and Christians surely formed a majority of the population of the Roman Empire by the end of the period. Only Islam, three centuries later, would uproot the faith in the Middle East and North Africa, and then, initially, by force of arms. But by then the Church had inherited the state in regions where it had collapsed, so that, as Goodenough says, "at the complete collapse of the state [the Church] would begin to dream of being itself the ideal rulership for the world, though such a thought was utterly foreign to the Church of the first three centuries" (1970, 41).

Constantine's sons took an active interest in the Church (Aland 1985, 79). The Christian empire undertook a long war against its pagan enemy, tearing down temples and ultimately curtailing pagans' rights of worship (Burckhardt 1958, 293 [for Constantine]). Constantine's sons and successors closed temples and destroyed idols, making ever more severe laws (Labriolle 1953, 224–27). Of greater consequence, the Christian emperors also assumed responsibility for the governance of the Church of Christ triumphant. At Nicaea in 325 Constantine called a council to settle the issues of Arianism that had vexed the Church (Frend 1984, 498–501). At issue was the nature of Christ in relationship to God. The upshot: "Christ cannot have the identical nature of God; he is God, but he is distinct from God and can be described only in a distinctive way" (Aland 1985, 192). But the matter remained subject to dispute for another century or more. The importance from our perspective is simple. The state now vigorously entered the life of the Church, and none could doubt that the empire had turned Christian. Not only that, but the head of state, from Constantine onward, besides favoring Christianity, despised Judaism. Constantine, for example, saw the Jews as "a hostile people, a nation of parricides, who slew their Lord" (Frend 1984, 499).

With the emperor Julian, Christianity faced a serious reverse, for Julian intended a revolution from above to lead the state to paganism, as he reopened pagan temples and fostered pagan culture. But his brief reign, 361–63, brought in its wake a ferocious counterrevolution, with the Christian state now suppressing the institutions of paganism, and Christian men in the streets of the towns and villages acting on their own against those institutions. Julian's successors also persecuted pagan philosophy. Valentinian I (364–75) and Valens (364–78) took an active role in the campaign against Neoplatonism. In 380 the emperor Theodosius (379–95) decreed the end of paganism: "It is our desire that all the various nations which are subject to our clemency and moderation should continue in the profession of that religion which was delivered to the Romans by the divine Apostle Peter (Aland 1985, 82). Paganism found itself subjected to penalties. The state church—a principal indicator of the

Christian civilization that the West was to know—now came into being. In 381 Theodosius forbade sacrifices and closed most temples. In 391–92 a new set of penalties imposed sanctions on paganism.

We know the fourth century as the decisive age in the beginning of the West as Christian. But to people of the time, the outcome was uncertain. The vigorous repression of paganism after Julian's apostasy expressed the quite natural fear of Christians that such a thing might happen again. Bickerman states matters in a powerful way:

> Julian was yesterday, the persecutors the day before yesterday. Ambrose knew some magistrates who could boast of having spared Christians. At Antioch the Catholics had just endured the persecution of Valens . . . and unbelievers of every sort dominated the capital of Syria. The army, composed of peasants and barbarians, could acclaim tomorrow another Julian, another Valens, even another Diocletian. One could not yet, as Chrysostom says somewhere, force [people] to accept the Christian truth; one had to convince them of it. (In Wilken 1984, 32–33)

Although matters remained in doubt, the main fact is unmistakable: In the beginning of the fourth century Rome was pagan; by the end of the century, it was Christian. In the beginning Jews in the Land of Israel administered their own affairs. In the end, their institution of self-administration lost the recognition it had formerly enjoyed. In the beginning Judaism enjoyed entirely licit status, and the Jews had the protection of the state. In the end Judaism suffered abridgement of its former liberties, and the Jews of theirs. In the beginning, the Jews lived in the Land of Israel, and in some numbers. In the end they lived in Palestine, as a minority. Constantine and his mother built churches and shrines all over the empire (Aland 1985, 181ff.), but especially in Jerusalem, so the Land of Israel received yet another name, for another important group, now becoming the Holy Land. To turn to the broader perspective, from the beginning of the fourth century we look backward over an uninterrupted procession of philosophers and emperors, Aristotle and Plato and Socrates and Alexander and Caesar upon Caesar. From the end of the fourth century we look forward to Constantinople, Kiev and Moscow, to Christian Rome, Paris and London, to cathedrals and saints, to an empire called Holy and Roman and a public life infused with Christian piety and Christian sanctity, to pope after pope after pope. Before Constantine's conversion in 312 Christianity scarcely imagined a politics; its collective life was lived mostly in private. Afterward Christianity undertook to govern, shaped the public and political institutions of empires, and through popes and emperors alike defined the political history of the world for long centuries to come.

From the viewpoint of the Jews, the shift signified by the conversion of Constantine marked a caesura in history. For Christians, the meaning of history, commencing at Creation, pointed toward Christ's triumph through the person of the emperor and the institution of the Christian state. To Israel, the Jewish people, what can these same events have meant? The received Scriptures of ancient and recent Israel—both Judaic and Christian Scriptures—

now awaited that same sort of sifting and selection that had followed earlier turnings of a notable order, in 586 B.C. and after 70, for example: which Scriptures had now been proved right, which irrelevant? So Christians asked themselves, as they framed the canon of the Bible, both Old and New Testaments. Then to Israel, the Jewish people, what was the role and what was the place for the received Torah of Sinai, in its diversity of scrolls? The dogged faith that Jesus really was Christ, Messiah and King of the world, now found vindication in the events of the hour. What hope endured for the salvation of Israel in the future? In the hour of vindication the new Israel confronted the old, the one after the spirit calling into question the legitimacy of the one after the flesh: What now do you say of Christ? For Israel, the Jewish people, what was there to say in reply, not to Christ but to Christians? These three issues frame our principal concerns: the meaning of history, the realization of salvation, the definition of one's own group in the encounter with the other.

The Jews in the Land of Israel in the Fourth Century

The crisis of the age—and there assuredly was a crisis for Jews—began in politics but extended to matters of the mind: psychology, theology, and myth gone wrong, most of all. For what happened was something that Jews did not anticipate, the rise to power of the Christian faith, seen by Jews until then as a mere aberration and a heresy. What Jews did anticipate was never to come to pass: in the enormous shift of history and politics, the opportunity to rebuild the Temple came—and went. These two then, the rise to power of the formerly unimportant sect, the failure of the messianic expectation at the moment of its best hope—define the contours of the difficult and decisive century, the first in the history of the Christian—and Judaic—West as it would come into being, and the last in the history of the classical Mediterranean world.

While the Christian empire outlawed paganism, policy toward the Jews accorded limited toleration. We err if we identify the systematic destruction of Jews' lives and property in the Christian West, which took place after the Crusades, with the Roman policy of Constantine's age. Overall, the Jews of the land and of the Roman Empire in general continued to enjoy state recognition and protection. Worship was protected and not to be interrupted; synagogues were exempt from billeting; synagogue staffs were exempt from curial charges just as were Christian clergy; Jews did not have to go to court on the Sabbath; Jewish courts settled civil disputes (Jones 1966, 945–46). On the other hand, there were also disabilities:

> Intermarriage between Jews and Christians was declared by Theodosius to be tantamount to adultery and subjected to the same penalties. . . . Constantine forbade Jews to circumcise their slaves, [violation being] a capital offense and furthermore forbade Jews to buy slaves of any religion but their own. . . .
> Christianity added theological animus to the general dislike of the Jews, and the

numerous diatribes against them, in the form of sermons or pamphlets, which Christian leaders produced, must have fanned the flames. It is surprising indeed that the emperors, most of whom shared the popular view, maintained such moderation in their legal enactments . . . the attitude of the emperors seems to have been mainly inspired by respect for the established law. The Jews had since the days of Caesar been guaranteed the practice of their ancestral religion and the government shrank from annulling this ancient privilege. (Jones 1966, 946–47)

Still, Jones's judgment for the period at hand is positive: "Except for their exclusion from the public service and the bar the Jews . . . incurred no serious civil disabilities until the reign of Justin." True, on occasion mobs took over and burned down synagogues. But when that happened the government exacted compensation. Mass baptisms by force occurred only after this period and far from the land of Israel. In *The Decline of the Ancient World* Jones further comments, "The imperial government . . . consistently maintained and enforced their [the Jews'] religious liberty. . . . Most responsible bishops supported governmental policy. Some firebrands invited their congregations to burn down synagogues and forcibly baptize their congregations, but the church councils and popes condemned such actions" (1966, 342). So, in all, the problems of the age of Constantine affected morale more than they did the political or material welfare and well-being of the Jews of the land. But the changes that affected morale were of a political character. Given the Jews' long history of enjoying political toleration in the Roman Empire, the shifts made an enormous difference, even though, in light of what would happen centuries beyond, they do not appear intolerable.

The triumph of Christianity, as it unfolded through the fourth century, by no means provided Christians with a certainty of what was to come. For a long time the outcome was unsure, as Bickerman stresses. And, overall, the Jews' legal status remained secure. So the issues of the age, so far as they pressed, turn out to concern intellectual, not political or economic, problems.[2] The matter of meaning predominated, because the condition of politics and social and material circumstances stood essentially unaffected (Wilken 1983, 49–53; cf. Ari-Yonah 1976, 161–74). Changes to the Jews' detriment mainly affected narrowly religious matters, such as proselytism and, in particular, conversion of slaves. Constantine, to be sure, inaugurated a tradition of verbal abuse of Judaism and of Jews, and later in the century political change did take place. But, overall, we find slight evidence of a change in the Jews' legal rights and status in the fourth century (Wilken 1983, 53). Meyers, Kraabel, and Strange state: "The great flowering of Jewish material culture in this same period— usually thought to be a time of stress and growing tension between Jews and Christians—seems to suggest that the restrictive legislation against Jews had a far more limited impact than was thought heretofore" (in Wilken 1983, 55). What happened in the fourth century that can have made a difference to the sages of Judaism, living in the Land of Israel ("Palestine")? First, the Christians took a keen interest in the Land of Israel, now become the Holy Land

(Avi-Yonah 1976, 160). Second, the Christian church emerged "as an organization competing with the State itself . . . attractive to educated and influential persons." The bishops of the Church formed the center of large voluntary organizations, in politics, in charitable tasks, even in defending towns against attach (Momigliano 1963a, 9, 10). So Christianity attained prominence on the local scene.

As Christians gained firm control of the government of the empire, Jews in the Land of Israel entered a situation formerly scarcely known, as Baron characterizes it: "For the first time since the brief outburst under Hadrian, their inner life, religious observance, community organization, and nonpolitical public utterances became an important concern of the central government. . . . The Jewish question clearly was of religious concern to the Christian state" (1952, 172). Three important events stand out: first, the abortive rebuilding of the Temple, promised by Julian; second, the inclusion, in the law code of Theodosius, of provisions hostile to the Jews and Judaism; third, the end, in 429, of the patriarchate, political institution of Jewish self-administration in the Land of Israel and abroad (Jones 1966, 944). But the change in the Jews' status found its mark in no such dramatic events. The policy, applied by emperors beyond Constantine, was "that no Jew should exercise authority over a Christian . . . Jews, for example, not being allowed to own Christian slaves" (Baron, 1952, 181). That prohibition of "Jewish lordship over Christians had a severe effect on Jewish economic life," for, as Ruether further points out, "In a slave economy, it was impossible to operate any large-scale manufacturing or agricultural enterprise without slaves" (1972, 187). With the Christianization of much of the population, a normal labor force was denied to Jewish entrepreneurs. Jews also could not proselytize and could not prevent Jews from converting to Christianity. Theodosius made it a crime for a Christian to marry a Jew. In all, as Ruether says, "By the late fourth century, new types of laws began to be added which drastically reduced Jewish social standing. Jews were excluded from all civil and military ranks and were gradually excluded from holding any type of public office" (1972, 189). Still, in the Theodosian code Jews did retain the right to govern their own religious affairs (Baron 1952, 191). They could not be forced to come to court on the Sabbath or to carry out forced labor on holy days. In 398 Theodosius I wrote:

> It is sufficiently evident that the Jews' sect has not been prohibited by any law. Hence we are seriously aroused over the fact that their assemblies have been forbidden in various places. Your sublime Excellency will, therefore, upon receipt of this order, check with appropriate severity the overzealousness of those who, in the name of the Christian faith, arrogate to themselves illegal [powers] and attempt to destroy and despoil synagogues. (Baron 1982, 192)

The Christian emperors joined a policy of protection of Jews' rights and property and limited the exercise of Judaism to Jews alone. Baron maintains that the Jewish population of the Land of Israel declined. He cites Jerome: "In comparison to their previous multitude there hardly remained a tenth of them" (1952, 210). So much for trends, latent and manifest, in the changing status of the Jews and of Judaism in the age of Constantine. What of events? Only a single noteworthy event took place in the public history of Judaism in the fourth century. That was the fiasco of Emperor Julian's plan of rebuilding the Temple. To state what happened simply, the Emperor encouraged the Jews to rebuild the Temple in Jerusalem and to restore the animal sacrifices there. After a brief effort, the structure collapsed, and nothing came of the plan. What was at issue, and why did it matter to both Judaic sages and Christian theologians?

Christians had long cited the destruction of the Temple of Jerusalem as proof of the prophetic powers of Jesus, who, in the Christian record, had predicted the matter before it happened. The ruin of Jerusalem had served for three centuries to testify to the truth of Christianity. The emperor Julian, as part of his policy of opposing Christianity, gave orders to permit the Jews to rebuild their Temple and to resume animal sacrifices, just as the pagan temples were to be restored and their animal sacrifices renewed. Julian in general favored Jews, remitted taxes that had applied to them in particular, and as part of that broader policy undertook to rebuild the Jews' Temple. Forbidden to worship in Jerusalem for the preceding two hundred years, the Jews took the emperor's decree as a mark of friendship. Some may have assumed that the emperor's action forecast the coming of the Messiah. Julian had moreover issued edicts of toleration, but, singling out Christianity, he pressured Christians to give up the faith and revert to paganism. He further declared war on Christianity by forbidding Christians to teach in the schools; Christians could not teach the classical authors, for Christians "despise the gods the [classics] honored." He took away the clergy's former legal power, withdrew recognition of bishops as judges in civil matters, and subjected the clergy to taxation. So, as Bowersock says, "Julian and the Jews had a common enemy in the Christians; their allegiance could be valuable in the Near East, particularly in Mesopotamia, where the emperor was going to conduct his campaign against the Persians." Julian undertook a more general policy of restoring temples Christians had closed, and, for their part, the Christians had turned Jerusalem into a Christian city. Constantine and his mother had built churches and shrines there. Since, moreover, Julian had in mind to restore sacrifices as part of normal prayer, he wanted the Jews to restore their cult as well. By securing the restoration of the Temple, he moreover would invalidate the prophesy of Jesus that not one stone of the Temple would be left upon another. But when Julian died in battle, in 363, nothing had been accomplished (Lietzmann 1950, 282; Bowersock 1978, 87–90; Jones 1966, 60; Frend 1984, 606; Labriolle 1953, 232–36). Frend explains the matter very simply: "His aim may have been . . . to strike at the heart of Constantinian Jerusalem, to upstage the Holy Places by a new, rebuilt 'sacred city of Jerusalem.' Unfortunately workers struck hidden gaseous deposits when they began to lay the new foundations. Explosions and fire greeted their efforts, and the attempt was abandoned in confusion (1984, 606). So ended the last attempt to rebuild the Temple of Jerusalem from then to now. Julian's successors dismantled all of his programs and restored the privileges the Church had lost (Goodenough 1970, 61). We need hardly speculate on the profound disappointment that overtook the Jews of the empire and beyond. The seemingly trivial incident—a failed project of restoring a building—proved profoundly consequential for Judaic and Christian thinkers. We know that a quarter of a century later, John Chrysostom dwelt on the matter of the destruction of the Temple—and the Jews' failure to rebuild it—as proof of the divinity of Jesus.

Whether some, or many, Jews reached the same conclusion in the aftermath of the fiasco, we do not know. All we know is the sages' response to the messianic question, to which we shall turn in due course. We have no reference in the sages' writings to the matter. But we can readily reconstruct an appropriate response, if not one particular to the event: the Temple will be rebuilt when the Messiah comes, not before; the Messiah will come when Israel attains that sanctification that the Torah requires, and the model of the sage provides the ideal for which Israel should strive. The attitude of mind required of Israel was humility and acceptance, humility before God and acceptance of the sages' authority. These attitudes, joined with actions aimed at living the holy life, will in due course prove Israel worthy of receiving the Messiah. That message, written across the pages of the Talmud of the Land of Israel but so far as we know not in any prior document in the sages' movement, assuredly addressed the crisis of disappointment (see Neusner 1984).

After Julian, the Christian restoration intensified the prior abridgement of the civil status of the Jews. Referring to the view that the Jews should be kept in a condition of misery but should not be exterminated, Ruether says, "Between 315 and 439 (from the reign of Constantine to the promulgation of the Theodosian Code), this view of the Jew was enforced through a steadily worsening legal status" (1972, 186). Avi-Yonah divides the period after Julian into three parts, the first, 363–83, until the accession of Theodosius, a period of "a truce between the hostile religions." The second, from the accession of Theodosius I to the death of his son, Arcadius, was marked by an "energetic attack on Judaism by the leaders of the church, mainly through pressure on the imperial government. The government ceded here and there but did not cause serious injury to the Jewish community as a whole or to Jews as individuals. This campaign against Judaism was part of a larger program of physical attacks on paganism and pagans and their places of worship, which sharpened after 380" (MacMullen 1984, 186). The third subperiod lasted from the accession of Theodosius II till the publication of his third Novella (408–38). "During this time the power of the church overcame the scruples of the government and both turned against the Jews" (Avi-Yonah 1976, 208). So, through to the end of the period at hand, the judgment with which we began, that the problems were those of morale, not of politics and economics, remains valid. Of interest in relation to this judgment are a few facts.

The first involved the official recognition of Christianity as the religion of the state. In 395 Theodosius declared the empire a Christian state and abolished paganism. Theodosius' suppression of paganism and of Christian deviation made its impact, also, on Judaism, as we have noted, but the success of the bonding of religion and patriotism, "welded into an unbreakable alliance that was to last as long as Byzantium, indeed as long as 'Holy Russia' lasted" (Frend 1984, 745), would preserve the Christian Roman Empire in the East long after Rome in the West faded from sight. And it was there, in the East, that the Judaism of the Christian West found definition. A second event of importance marking the end of the period was the last of the line of hereditary patriarchs in 429. The patriarchs had nominated the clergy of synagogues (Jones 1966, 945), sent out agents to collect dues and supervise synagogues, and, in general, had enjoyed high public standing (Ari-Yonah 1976, 225–29). So far as we know, many sages known from the rabbinic writings served in the administration of the patriarch, but they assuredly did not control that administration or its head. They were clerks and useful because they knew the law. In 429 the patriarchate came to an end, when the emperor declined to approve a new holder of the post. A third important event, though long in the unfolding, was the formation of a Christian majority in the Land of Israel. Between the mid-fourth and the mid-fifth centuries, the Jews became a minority in their own country (Avi-Yonah 1976, 220). This was the most profound change marked by the age of Constantine, and nothing in the history of Scripture had prepared Israel for that astonishing change.

Judaism in the Land of Israel

The documents that record the Judaism we consider, that is, the system of views held at the end of the fourth century, report the opinions of a single, small sector of Israel, the Jewish people, in the Land of Israel. That sector bears the honorific title "rabbi," and falls into the category of sage or clerk: it was the learning of men (no women among them) that qualified them for positions of authority within the Jewish nation in the Land of Israel. What sort of government did sages staff? It was an ethnic regime, with some rather limited, on the whole trivial, authority over the Jewish populations in diverse communities. Jews did not live in territorial units, ethnically uniform and distinct from areas inhabited by other, equally distinct groups. Every page of the Talmud of the Land of Israel bespeaks a polyglot and multiform society. Even towns such as Sepphoris and Tiberias, with mainly Jewish populations, are described as sheltering non-Jewish populations, each one with its particular status and rights. What must follow is that the rabbinical courts ruled an ethnic, not a territorial, domain. Cases involving Jews alone would have come to these courts, with other courts doing an equivalent labor for other groups, and provision being made (the Talmud hardly hints at its character) for litigation and determination of other juridical questions between members of different ethnic or other political units. The rabbis' courts formed only one detail within a political system encompassing a great world beyond, and supporting the small world within, the frame of rabbinical authority. But of that larger structure of politics and government the Talmud tells us virtually nothing. We have therefore to conclude that the Talmud's perspective (its "Judaism") is that of a very low level of bureaucracy. In the larger political system, the rabbis' courts constituted a trivial detail. The courts in their hands, powerful though they were in affecting the lives of ordinary Israelites, took up minor matters with which the great powers of government and state—out there, way up and beyond—did not care to deal. Before us, then, is the world of power portrayed by ethnarchic clerks, minor players in the larger scheme of things.

Sages or rabbis are portrayed by the Talmud of the Land of Israel as exercising authority not only over their own circles, people who agreed with them, but over the Jewish community at large. This authority was practical and involved very specific powers. The first and most important of these was the power of a rabbi to sort out and adjudicate rights to property and personal status affecting property. The rabbi is described as able to take chattels or real estate from one party and to give them into the rightful ownership of another party. The second sort of power rabbis are supposed to have wielded was to tell people what to do, or not to do, in matters not involving property rights. A rabbi is presented as able to coerce someone to do what that ordinary Jew might otherwise not wish to do, or to prevent him from doing what he wanted. The first kind of authority may be called judicial, the second moral. But the distinction is ours, not theirs.

We must be struck by the difference in social role and function between the sages of Judaism and the theologians of Christianity. Eusebius was a monk and a scholar; Chrysostom was a preacher and a deacon; Aphrahat was a bishop, in some ways analogous to a rabbi in the higher ranks of the Judaic bureaucracy in that he carried out practical responsibilities of administration. But the sages who speak through our documents—so far as we know about them—both mastered the received tradition and also administered it in the community's government.[3] I cannot find instances, in the lives of Eusebius, Chrysostom, and Aphrahat, as these come to us, in which the theologians told people how to sort out practical issues, e.g., of marriage and of property. The Talmud takes for granted that rabbis could define the status of persons in such ways as to affect property and marital rights and standing. It is difficult to imagine a more effective form of social authority—and, in due course,

3. A labor of differentiation among the types of sages portrayed in the literature has yet to tell us how to distinguish one sage from another. All presently come to us within a single uniform paradigm, which requires more nuanced analysis than it has yet received.

Church courts would attain that same authority. But in his time, Chrysostom could only envy the prestige of the rabbinical (or, at least, the Jewish) courts among the common population.

The Talmud of the Land of Israel treats as settled fact a range of precedents, out of which the character of the law is defined. In those precedents, rabbis declare a woman married or free to marry; permit a priest's wife to eat food given as a leave-offering or prohibit her from doing so; give a woman the support of her husband's estate or deprive her of it; give a woman the right to collect a previously contracted marriage settlement or declare she lacks that right. In such ways, as much as in their control of real estate, commercial, and other material and property transactions, the rabbis governed the Jewish community as effective political authorities. Whatever beliefs or values they proposed to instill in the people, or realize in the collective life of the community, they effected not through moral suasion or pretense of magic, but through political power. They could tell people what to do and force them to do it. That is the type of social authority implicit in the Talmud; that is the system of politics attested and assumed in our documents.

When we ask about the ideological validation for the authority at hand, we turn from political questions to religious ones. But the Talmud of the Land of Israel, Genesis Rabbah, and Leviticus Rabbah are remarkably reticent about the basis for rabbis' power over the Jews' political institutions: who bestowed this legitimacy and supplied the force? To be sure, the systematic provision of biblical proof-texts for Mishnaic laws presents an ample myth for the law. Given by God to Moses at Mount Sinai, the Torah, including the Mishnah, is viewed as law and represents the will of Heaven. But with all the faith in the world, on the basis of such an assertion about God's will, the losing party to a litigation over a piece of real estate would surely have surrendered his property to the other side only with the gravest reservations—if at all. He more than likely would have complained to some other authority, if he could. Short of direct divine coercion, upon which a legal system cannot be expected to rely, there had to be more reliable means of making the system work. What these means were, however, the Talmud hardly tells us. So, for the present purpose, we cannot pretend to know. We only know rabbis held that they could run courts and make decisions for Jews who were not rabbis or disciples.[4]

4. What is striking, among other matters on which our document maintains a puzzling silence, is not only the relationship of the rabbinical courts to the larger political structure upon which the actions of those courts had to depend. Equally striking is the relationship of the rabbis as judges and administrators to other Jewish community judges and administrators who may have carried out the same tasks and exercised the same responsibilities in regard to the Jewish nation of the Land of Israel. While, to be sure, unlike the case of Babylonian rabbinism, we hear no complaints about unqualified judges, people executing decisions not based upon sound knowledge of the law, hence, nonrabbinic Jewish judges at work in the Jewish nation, we hardly may take for granted that the Talmud tells us all of the facts about the Jewish political structure of the Land of Israel. So on what basis was the Mishnah adopted as the sole legitimate law of the Jewish nation

We cannot differentiate the rabbi as judge, local authority, and administrator from the rabbi as moral authority and supernatural figure. True, in the world in which the rabbi encompassed all of these roles, we find a measure of specialization and differentiation within other religious-social groups. The same Christian saint who sat on a pillar was not apt, in general, to be the one who wrote theological books, though the scholars aspired to the life of the stylite and asceticism was a generally held ideal. Jerome worked in a library, not in a cave, though, to be sure, he had once had the ambition to live as a solitary. The bishop who ran affairs of his Christian diocese was unlikely also to write theological works (though some did). True, Augustine was a bishop—but most bishops were not Augustines. Only after death were the persons—bodies and bones—of the great theologians treated as supernatural. In their lives, hermits and stylites tended to monopolize people's hope for holiness incarnate. Accordingly, we should imagine, points of specialization and expert knowledge or ability, also, were differentiated within the rabbinic estate. But our Talmud (all the more so the scriptural-exegetical compilations) does not allow us to recognize this, giving us lawyer-magicians, philosopher-politicians. We meet teachers worried bout controlling the weather and administering healing to the sick, while also telling Mrs. Cohen she may eat her husband's holy rations for breakfast, and Mr. Levi to support his stepmother, Mr. Isaac to hand over his back lot to his neighbor, the rightful owner, and Mr. Jacob to fulfill his contract. The same names appear in every context in which the exercise of authority is at issue. But to make sense of that authority, as I said, we have to sort out its types, attempt to classify each story in which one party told another party what to do and made his instructions stick.

So, in all, the rabbi as clerk and bureaucrat dealt with matters of surpassing triviality, a fair portion of them of no interest to anyone but a rabbi, I should imagine. He might declare which dog a flea might bite. But would the fleas listen to him? Accordingly, as we review the principal expressions, the sages' writings, in which we find voluminous evidence of rabbis' quest for authority over the Jewish nation, turn out to present ambiguities about inconsequentialities. On the one side, the rabbi could make some practical decisions. On the other, he competed for authority over Israel with the patriarch and with local village heads. And, in general, no Jew decided much. From the viewpoint of the Roman Empire, moreover, the rabbi was apt to have been one among many sorts of invisible men, self-important nonentities, treating as consequential those things that concerned no one but themselves, doing little, changing nothing. After all, in the very period in which the tales before us were coming to closure and beginning to constitute the documents as we have

---

in its Land (if indeed all law derived from the Mishnah)? And at what time did the Jewish political agency (the court, administration, school), established by the imperial government to take charge of the Jewish nation, hand over authority to a bureaucracy of clerks made up solely of people trained in the Mishnah? These are pressing questions to which we have no answers at all.

them, the power of the Jewish nation to govern itself grew ever less. Even the authority of the patriarch supposedly ended within the very period at hand, leaving only rabbis and their Talmud, legal theory in abundance but legal standing that was slight indeed. So we discern a certain disproportion between the insistence of the Talmud that rabbis really decided things and established important precedents, and the Talmud's context—both the actual condition of Israel, whom rabbis ruled, and the waning authority of the government of Israel, by whom rabbis were employed.

One of the Talmud's principal points of emphasis therefore turns out, upon closer inspection, to address head-on, but in a perverse way, the reality of Israel within the now-Christian Roman Empire. In the Talmud of the Land of Israel, Genesis Rabbah, and Leviticus Rabbah, we find not the slightest hint that anything noteworthy has happened in the Christian world. The Talmud's puzzling indifference to the stunning, world-historical events of the age, which it never mentions at all, should not deceive us. For silence is also a response. It is not possible to suppose that the Talmud's framers, by the end of the fourth century, in the aftermath of nearly a century of Christian rule and pagan disaster, of Jewish messianic fervor followed by a heart-breaking debacle, had nothing to say. The people who made the Talmud of the Land of Israel and the great compilations of scriptural exegesis could not have failed to realize that things had changed for the worse.

They knew. They cared. They judged. But if so, we can suppose only one of two alternatives. Either the rabbis of the Talmud framed their document in total disregard of the issues of the day, or they composed their principal literary monument in complete encounter with those issues and in serene certainty of their mastery. By putting emphasis on how *they* decided things, by inserting into the processes of legal theory precedents established in their courts, and by representing the life of Israel in such a way that the government of the nation was shown to be entirely within the hands of the nation's learned, legitimate authorities, the Talmud's sages stated quite clearly what they thought was going on. Israel remained Israel, wholly subject to its own law, entirely in control of its own destiny, fully possessed of its own land. Testimony to and vindication of the eternity of Israel lay in the continuing authority of Israel's sages, fully in control of God's light and law for Israel.

The Talmud of the Land of Israel turns out to lay its principal emphases precisely upon those things that the traits of the age and social setting should have led us to expect. The Talmud's message speaks of how to attain certainty and authority in a time of profound change. The means lie in the person of the Talmudic sage. Salvation consists in becoming like him. The power to change the world, not merely judge or describe it, was the rabbi's. The power of the rabbi extended backward to Moses' Scripture, forward to the Messiah. He was the link, his word the guarantee. The most important fact in the Talmud is its anonymous, monotonous, uniform voice, its "rabbi." The critical actor is the rabbi as authority on earth and intermediary of supernatural power. The rabbi, mediating divine power, yet highly individual, became the center and the focus of the supernatural life of Israel. The rabbi would become Israel's model of sanctification, the Jews' promise of ultimate salvation. That is why from then to nearly now, whatever Judaism there would ever be properly came to be called rabbinic. So in dealing with the viewpoint—the Judaism—of the sages' writings alone, we retrospectively focus upon positions that, for many centuries to come, would define the position of Judaism—whole and complete.

2

Genesis Rabbah and Israel's History: Christian and Judaic Theories of History and Its Meaning

The Issue of History: Events, Patterns, Proofs

The scriptural record of Israel, shared by both parties to the dispute, took as its premise a single fact. When God wished to lay down a judgment, God did so through the medium of events. History, composed of singular events, therefore spoke God's message. Prophets found vindication through their power to enunciate and even (in the case of Moses) to make, and change, history. Revealing God's will, history moreover consisted of a line of one-time events, all of them heading in a single direction, a line that began at creation and will end with salvation.

No stoic indifference, no policy of patient endurance could shelter Israel, the Jewish people, from the storm of doubt that swept over them. For if Constantine had become a Christian, if Julian's promise of rebuilding the Temple had produced nothing, if Christian emperors had secured control of the empire for Christ and even abridged long-standing rights and immunities of Israel, as they did, then what hope could remain for Israel? Of greater consequence, was not history vindicating the Christian claim that God had saved humanity through the suffering people of God, the Church? Christians believed that the conversion of Constantine and the Roman government proved beyond a doubt that Christ was King-Messiah. For Israel the interpretation of the political happenings of the day required deep thought about the long-term history of humanity. Conceptions of history carried with them the most profound judgments on the character of the competing nations: the old people, Israel, and the Christians, a third race, a no-people—as some called themselves—now become the regnant nation, the Church. We do not know that the conversion of Constantine and events in its aftermath provoked sages to devote thought to the issues of history and its meaning. We know only that they compiled documents rich in thought on the subject. What they said, moreover, bore remarkable pertinence to the issues generated by the history of the period.

We turn to the substance of sages' and theologians' doctrine of history as expressed in Genesis Rabbah and in the histories of Eusebius. The program of the two parties was essentially uniform, and we can therefore presume that a confrontation of ideas on the same issue took place. When sages and theologians debated history, three separate matters came under discussion. The first involved the identification of important events, things that had happened that made a difference. The second required discerning the patterns of events, thus raising questions of the meaning and end of history. The third range of discourse, of course, focused upon the difference history made; what mattered in history or, in other words, what history proved.

Christian theologians joined the issue with the claim that what had happened proved that Jesus was Christ. The empire that had persecuted Christians now had fallen into their hands. What better proof than that. Eusebius, for example, started his account of the age of Constantine with the simple statement: "Rejoicing in these things which have been clearly fulfilled in our day, let us proceed to the account. . . . And finally a bright and splendid day, overshadowed by no cloud, illuminated with beams of heavenly light the churches of Christ throughout the entire world" (Eusebius 1961, 1:369). Christians entered the new age, as Eusebius says, with the sense that they personally witnessed God's kingdom come: not "by hearsay merely or report, but [we] observe . . . in very deed and with our own eyes that the declarations recorded long ago are faithful and true . . . 'as we have heard, so have we seen, in the city of the Lord of hosts, in the city of our God.' And in what city but in this newly built and god-constructed one, which is a 'church of the living God'. . . ." The events that mattered at the time were those pointing toward the end-result, the one at hand. The pattern of events presented a more complex exercise, since a great many matters had to fit into one large picture.

The Judaic sages, for their part, constructed their own position, which implicitly denied the Christian one. They worked out a view of history that consisted of a rereading of the book of Genesis in light of the entire history of Israel, read under the aspect of eternity. Genesis then provided a complete, profoundly typological interpretation of everything that had happened as well as a reliable picture of what, following the rules of history laid down in Genesis, was going to happen in the future. Typological in what sense? The events of Genesis served as types, prefiguring what would happen to Israel in the future. Just as the Christians read stories of the Old Testament as types of the life of Christ, so the sages understood the tales of Genesis in a similarly typological manner. For neither party can history have retained that singular and one-dimensional, linear quality that it had had in Scripture itself.

Eusebius for his part also began his history of humanity from Genesis. He undertook to describe the history of the world from its very beginnings to its climactic moment, in which he lived. Sages in Genesis Rabbah did the same thing. Sages in fact had inherited two conflicting ways of sorting out events and declaring some of them to add up to history, to meaning. From the biblical prophets they learned that God made God's will known through what happened, using pagan empires to carry out a plan. So some events formed a pattern and proved a proposition. The sages did not propose to deny this. They inherited, also from Scripture, a congruent scheme for dealing with history. This scheme involved differentiating one period from another, one empire from another, assigning to each a symbol, e.g., an animal, and imputing to each animal traits characteristic of the empire, and of the age. This apocalyptic approach to history did not contradict the basic principles of the prophetic view of events but expressed that view in somewhat different, more concrete terms. But, as we shall see, there was a separate, conflicting theory of events and how to discern their meaning, and that was the Mishnah's. In due course we shall take up this other approach to deciding which events make history, determining the pattern of history, and, finally, undertaking to express the proposition or principle that history proved. For the moment, however, it suffices to make a simple point. Both parties—Judaic sages, Christian theologians—did propose to answer one and the same question: What does it all mean? Specifically, for the age of Constantine, how shall we interpret the momentous events of the day? Which events matter? What patterns do we discern in them? And what, finally, do they prove?

Eusebius and the Beginnings of Christian Historiography

If Eusebius lived today in an American university, he would occupy professorships in departments of political science, sociology, history, religious and theological studies, and, of course, classics. But I think his particular department would be political science. For Eusebius, though the founder of Christian historiography, confronted an essentially political problem and organized his thought in response to it. He turned to history for the same reason that people today study history: to understand how things have come to their present pass. As Chesnut explains, Eusebius wrote history in order to develop a poltical theory:

> The reformulation of Christian political theory necessitated by the legitimization of Christianity under Constantine was given official form in the writings of Eusebius. . . . The Roman empire suddenly became a government within which Christians could take more active part, but for which they had to take more active responsibility. Some set of ideals for the Christian monarch had to be developed and given shape, by which men could live their lives in the new Christian world. (Chesnut 1977, 34)

Eusebius saw his work as fresh, the first of its kind. He says he has no antecedents, no models. That is so not only of his profession but also of his life. Eusebius saw himself as living in a new era, one without precedent. So von Campenhausen says: "The victory of the Emperor Constantine, friend of Christians and beloved of God, and the beginning of his reign of absolute power in East and West alike, brought the previous development to its goal and a new epoch opened. For Eusebius too a new era began in his own life" (1959, 62–63). It is this deep sense that a fresh phase in human history was beginning that makes Eusebius interesting. He created history as a Christian science and addressed questions of historical meaning, answering them in terms of the epochs into which time was to be divided.

Eusebius was born in Caesarea about 260, survived the final persecutions of the Church, from 303 to 308, and also witnessed the advent of the Christian emperor after 310. He saw the whole as a divine plan, which he would uncover and record, seeing himself as the first Christian historian: "I am not aware that any Christian writer has until now paid attention to this kind of writing." He provided a narration of how humanity had moved inexorably from the beginning to the remarkable moment at which he lived. He was the first historian of the Church, but that meant that he had to invent history all over again, since, until his time, the Church was not a factor in the history of nations. What Eusebius did was to retell the history of the Church in relationship to the age in which it lived, down to the present, and in this way he created a theology of history, explaining the movement through persecution to the ascent to the throne of a Christian emperor. His was the first full-length narrative history written from a Christian viewpoint. What he contributed, in Kelly's words, was "a chronologically framed compendium of world history from the birth of Abraham down to 325 . . . showing that the Jewish-Christian tradition stretched back farther than any other" (Kelly 1975, 72–73; see also Chesnut 1977, 31; Jackson 1933, 56; Luibheid 1966, 13).

Eusebius drew on history to derive proof for rules of theology. He organized facts in order to make points that transcended specific instances. Accordingly, he worked as a kind of social scientist, in that the concrete instance demonstrated a general rule. The rules, of course, derived from theology. But the historical method was rigorous and consistently applied. His account of Constantine, for example, proved the point that God honors pious princes but destroys tyrants (*Life of Constantine* 1:3). But his main interest was to demonstrate that, from the creation of the world, all events formed a single pattern, leading up to the moment at which the Church would inherit the universal empire: "It is my purpose to write an account of the successions of the holy apostles, as well as of the times which have elapsed from the days of our Savior to our own; and to relate the many important events which are said to have occurred in the history of the Church." (1961, 1:1,1).

To carry out his purpose, however, Eusebius starts with the time before the creation of the world, with the preexistence and divinity of "our savior and Lord Jesus Christ." His name was known from the beginning and honored by the prophets. His religion was not new. In these arguments, Eusebius provides the Church with a history from the very beginnings of the world. He stresses the fact that the Christians formed a new nation, most numerous: "But although it is clear that we are new and that this new name of Christians has really but recently been known among all nations, nevertheless our life and our conduct, with our doctrines of religion, have not been lately invented by us, but from the first creation of man . . . have been established by the natural understanding of divinely favored men of old" (1961, 1:4). Eusebius therefore links the Christian nation to the ancients, some before the flood, others descendants of Noah, Abraham, and onward. Christian religion begins with Abraham:

> But that very religion of Abraham has reappeared at the present time, practiced in deeds, more efficacious than words, by Christians alone throughout the world. What then should prevent the confession that we who are of Christ practice one and the same mode of life and have one and the same religion as those divinely favored men of old? Whence it is evident that the perfect religion committed to us by the teaching of Christ is not new and strange . . . but it is the first and the true religion. (1961, 1:4)

Abraham provides more than precedent. In the view of the historian, he proves social rules. He lived that life of virtue that produced in God the response of blessing. What is striking in Eusebius' picture is his powerful faith that Christianity began with the beginning of history and made its original statement through Abraham. No wonder then that sages too turned back to the same story and found in it the foundations for their faith.

His principal stress was on the creation of a political philosophy based on the unity of the Church and the empire under the providence of God. In the year of Constantine's conversion, Eusebius published his *Ecclesiastical History* (312), and in 337 his *Life of Constantine*. Other lives of holy men followed in sequence. Hagiography and pagan historical works alternate, according to Momigliano: "The Christians attack. The pagans are on the defensive" (1963b, 81). But with power and responsibility, Christian historians had to account for the past. So Momigliano characterizes matters:

> The new history could not suppress the old. Adam and Eve and what follows had in some way to be presented in a world populated by Deucalion, Cadmus, Romulus, and Alexander the Great. This created all sorts of new problems. First, the pagans had to be introduced to the Jewish version of history. Secondly, the Christian historians were expected to silence the objection that Christianity was new. . . . Thirdly, the pagan facts of life had to get into the Jewish-Christian scheme of redemption. . . . It soon became imperative for the Christians to produce a chronology which would satisfy both the needs of elementary teaching and the purposes of higher historical interpretation. . . . Christian chronology was also a philosophy of history. . . . Christian elementary teaching of history could not avoid touching upon the essentials of the destiny of man. (1963b, 81)

Accordingly, as I have already stressed, no one can imagine that Christians began writing history only in the aftermath of the conversion of Constantine. A Christian scheme for describing the history of the world, beginning to end, did not await Eusebius. On the contrary, he reworked what he had in hand. But he laid stress on the pattern of history (Momigliano 1963b, 85), and that is why he is important. For it was in the discerning of patterns that history crossed the border into theology, and theology in the form of apocalypse at that.

The new historiography was old in two senses. First, it drew upon available

Christian materials, and, second, it drank richly from the apocalyptic heritage of Daniel in the Old Testament, Revelation in the New, and much else. What, in fact, did the Christian historians do? Momigliano points out, "The Christians invented ecclesiastical history and the biography of the saints, but they did not try to christianize ordinary political history" (1963b, 88). But, as we have seen, this is precisely what Eusebius did, for he was writing a national history and saw the Christians as the nation. But what sort of nation? It was *sui generis*, beginning in heaven, warring for God and Christ against the devil. In chapter 4 we shall see this viewpoint worked out in detail, with Aphrahat characterizing the Christians as a people born out of the peoples, a no-people, a people with no past—yet with the past that (Jews thought) was Israel's. This was a new kind of history indeed, appropriate to the enormous event that had come about. Now history told the story of persecution on the one side, and heresy on the other. And the principal form in the writings of Eusebius was the saint's biography (Momigliano 1963b, 93). The special interest of sages in the lives of the patriarchs and matriarchs forms the corresponding statement. They found in those lives the models not merely for personal conduct but for the history of the nation, Israel. The task, for Eusebius, lay in the writing of the national history of the Church through the lives of the saints and martyrs.

Von Campenhausen characterizes Eusebius' picture of history in this way:

> Christianity was the decisive power behind the moral progress of the world, the crowning consummation of the history of thought and religion, and its prophecies and commandments had become the basis of a program of human renewal. Monotheism and the new idealistic morality, which constituted the heart of the gospel of Jesus for Eusebius, were unable to rule the world from the beginning . . . "life, which was still so to some extent animal and unworthy had to be tamed and molded by the beginnings of philosophy and civilization." When the Roman Empire brought peace to the world and overcame the multiplicity of governments, the hour for the Christian people had come, according to the will of God. . . . God has protected his Church in the world from all the demonic onslaughts of its enemies and has led it to victory and success as the shining light of all people. (1959, 59)

So history presents the unfolding of God's will. Like Aphrahat, whom we shall meet presently, Eusebius was a scholar working with facts.

The picture of history drawn by Eusebius laid stress on the divine promise to the seed of Abraham, meaning "all who lived according to the standards of piety that would be reestablished and renewed in the world by the coming of Christ." The Mosaic law had its place as "prologue to the event which would restore that friendship" between God and man, namely, "the coming of the Messiah." Christianity was not "the upstart religion . . . but the republication of a standard and a code which long predated the Homeric or Mosaic past." This was addressed to all humanity, and the expansion of the Roman Empire, "coincident with the coming of Christ . . . was no accident but had to be seen as part of the divine plan long ago revealed in the promise to Abraham. . . . The increase in Roman power meant an increase in the potential area of Christian activity." With the conversion of Constantine, therefore, the Church "had at last caught up with the expanding Empire. The growing power of Rome had been preparing the way to be followed by the spreading movement of Christianity . . . the fact that [Constantine] had become a Christian was so extraordinary, so overwhelming in its implications and in its results, that it could be explained only as the outcome of a specific ordinary ordinance of God" (Luibheid 1966, 13–15). Eusebius had a very specific interest in the Jews and Judaism, of course. He wished to answer Jews' objections to the Gospel and to retrieve the Hebrew Scriptures from Judaism and demonstrate that the Old Testament validates the New. That accounts for his notion of a worldwide religion before Moses, a religion now fully worked out in Christianity. Eusebius gave full expression to the idea "of a world-conquering Christian civilization" (Leitzmann 1950, 166, 169).

As we shall note, the sages produced no writing like that of Eusebius. They responded to historical events in a different idiom, often putting forth ideas of the same sort (though with opposite propositions, to be sure). What made Eusebius different from sages in this regard? If we wish to understand why, in the canon of Judaism, Eusebius has no counterpart of any kind, we find the explanation in the problem confronting the Christian historians. Chesnut explains:

> In the histories of this period, the ruler of the Roman state, due to his enormous power, often played the single most important role in determining the course of human events. He had traditionally been regarded by many ancient men as a divine being. . . . It will be necessary to explore the attempts of the first Christian historians to deal with both the sacred king and the philosophical king and the gradual emergence in their writings of a combination of the old pagan theory of rulership with a new, medieval understanding of the ideal monarch as a pious, ascetic soldier-monk. . . . It was necessary to confront the pagan idea of Eternal Rome with some more Christian concept, while dealing as well with the quite different pagan historiographical motif of the decline and fall of the Roman Empire. (1977, 33)

These motifs in no way affected Jews' understanding of themselves and their history. As we noted in the opening chapter, Israel and the Christian nation had changed places, the one beginning as a state but now no longer a political entity, the other beginning as a religious group and now entering upon a long political existence. Israel now had no kings, no state, no theory of eternal Jerusalem to translate into this-worldly narrative. The problems and motifs of Christian history derived from Christian theology, on the one side, and the Christians' remarkable situation in the new world, on the other. So Christian historians had to produce, as Chesnut says, a "new kind of history" to deal with a pressing situation and urgent questions. The task proved in no way narrowly historical. Eusebius did not merely have the work of preserving information or received traditions. For those out of touch with politics and affairs of state, history took a different form. It required deep reflection on the signs and trends of time, with special interest in the reading of Scripture as the guide not to what had been but to what would be. This search, within Scripture, for the meaning of the affairs of the day carried thinkers far from the political agenda of Eusebius and his co-workers. Scripture opened its doors to this other kind of historian and supplied the wherewithal for this different kind of history.

Israel's sages, in Genesis Rabbah, and Eusebius, the great Church historian, bear much in common. Both parties went back to the beginnings. From the history of former times both wanted to draw lessons for present and future history. From the story of the beginnings of the world and of Israel they sought meaning for their own times. For that purpose they proposed to identify the patterns in events that would convey the will of God for Israel. The issue was the same, the premise the same, the facts the same. Only the conclusions differed. In the initial encounter, in the age of Constantine, therefore, the Judaic philosophers of history and the Christians represented by Eusebius conducted a genuine argument: different people talking to different people about essentially the same thing.

It was the book of Genesis. In looking to the past to explain the present, the Judaic sages turned to the story of the beginnings of creation, humanity, and Israel, that is, to the book of Genesis. In doing so, they addressed precisely that range of historical questions that occupied Eusebius: where did it all start? Both parties shared the supposition that if we can discern beginnings, we can understand the end. The Israelite sages took up the beginnings that, for Eusebius too, marked the original pattern for ongoing history. Sages, of course, would not have added what to Eusebius was critical: "Where did it all start—*now that we know where it was all heading all the time?*" Sages could not imagine, after all, that what had happened in their own day marked the goal and climax of historical time. Rome formed an episode, not the end. But, then, sages had to state what they thought constituted the real history of the world and of Israel.

The book of Genesis became the principal mode of historical reflection and response for the sages of the time. They chose that book in order to deal in precisely the same manner and setting with exactly the same questions that occupied Eusebius: to understand the (to Eusebius) end or (to sages) critical turning, look back to the beginning. In fact, in the present context of debate, only the book of Genesis could have served both parties so well. For Eusebius, the end would impart its judgment of the meaning of the beginning: this is where things all along had been heading. For the sages of Genesis Rabbah the beginning would tell us where, in time to come, things will end up. That is the point on which the parties differed, making possible our reconstruction of their genuine argument, within agreed-upon limits.

Genesis Rabbah and Israel's Historical Crisis

To place into proper perspective the sages' thought, expressed in Genesis Rabbah, on the nature and meaning of history, we had best begin with a look backward, toward the place and meaning of history as expounded in the pages of the Mishnah.[1] The Mishnah, promulgated two hundred years prior to the composition of Genesis Rabbah, set forth a theory of how events are to be interpreted and what meaning is to be inferred from them. That theory lay in the background of all thought on the same subject, given the Mishnah's authority in the thought of the sages. Accordingly, we shall not understand what sages accomplished in Genesis Rabbah (and in the other documents of the age) without first reviewing the context in which their thought went forward.

The framers of the Mishnah explicitly refer to very few events, treating those they do mention with a focus quite separate from the unfolding events themselves. They rarely create narratives; historical events do not supply organizing categories or taxonomic classifications. We find no tractate devoted to the destruction of the Temple, no complete chapter detailing the events of Bar Kokhba, nor even a sustained celebration of the events of the sages' own historical lives. When things that have happened are mentioned, it is neither to narrate nor to interpret and draw lessons from the events. It is either to illustrate a point of law or to pose a problem of the law—always in passing, never in a pointed way. Narrative, in the Mishnah's limited rhetorical repertoire, is reserved for the narrow framework of what priests and others do on recurrent occasions and around the Temple. That staple of history, stories about dramatic events and important deeds, provides little nourishment in the minds of the Mishnah's jurisprudents. Events, if they appear at all, are treated as trivial. They may be well known, but they are consequential in some way other than is revealed in the detailed account of what actually happened.

The Mishnah absorbs into its encompassing system all events, small and large. With them the sages accomplish what they accomplish in everything else: a vast labor of taxonomy, an immense construction of the order and rules governing the classification of everything on earth and in heaven. The disruptive character of history—one-time events of ineluctable significance—scarcely impresses the philosophers represented by the Mishnah. They find no difficulty in showing that what appears unique and beyond classification has in fact happened before and so falls within the range of trustworthy rules and known procedures. Once history's components, one-time events, lose their distinctiveness, then history as a didactic intellectual construct, as a source of lessons and rules, also loses all pertinence. Working like social scientists, much as did Eusebius, sages sorted out events and classified them. In that way they looked for points of regularity—lessons, laws, and rules—which would explain and make sense of new episodes. In discovering out of anecdotes a larger system of historical—we would say, theological—laws, sages treated history as the raw material for social science. The parallel to the mode of thought displayed by Eusebius is clear.

To this labor of taxonomy, the historian's way of selecting data and arranging

---

1. I draw here on my *Messiah in Context* (1984a).

them into patterns of meaning to teach lessons proves inconsequential. For history-writing, by contrast, what is important is to describe what is unique and individual, not what is ongoing and unremarkable. History is the story of change, development, movement, not of what does not change, develop, or move. For the thinkers of the Mishnah, on the other hand, historical patterning emerges through taxonomy, the classification of the unique and individual, the organization of change and movement within unchanging categories. In the Mishnah's system one-time events are not important. The world is composed of nature and supernature. The laws that count are those to be discovered in heaven and, in heaven's creation and counterpart, on earth. Keep those laws and things will work out. Break them, and the result is predictable: calamity of whatever sort will supervene in accordance with the rules. But just because it is predictable, a catastrophic happening testifies to what has always been and must always be, in accordance with reliable rules and within categories already discovered and well explained. That is why the lawyer-philosophers of the mid-second century produced the Mishnah—to explain how things are.

The events of the fourth century directed attention to trends and patterns, just as the framers of the Mishnah would have wanted. But in search of those trends, the detailed record of history—so far as the record made trends visible and exposed the laws of social history—demanded close study. That is why the sages' response to the historical crisis of the fourth century required them to reread the records of history, much as Eusebius resifted the facts of the past. The sedulous indifference to concrete events, except for taxonomic purposes, characteristic of the Mishnaic authorship, provided no useful model. Concrete, immediate, and singular events now made a difference.

Like Eusebius, sages turned to the story of the beginning to find out the meaning of the present moment. Genesis Rabbah, a work that came to closure sometime after 400, forms a striking counterpart to the writing of Eusebius for one important reason. Its authors not only lived through that same period of radical political change but also reconsidered the historical question, and they did so in the same way, by reverting to the record of creation, the beginnings of Israel in particular. Once more I enter the necessary warning: whether sages found themselves impelled to do so by the triumph of Christianity, we cannot show. We only know what they did, which turns out to be precisely the same thing that Eusebius did. I see no inherent difference between the inquiry of Genesis Rabbah and the question of Eusebius: What patterns do we discern, now that (from Eusebius's perspective) we know where, all the time, things where heading? Since the method of the two parties proved identical, and the sources on which they drew were the same, we may proceed to examine the arguments adduced by parties who, we realize, shared one and the same issue and also concurred upon the premises and the proofs for the propositions that, in the mind of each, would settle the issue. Here, therefore, we see how a genuine and authentic argument could have been carried on by two parties to a single dispute.

In Genesis Rabbah, a commentary on the book of Genesis made up of episodic comments on verses and their themes, the Judaic sages who framed the document presented a profound and cogent theory of the history of Israel, the Jewish people. Let me briefly characterize their mode of thought in doing the work. In contrast to the approach of Eusebius, the framers of Genesis Rabbah interpreted contemporary history in the light of the past, while Eusebius read the past in light of the present. So the Israelite sages invoked the recurring and therefore cyclical patterns of time, finding in their own day meaning imparted by patterns revealed long ago. Eusebius, for his part, stood squarely in the tradition that saw events not as cyclical but as one-time and remarkable, each on its own. So the one side looked for rules, somewhat like the social scientist–philosopher, asking how events form patterns and yield theories of a deeper social reality. The other side looked not for rules but for the meaningful exceptions: What does this event, unique and lacking all precedent, tell us about all that has happened in the past?[2] But the two sides met with a single concern: What do the events of the day mean for tomorrow?

Accordingly, the framers of Genesis Rabbah intended to find those principles of society and of history that would permit them to make sense of the ongoing history of Israel. They took for granted that Scripture speaks to the life and condition of Israel, the Jewish people. God repeatedly says exactly that to Abraham and to Jacob. The entire narrative of Genesis is so formed as to point toward the sacred history of Israel, the Jewish people: its slavery and redemption; its coming Temple in Jerusalem; its exile and salvation at the end of time. In the reading of these sages, therefore, the powerful message of Genesis proclaims that the world's creation commenced a single, straight line of events, leading in the end to the salvation of Israel and through Israel all humanity. That message—that history heads toward Israel's salvation—the sages derived from the book of Genesis and contributed to their own day. Therefore in their reading of Scripture a given story will bear a deeper truth about what it means to be Israel, on the one side, and what in the end of days will happen to Israel, on the other. But their reading makes no explicit reference to what, if anything, had changed in the age of Constantine. But we do find repeated references to the four kingdoms, Babylonia, Media, Greece, Rome—and beyond the fourth will come Israel, fifth and last. So the sages' message, in their theology of history, was that the present anguish prefigured the coming vindication of God's people.[3]

Accordingly, sages read Genesis as the history of the world with emphasis on Israel. The lives portrayed, the domestic quarrels and petty conflicts with

---

2. I think we go too far if we impute to Eusebius the notion that, just as the resurrection put all of history into a new light, so the advent of the Christian emperor likewise required the rereading of the entire past. But the point of contact in the otherwise extravagant comparison is simple. Both events were one-time, unique, and, for that reason, enormously important.

3. As I said, we do not know that it was in response to the crisis of Constantine's Christian empire that sages composed Genesis Rabbah—their vast expansion of the book of Genesis to encompass their own time. We only know what they said and the context in which they said it.

the neighbors, all serve to yield insight into what was to be. Why so? Because the deeds of the patriarchs taught lessons on how the children were to act, and, it followed, the lives of the patriarchs signaled the history of Israel. Israel constituted one extended family, and the metaphor of the family, serving the nation as it did, imparted to the stories of Genesis the character of a family record. History become genealogy conveyed the message of salvation.[4] All of the sages' propositions really laid down the same judgment, one for the individual and the family, the other for the community and the nation, since there was no differentiating. Every detail of the narrative therefore served to prefigure what was to be, and Israel found itself, time and again, in the revealed facts of the history of the creation of the world, the decline of humanity down to the time of Noah, and, finally, its ascent to Abraham, Isaac, and Israel.

So sages read Genesis as history. It was literally and in every detail a book of facts. Genesis constituted an accurate and complete testimony to things that really happened just as the story is narrated. While, therefore, sages found in Genesis deeper levels of meaning, uncovering the figurative and typological senses underlying a literal statement, they always recognized the literal facticity of the statements of the document. In the fourth century the two heirs of ancient Israel's Scriptures, Judaism and Christianity, laid claim to the Land of Israel/the Holy Land. Constantine and his mother dotted the country with shrines and churches, so imparting to the geography of the land a Christian character. Israel, for its part, was losing its hold on the Land of Israel, as the country gained a Christian majority. Here, in Genesis, sages found evidence for Israel's right to hold the land.

The following picture, deriving from Genesis Rabbah LXI:VII.1, of the way in which facts of Scripture settled claims of living enemies makes the matter clear.

B.   In the time of Alexander of Macedonia the sons of Ishmael came to dispute with Israel about the birthright, and with them came two wicked families, the Canaanites and the Egyptians.

C.   They said, "Who will go and engage in a disputation with them?"

D.   Gebiah b. Qosem [the enchanter] said, "I shall go and engage in a disputation with them."

E.   They said to him, "Be careful not to let the Land of Israel fall into their possession."

F.   He said to them, "I shall go and engage in a disputation with them. If I win over them, well and good. And if not, you may say, 'Who is this hunchback to represent us?'"

G.   He went and engaged in a disputation with them. Said to them Alexander of Macedonia, "Who lays claim against whom?"

H.   The Ishmaelites said, "We lay claim, and we bring our evidence from

---

4. In chapter 4 this metaphor for Israel will form the center of our discussion on who is Israel from sages' viewpoint. Genesis Rabbah supplies the *locus classicus* for the metaphor.

their own Torah: 'But he shall acknowledge the firstborn, the son of the hated' (Deut. 21:17). Now Ishmael was the firstborn. [We therefore claim the land as heirs of the first-born of Abraham.]"

I.   Said to him Gegiah b. Qosem, "My royal lord, does a man not do whatever he likes with his sons?"

J.   He said to him, "Indeed so."

K.   "And lo, it is written, 'Abraham gave all that he had to Isaac' (Gen. 25:2)."

L.   [Alexander asked,] "Then where is the deed of gift to the other sons?"

M.   He said to him, "But to the sons of his concubines, Abraham gave gifts, [and while he was still living, he sent them away from his son Isaac, eastward to the east country]' (Gen. 25:6)."

N.   [The Ishmaelites had no claim on the land.] They abandoned the field in shame.

Israel's later history is prefigured in the gift to Isaac and the rejection of the other sons. Scripture contains the evidence, and, moreover, points to the rules of history.

As we can see, sages looked in the facts of history for the laws of history. We may compare the sages to social scientists or social philosophers, trying to turn anecdotes into insight and to demonstrate how we may know the difference between impressions and truths. Accordingly, just as we study nature and derive facts demanding explanation and yielding law, so we study Scripture and find facts susceptible of explanation and yielding truth. We therefore read the Judaic sages who stand behind Genesis Rabbah as social scientists, not narrative historian-storytellers. For the sages looked in history for social laws to guide them in their governance of Israel as they led the people to the end of history. Let us begin with an exemplary case (drawn from Genesis Rabbah LV:VIII.1) of how sages discovered social laws of history in the facts of Scripture. What Abraham did corresponds to what Balaam did, and the same law of social history derives proof from each of the two contrasting figures.

LV:VIII

1.   A.   "And Abraham rose early in the morning, [saddled his ass, and took two of his young men with him, and his son Isaac, and he cut the wood for the burnt offering and arose and went to the place which God had told him]" (Gen. 22:3):

      B.   Said R. Simeon b. Yohai, "Love disrupts the natural order of things, and hatred disrupts the natural order of things.

      C.   "Love disrupts the natural order of things we learn from the case of Abraham: '. . . he saddled his ass.' But did he not have any number of servants? But that proves love disrupts the natural order of things.

      D.   "Hatred disrupts the natural order of things we learn from the case of Balaam: 'And Balaam rose up early in the morning and saddled his ass' (Num. 22:21). But did he not have any number of servants? But that proves hatred disrupts the natural order of things. . . ."

2. A. Said R. Simeon b. Yohai, "Let one act of saddling an ass come and counteract another act of saddling the ass. May the act of saddling the ass done by our father Abraham, so as to go and carry out the will of him who spoke and brought the world into being counteract the act of saddling that was carried out by Balaam when he went to curse Israel.

    B. "Let one act of preparing counteract another act of preparing. Let Joseph's act of preparing his chariot so as to meet his father serve to counteract Pharaoh's act of preparing to go and pursue Israel."

We see that the narrative is carefully culled for probative facts, yielding laws. One fact is that there are laws of history. The other is that laws may be set aside, by either love or hatred. Yet another law of history applies in particular to Israel, deriving from the life of both Israel and the nations, Abraham and Balaam. The fundamental syllogism, not stated at all, is that Israel's history follows rules that can be learned in Scripture. Nothing is random, all things are connected, and fundamental laws of history dictate the sense and meaning of what happens. These laws are stated in the very language of Scripture.

Once we recognize the mode of inquiry, we ask about the results. What are the laws of history, and, more important, how do they apply to the crisis at hand? The principal message of the story of the beginnings, as sages read Genesis, is that the world depends upon the merit of Abraham, Isaac, and Jacob; Israel, for its part, enjoys access to that merit, being today the family of the patriarchs and matriarchs. That sum and substance constitutes the sages' doctrine of history: the family forms the basic and irreducible historical unit. Israel is not so much a nation as a family, and the heritage of the patriarchs and matriarchs sustains that family from the beginning even to the end. So the sages' doctrine of history transforms history into genealogy, just as Eusebius's doctrine of history turns history into chronology. The consequence, for sages, will take the form of the symbolization through family relationships of the conflict between (Christian) Rome and eternal Israel. As we shall see later in this chapter as well as in chapter 4, the rivalry of brothers, Esau and Jacob, contains the history of the fourth century—from the sages' viewpoint a perfectly logical mode of historical reflection. That, in detail, expresses the main point of the system of historical thought yielded by Genesis Rabbah.

Israel therefore endures, whatever happens. The relevance of that message to the time of the document is self-evident, but no one can maintain that the framers made up, or selected, the items treated by them with the victory of Christianity in mind. The way in which the merit of the patriarchs and matriarchs protects their grandchildren finds abundant exemplification. Here is a brief instance:

XLIII:VIII

2. A. "And Abram gave him a tenth of everything" (Gen. 14:20):

   B. R. Judah in the name of R. Nehorai: "On the strength of that blessing the three great pegs on which the world depends, Abraham, Isaac, and Jacob, derived sustenance.

   C. "Abraham: 'And the Lord blessed Abraham in *all* things' (Gen. 24:1) on account of the merit that 'he gave him a tenth of *all* things' (Gen. 14:20).

   D. "Isaac: 'And I have eaten of *all*' (Gen. 27:33), on account of the merit that 'he gave him a tenth of *all* things' (Gen. 14:20).

   E. "Jacob: 'Because God has dealt graciously with me and because I have all' (Gen. 33:11) on account of the merit that 'he gave him a tenth of *all* things'" (Gen. 14:20).

3. A. Whence did Israel gain the merit of receiving the blessing of the priests?

   B. R. Judah said, "It was from Abraham: '*So* shall your seed be' (Gen. 15:5), while it is written in connection with the priestly blessing: '*So* shall you bless the children of Israel' (Num. 6:23)."

   C. R. Nehemiah said, "It was from Isaac: 'And I and the lad will go *so* far' (Gen. 22:5), therefore said the Holy One, blessed be he, '*So* shall you bless the children of Israel' (Num. 6:23)."

   D. And rabbis say, "It was from Jacob: 'So shall you say to the house of Jacob' (Ex. 19:3) (in line with the statement, '*So* shall you bless the children of Israel' (Num. 6:23)."

No. 2 links the blessing with the history of Israel. Now the reference is to the word "all," which joins the tithe of Abram to the blessing of his descendants. Since the blessing of the priest is mentioned, No. 3 treats the origins of the blessing.

Historical study commonly leads to the periodization of history, the division of time into a number of distinct epochs. This patterning of history, its division in eras, each with its own definitive traits, constitutes one important exercise of historical thought of a social-scientific order. Eusebius of course understood the importance of periodization. Reading Scripture, for example, he identified a number of distinct periods, each leading to the next and culminating in his own time. As we shall see in chapter 4, a principal mode of explaining the identification and status of Israel, the Jewish people, involved the periodization of history among four monarchies, as specified by Daniel. Leviticus Rabbah identifies with the four empires animals in Leviticus 11 and other texts. Rome then stands as the penultimate epoch; Israel for the end. For the present topic, we consider how the patriarchs, for their part, contribute to the periodization of history—itself a source of comfort to doubting Israel even now. For if there is a well-defined sequence, then we can understand where we are and wait patiently until we reach the next, and better, age. Time and again events in the lives of the patriarchs prefigure the four monarchies, among which, of course, the fourth, last (but for Israel), and most intolerable was Rome. Here (Genesis Rabbah XLIV:XVII) is an exercise in the recurrent proof of that single proposition.

XLIV:XVII

4. A. "[And it came to pass, as the sun was going down,] lo, a deep sleep fell on Abram, and lo, a dread and great darkness fell upon him" (Gen. 15:12):

   B. ". . . lo, a dread" refers to Babylonia, as it is written, "Then was Nebuchadnezzar filled with fury" (Gen. 3:19).

   C. ". . . and darkness" refers to Media, which darkened the eyes of Israel by making it necessary for the Israelites to fast and conduct public mourning.

   D. ". . . great . . ." refers to Greece.

   G. ". . . fell upon him" refers to Edom, as it is written, "The earth quakes at the noise of their fall" (Jer. 49:21).

   H. Some reverse matters:

   I. ". . . fell upon him" refers to Babylonia, since it is written, "Fallen, fallen is Babylonia" (Is. 21:9).

   J. ". . . great . . ." refers to Media, in line with this verse: "King Ahasuerus did make great" (Est. 3:1).

   K. ". . . and darkness" refers to Greece, which darkened the eyes of Israel by its harsh decrees.

   L. ". . . lo, a dread" refers to Edom, as it is written, "After this I saw . . . a fourth beast, dreadful and terrible" (Dan. 7:7).

The fourth kingdom is part of that plan, which we can discover by carefully studying Abraham's life and God's word to him. The inevitable and fore-ordained salvation follows this same pattern of historical epochs:

XLIV:XVIII

1. A. "Then the Lord said to Abram, 'Know of a surety [that your descendants will be sojourners in a land that is not theirs, and they will be slaves there, and they will be oppressed for four hundred years; but I will bring judgment on the nation which they serve, and afterward they shall come out with great possessions']" (Gen. 15:13–14):

   B. "Know" that I shall scatter them.

   C. "Of a certainty" that I shall bring them back together again.

   D. "Know" that I shall put them out as a pledge [in expiation of their sins].

   E. "Of a certainty" that I shall redeem them.

F.   "Know" that I shall make them slaves.
G.   "Of a certainty" that I shall free them.

Reading the verse as a paradigm for all time, we recognize its immediate relevance to the age of the document in which it occurs. There is oppression, but redemption is coming. The lives of the patriarchs bring reassurance. The proposition is that God has unconditionally promised to redeem Israel; but, if Israel repents, then the redemption will come with greater glory. If Abraham, Isaac, and Jacob stand for Israel later on, then Ishmael, Edom, and Esau represent Rome. Hence whatever sages find out about those figures tells them something about Rome and its character, history, and destiny.

So Genesis is read as a literal statement and also as an effort to prefigure the history of Israel's suffering and redemption. Ishmael, standing now for Christian Rome, claims God's blessing, but Isaac gets it, as Jacob will take it from Esau. Details, as much as the main point, yielded laws of history. In the following passage, the sages take up the detail of Rebecca's provision of a bit of water, showing what that act had to do with the history of Israel later on. The passage is somewhat protracted, but it contains in a whole and cogent way the mode of thought and the results: salvation is going to derive from the merit of the matriarchs and patriarchs.

XLVIII:X

2. A.   "Let a little water be brought" (Gen. 18:4):
    B.   Said to him the Holy One, blessed be he, "You have said, 'Let a little water be brought' (Gen. 18:4). By your life, I shall pay your descendants back for this: 'Then sang Israel this song,' " 'spring up O well, sing you to it'" (Num. 21:7)."
    C.   That recompense took place in the wilderness. Where do we find that it took place in the Land of Israel as well?
    D.   "A land of brooks of water" (Deut. 8:7).
    E.   And where do we find that it will take place in the age to come?
    F.   "And it shall come to pass in that day that living waters shall go out of Jerusalem" (Zech. 14:8).
    G.   ["And wash your feet" (Gen. 18:4)]: [Said to him the Holy One, blessed be he,] "You have said, 'And wash your feet.' By your life, I shall pay your descendants back for this: 'Then I washed you in water' (Ez. 16:9)."
    H.   That recompense took place in the wilderness. Where do we find that it took place in the Land of Israel as well?
    I.   "Wash you, make you clean" (Is. 1:16).
    J.   And where do we find that it will take place in the age to come?
    K.   "When the Lord will have washed away the filth of the daughters of Zion" (Is. 4:4).
    L.   [Said to him the Holy One, blessed be he,] "You have said, 'And

rest yourselves under the tree' (Gen. 18:4). By your life, I shall pay your descendants back for this: 'He spread a cloud for a screen' (Ps. 105:39)."

M. That recompense took place in the wilderness. Where do we find that it took place in the Land of Israel as well?

N. "You shall dwell in booths for seven days" (Lev. 23:42).

O. And where do we find that it will take place in the age to come?

P. "And there shall be a pavilion for a shadow in the day-time from the heat" (Is. 4:6).

Q. [Said to him the Holy One, blessed be he,] "You have said, 'While I fetch a morsel of bread that you may refresh yourself' (Gen. 18:5). By your life, I shall pay your descendants back for this: 'Behold I will cause to rain bread from heaven for you' (Ex. 16:45)."

R. That recompense took place in the wilderness. Where do we find that it took place in the Land of Israel as well?

S. "A land of wheat and barley" (Deut. 8:8).

T. And where do we find that it will take place in the age to come?

U. "He will be as a rich cornfield in the land" (Ps. 82:16).

V. [Said to him the Holy One, blessed be he,] "You ran after the herd ['And Abraham ran to the herd' (Gen. 18:7)]. By your life, I shall pay your descendants back for this: 'And there went forth a wind from the Lord and brought across quails from the sea' (Num. 11:27)."

W. That recompense took place in the wilderness. Where do we find that it took place in the Land of Israel as well?

X. "Now the children of Reuben and the children of God had a very great multitude of cattle" (Num. 32:1).

Y. And where do we find that it will take place in the age to come?

Z. "And it will come to pass in that day that a man shall rear a young cow and two sheep" (Is. 7:21).

AA. [Said to him the Holy One, blessed be he,] "You stood by them: 'And he stood by them under the tree while they ate' (Gen. 18:8). By your life, I shall pay your descendants back for this: 'And the Lord went before them' (Ex. 13:21)."

BB. That recompense took place in the wilderness. Where do we find that it took place in the Land of Israel as well?

CC. "God stands in the congregation of God" (Ps. 82:1).

DD. And where do we find that it will take place in the age to come?

EE. "The breaker is gone up before them . . . and the Lord at the head of them" (Mic. 2:13).

The passage presents a sizable and beautifully disciplined construction, making one point again and again. Everything that the matriarchs and patriarchs did brought a reward to Abraham's descendants. The enormous emphasis on the way in which Abraham's deeds prefigured the history of Israel, both in the wilderness and in the Land, and, finally, in the age to come, provokes us to wonder who held that there were children of Abraham beside Israel. The answer, then, is clear. We note that there are five statements of the same proposition, each drawing upon a clause in the base verse. The extended statement, moreover, serves as a sustained introduction to the treatment of the individual clauses that follow, item by item. When we recall how Christian exegetes imparted to the Old Testament the lessons of the New, we realize that sages constructed an equally epochal and encompassing reading of Scripture. They now understand the meaning of what happened then, and, therefore, they also grasped from what had happened then the sense and direction of events of their own day. So history yielded patterns, and patterns proved points, and the points at hand indicated the direction of Israel. The substance of historical doctrine remains social in its focus. Sages present their theory of the meaning of history within a larger theory of the identification of Israel. Specifically, they see Israel as an extended family, children of one original ancestral couple, Abraham and Sarah. Whatever happens, then, constitutes family history, which is why the inheritance of merit from the ancestors protects their children even now, in the fourth century.

What, one asks, did sages find to validate their insistence that the biblical story, in Genesis, told the tale of Israel's coming salvation? Obviously, it is the merit of the ancestors that connects the living Israel to the lives of the patriarchs and matriarchs of old. The reciprocity of the process of interpreting Israel's history in light of the founders' lives, and the founders' lives through the later history of Israel, infuses the explanation of the debate over Sodom. Never far from the sages' minds is the entire sweep and scope of Israel's long history. Never distant from the lips of the patriarchs and matriarchs is the message of Israel's destiny. Israel's history takes place in eternity, so considerations of what comes first and what happens later—that is, priority and order—do not apply. The lives of the patriarchs and matriarchs therefore prefigure the life of Israel, as we have seen throughout. The entire history of Israel takes place in each of the great events of the lives of the patriarchs, as in No. 2 of the following composition:

LIII.X

2. A. ". . . and Abraham made a *great* feast on the day that Isaac was weaned" (Gen. 21:8):

   B. R. Judah said, "The *Great* One of the ages was there."

   C. R. Yudan in the name of R. Yose bar Haninah: " 'The king made a great feast' (Est. 2:18). The *Great* One of the ages was there. That is in line with this verse: 'For the Lord will again rejoice over you for good' (Deut. 30:9), in the days of Mordecai and Esther, 'As he rejoiced over your fathers' (Deut. 30:9), in the days of Abraham, Isaac, and Jacob."

We see that in this typological reading Israel's history takes place under the aspect of eternity. Events do not take place one time only. Events, to make a difference and so to matter, constitute paradigms and generate patterns. Salvation is always the same; its particularization is all that history records. So we can move in uninterrupted flow from Abraham to Esther to David. The lessons of history, therefore, do not derive from sequences of unique moments but from patterns that generate recurring and reliable rules. That is what I meant when I said that sages read the present in light of the past, rather than following the way of reading the past in light of the present. Given their present, they had little choice. No. 2 explicitly links Isaac's feast with the miracle in the time of Esther, and, should we miss the point, further links the two matters explicitly. The recurrent appeal to the events of the book of Esther should not be missed. The feast for Isaac prefigures the redemption of Israel. The reciprocal flow of merit found its counterpart in the two-way exchange of penalty as well. When Abraham erred, his descendants would pay the price. The merit of the patriarchs and matriarchs sustains, and the failures exact a cost, because the history of the nation and the ongoing life of the family form a single entity in history. That is a point we should not miss.

LIV:IV

1. A. "Abraham set seven ewe lambs of the flock apart" (Gen. 21:28):
   B. Said the Holy One, blessed be he, to him, "You have given him seven ewe lambs. By your life I shall postpone the joy of your descendants for seven generations.
   C. "You have given him seven ewe lambs. By your life matching them his descendants [the Philistines] will kill seven righteous men among your descendants, and these are they: Hofni, Phineas, Samson, Saul and his three sons.
   D. "You have given him seven ewe lambs. By your life, matching them the seven sanctuaries of your descendants will be destroyed, namely, the tent of meeting, the altars at Gilgal, Nob, Gibeon, Shiloh, and the two eternal houses of the sanctuary.
   E. "You have given him seven ewe lambs. [By your life, matching them] my ark will spend seven months in the fields of the Philistines."

No. 1 reverts to the theme of indignation at Abraham's coming to an agreement with Abimelech, forcefully imposing the theme of the later history of Israel upon the story at hand. A much more exemplary case derives from the binding of Isaac, the point from which the merit of Abraham flows. The aptness of the incident derives from its domestic character: relationship of mother, father, and only child. What Abraham and Isaac were prepared to sacrifice (and Sarah to lose) won for them and their descendants—as the story itself makes explicit—an ongoing treasury of merit. So Abraham's and Isaac's children through history will derive salvation from the original act of binding Isaac to the altar. The reference to the third day at Genesis 22:2 then invokes the entire panoply of Israel's history. The relevance of the composition emerges at the end. Prior to the concluding segment, the passage forms a kind of litany and falls into the category of a liturgy. Still, the recurrent hermeneutic which teaches that the stories of the patriarchs prefigure the history of Israel certainly makes its appearance. Because of the importance of the treatment of the story under discussion, we dwell on a protracted passage.

LVI:II

2. A.   Said R. Isaac, "Will this place [the Temple mount] ever be distant from its owner [God]? Never, for Scripture says, 'This is my resting place for ever; here I will dwell, for I have desired it' (Ps. 132:14).

    B.   "It will be when the one comes concerning whom it is written, 'Lowly and riding upon an ass'" (Zech. 1:9).

3. A.   "I and the lad will go thus far [and worship and come again to you]" (Gen. 22:5):

    B.   Said R. Joshua b. Levi, "[He said,] 'We shall go and see what will be the end of "thus."'" [Freedman, p. 492, n. 5: God had said, "Thus shall your seed be" (Gen. 15:5). So the sense is, "We will see how that can be fulfilled, now that I am to lose my son."]

4. A.   ". . . and we will worship [through an act of prostration] and come again to you" (Gen. 22:5):

    B.   He thereby told him that he would come back from Mount Moriah whole and in peace [for he said that *we* shall come back].

5. A.   Said R. Isaac, "And all was on account of the merit attained by the act of prostration.

    B.   "Abraham returned in peace from Mount Moriah only on account of the merit owing to the act of prostration: '. . . and we will worship [through an act of prostration] and come [then, on that account] again to you' (Gen. 22:5).

    C.   "The Israelites were redeemed only on account of the merit owing to the act of prostration: And the people believed . . . then they bowed their heads and prostrated themselves' (Ex. 4:31).

    D.   "The Torah was given only on account of the merit owing to the act of prostration: 'And worship' [prostrate themselves] you afar off' (Ex. 24:1).

    E.   "Hannah was remembered only on account of the merit owing to the act of prostration: 'And they worshipped before the Lord' (1 Sam. 1:19).

    F.   "The exiles will be brought back only on account of the merit owing to the act of prostration: 'And it shall come to pass in that day that a great horn shall be blown and they shall come that were lost . . . and that were dispersed . . . and they shall worship the Lord in the holy mountain at Jerusalem' (Is. 27:13).

G.   "The Temple was built only on account of the merit owing to the act of prostration: 'Exalt you the Lord our God and worship at his holy hill' (Ps. 99:9).

H.   "The dead will live only on account of the merit owing to the act of prostration: 'Come let us worship and bend the knee, let us kneel before the Lord our maker' (Ps. 95:6)."

No. 2 takes up the language of "seeing the place from afar," and by a play on the words, asks whether this place will ever be made far from its owner, that is, God. The answer is that it will not. No. 3 draws a lesson from the use of "thus" in the cited verses. The sizable construction at No. 4 makes a simple point, to which our base verse provides its modest contribution. But its polemic is hardly simple. The entire history of Israel flows from its acts of worship ("prostration") and is unified by a single law. Every sort of advantage Israel has ever gained came about through worship. Hence what is besought, in the elegant survey, is the law of history. The Scripture then supplies those facts from which the governing law is derived.

LVI:IX

1. A.   "And Abraham lifted up his eyes and looked, and behold, behind him was a ram, [caught in a thicket by his horns. And Abraham went and took the ram and offered it up as a burnt offering instead of his son]" (Gen. 22:13):

    B.   What is the meaning of the word for "behind"?

    C.   Said R. Yudan, " 'Behind' in the sense of 'after,' that is, after all that happens, Israel nonetheless will be embroiled in transgressions and perplexed by sorrows. But in the end, they will be redeemed by the horns of a ram: 'And the Lord will blow the horn' (Zech. 9:14)."

    C.   Said R. Judah bar Simon, " 'After' all generations Israel nonetheless will be embroiled in transgressions and perplexed by sorrows. But in the end, they will be redeemed by the horns of a ram: 'And the Lord God will blow the horn' (Zech. 9:14)."

    D.   Said R. Hinena bar Isaac, "All through the days of the year Israelites are embroiled in transgressions and perplexed by sorrows. But on the New Year they take the ram's horn and sound it, so in the end, they will be redeemed by the horns of a ram: 'And the Lord God will blow the horn' (Zech. 9:14)."

    E.   R. Abba bar R. Pappi, R. Joshua of Siknin in the name of R. Levi: "Since our father, Abraham, saw the ram get himself out of one thicket only to be trapped in another, the Holy One, blessed be he, said to him, 'So your descendants will be entangled in one kingdom after another, struggling from Babylonia to Media, from Media to Greece, from Greece to Edom. But in the end, they will be redeemed by the horns of a ram: 'And the Lord God will blow the horn . . . the Lord of Hosts will defend them' (Zech. 9:14–5).

2. A.   ". . . And Abraham went and took the ram and offered it up as a burnt offering instead of his son]" (Gen. 22:13):

    B.   R. Yudan in the name of R. Benaiah: "He said before him, 'Lord of all ages, regard the blood of this ram as though it were the blood of Isaac, my son, its innards as though they were the innards of Isaac my son.'"

    D.   R. Phineas in the name of R. Benaiah: "He said before him, 'Lord of all ages, regard it as though I had offered up my son, Isaac, first, and afterward had offered up the ram in his place.'"

For sages it is quite natural to link the life of the private person, affected by transgression, and the history of the nation, troubled by its wandering among the kingdoms. For the nation is a family. From the perspective of the Land of Israel, the issue is not exile but the rule of foreigners. In both cases the power of the ram's horn to redeem the individual and the nation finds its origin in the binding of Isaac. The exegetical thrust, linking the lives of the patriarchs to the life of the nation, thus brings the narrative back to the paradigm of individual being, so from patriarch to nation to person. The path leads in both directions, of course, in a fluid movement of meaning. No. 2 works on the language of "instead," a technical term in the cult, and so links the binding of Isaac to the Temple cult.

While Abraham founded Israel, Isaac and Jacob carried forth the birthright and the blessing. This they did through the process of selection, ending in the assignment of the birthright to Jacob alone. The lives of all three patriarchs flowed together, each being identified with the other as a single long life. This immediately produces the proposition that the historical life of Israel, the nation, continued the individual lives of the patriarchs. Once more we see that the theory of who Israel is rested on genealogy: Israel is one extended family, all being children of the same fathers and mothers, the patriarchs and matriarchs of Genesis. This theory of Israelite society, and of the Jewish people in the time of the sages of Genesis Rabbah, we note once again, made of the people a family, and of genealogy a kind of ecclesiology. The importance of that proposition in countering the Christian claim to be a new Israel cannot escape notice, as we shall see in chapter 4. Israel, sages maintained, is Israel after the flesh, and that in a most literal sense. But the basic claim, for its part, depended upon the facts of Scripture, not upon the logical requirements of theological dispute. And, we see abundantly, that claim constituted not merely a social theory of the classification of Israel—a family, not a nation like other nations—but also the foundations of a historical theory of the past, present, and future of Israel.

Sages found a place for Rome in Israel's history only by assigning to Rome a place in the family. Their larger theory of the social identity of Israel left them no choice. But it also permitted them to assign to Rome an appropriately significant place in world history, while preserving for Israel the climactic role. Israel and Rome—these two contend for the world. Still, Isaac plays his part in the matter. Rome does have a legitimate claim, and that claim demands recognition—an amazing, if grudging, concession on the part of sages that Christian Rome at least is Esau.

LXVII:IV

1. A. When Esau heard the words of his father, he cried out with an exceedingly great and bitter cry [and said to his father, 'Bless me, even me also, O my father!']" (Gen. 27:34):
    B. Said R. Hanina, "Whoever says that the Holy One, blessed be he, is lax, may his intestines become lax. While he is patient, he does collect what is coming to you.
    C. "Jacob made Esau cry out one cry, and where was he penalized? It was in the castle of Shushan: 'And he cried with a loud and bitter cry' (Est. 4:1)."
2. A. "But he said, 'Your brother came with guile and he has taken away your blessing'" (Gen. 33:35):
    B. R. Yohanan said, "[He came] with the wisdom of his knowledge of the Torah."

So Rome really is Israel's brother. No pagan empire ever enjoyed an equivalent place; no pagan era ever found identification with an event in Israel's family history. The passage—and numerous others like it, which we shall see in chapter 4—presents a stunning concession and an astounding claim. The history of the two brothers forms a set of counterpoints, the rise of one standing for the decline of the other. I cannot imagine a more powerful claim for Israel: the ultimate end, Israel's final glory, will permanently mark the subjugation of Esau. Israel then will follow, the fifth and final monarchy. The point of No. 1 is to link the present passage to the history of Israel's redemption later on. In this case, however, the matter concerns Israel's paying recompense for causing anguish to Esau. No. 2 introduces Jacob's knowledge of Torah in place of Esau's view of Jacob as full of guile.

Apart from the struggle with Esau, Jacob still serves as a model and paradigm of Israel's history. For example, his dream of the ladder to heaven encompassed all of Israel's history, with stress not on Esau but on Sinai.

LXVIII:XII

3. B. " 'That there was a ladder:' refers to the ramp to the altar.

   C. " '. . . set up on the earth:' that is the altar, 'An altar of dirt you will make for me' (Ex. 20:24).

   D. " '. . . and the top of it reached to heaven:' these are the offerings, for their fragrance goes up to heaven.

   E. " '. . . and behold, the angels of God:' these are the high priests.

   F. " '. . . were ascending and descending on it:' for they go up and go down on the ramp.

   G. " 'And behold, the Lord stood above it:' 'I saw the Lord standing by the altar' (Amos 9:1)."

4. A. Rabbis interpreted the matter to prefigure Sinai: " 'And he dreamed:

   B. " '. . . that there was a ladder:' this refers to Sinai.

   C. " '. . . set up on the earth:' 'And they stood at the lower part of the mountain' (Ex. 19:17).

   D. " '. . . and the top of it reached to heaven:' 'And the mountain burned with fire into the hearts of heaven' (Deut. 4:11).

   E. " '. . . and behold, the angels of God:' these are Moses and Aaron.

   F. " '. . . were ascending:' 'And Moses went up to God' (Ex. 19:3).

   G. " '. . . and descending on it:' "And Moses went down from the mount' (Ex. 19:14).

   F. " '. . . And behold, the Lord stood above it:' 'And the Lord came down upon Mount Sinai' (Ex. 19:20)."

No. 3 reads the dream in terms of the Temple cult, No. 4 in terms of the revelation of the Torah at Sinai, and No. 5 has the dream refer to the patriarchs.

None of these modes of reading the book of Genesis presents surprises. Since both Jacob and Moses explicitly spoke of the sons of Jacob as paradigms of history, the sages understood the text precisely as the Torah itself told them to understand it. That is, the sages simply took seriously and at face value the facts in hand, as any scientist or philosopher finds facts and reflects upon their meaning and the implications and laws deriving from them. So the sages' mode of reading derived from an entirely inductive and scientific, philosophical mode of thought. The laws of history begin with the principle that the merit of the founders sustains the children to come. The model for the transaction in merit—which underlines and explains the theory of genealogy as the foundation of Israel's social entity—comes to expression in the life of Joseph.

The typology proves diverse, since Joseph, as much as Abraham, Isaac, and Jacob, provides a model for the future; reference to what Joseph did guides us to the later history of Israel. So the history of Israel here is compared to the life of Joseph:

LXXXVII:VI

1. A. "And although she spoke to Joseph [day after day, he would not lis-
       ten to her, to lie with her or to be with her. But one day, when he
       went into the house to do his work and none of the men of the house
       was there in the house, she caught him by his garment, saying, 'Lie
       with me.' But he left his garment in her hand and fled and got out of
       the house]" (Gen. 39:10–13):

   B. R. Yudan in the name of R. Benjamin bar Levi: "As to the sons of
       Levi, the trials affecting them were the same, and the greatness that
       they achieved was the same.

   C. ". . . the trials affecting them were the same: 'And although she
       spoke to Joseph [day after day.' 'Now it came to pass, when they
       spoke to him day by day' (Est. 3:4). [Mordecai, descended from
       Benjamin, was nagged every day.] 'He would not listen to her.' 'And
       he did not listen to them' (Est. 3:4).

   D. ". . . and the greatness that they achieved was the same: 'And Pha-
       raoh took off his signet ring from his hand and put it upon Joseph's
       hand' (Gen. 41:42). 'And the king took off his ring, which he had
       taken from Haman and gave it to Mordecai' (Est. 8:2).

   E. " 'And arrayed him in fine linen clothing and put a gold chain about
       his neck' (Gen. 41:42). 'And Mordecai went forth from the pres-
       ence of the king in royal apparel of blue and white, and with a great
       crown of gold and with a robe of fine linen and purple' (Est. 8:15).

   F. " 'And he made Joseph ride in the second chariot which he had'
       (Gen. 41:43). 'And cause Mordecai to ride on horseback through
       the street of the city' (Est. 6:9).

   G. " 'And they cried before him, Abrech' (Gen. 41:43). 'And pro-
       claimed before Mordecai, "Thus shall it be done to the man" ' (Est.
       6:11)."

The parallel drawn between Joseph and Benjamin, that is, Mordecai, per-
mits the exegete to draw a parallel between the life of Joseph and the history
of Israel. No. 2 expands on the base verse, and No. 3 presents an argument in
favor of its authenticity, at the same time linking the present story to the two
preceding ones. God of course governed Joseph's destiny, detail by detail, and
as this becomes clear, the Jewish reader concludes that God's providence and
benevolence continue to dictate what is to happen to Israel, even though that
fact does not always prove self-evident.

   Sages had also to account for the present condition of Israel, not only make
promises about future redemption. An established explanation held Israel responsible for its fate. When the nation did God's will, it enjoyed security, and
when it violated God's will, it suffered. That basic theological conviction, familiar from ancient times, translated into quite specific statements on what

sorts of sins had caused Israel to suffer in later times. The tribes would suffer punishment because of the misdeeds of their ancestors, a point we noted with reference to Abraham as well.

LXXXIV:XX

1. A. "Then Jacob tore his garments and put sackcloth upon his loins and mourned for his son many days" (Gen. 37:34):
   B. R. Phineas in the name of R. Hoshaiah: "The tribal fathers caused their father to tear his garments, and where were they paid back? In Egypt: 'And they tore their clothes' (Gen. 44:13).
   C. "Joseph caused the tribal fathers to tear their clothes. He was paid back in the case of the son of his son: 'And Joshua tore his clothes' (Josh. 7:6).
   D. "Benjamin caused the tribal fathers to tear their clothes. He was paid back in Shushan, the capital: 'Mordecai tore his clothes' (Est. 4:1).
   E. "Manasseh caused the tribal fathers to tear their clothes. He was paid back by having his inheritance divided into half, half on the other side of the Jordan, and half in the land of Canaan."
2. A. ". . . and put sackcloth upon his loins:"
   B. Said R. Aibu, "Because Jacob took hold of sackcloth, therefore sackcloth did not leave him or his children to the end of all generations:
   C. "Ahab: 'And he put sackcloth on his flesh and fasted' (1 Kgs. 21:27).
   D. "Joram: 'And the people looked, and behold, he had sackcloth within upon his flesh' (2 Kgs. 6:30).
   E. "Mordecai: 'And he put sackcloth and ashes' (Est. 4:1)."

Once more, what the brothers did, their descendants had to pay for. The premise of this entire account comes to explicit statement in the treatment of Jacob's blessing of the tribal ancestors. Here he reviews the entire future history of Israel.

XCVIII:II

7. A. "Then Jacob called his sons and said, 'Gather yourselves together, that I may tell you what shall befall you in days to come:"
   B. R. Simon said, "He showed them the fall of Gog, in line with this usage: 'It shall be in the end of days . . . when I shall be sanctified through you, O Gog' (Ez. 38:15). 'Behold, it shall come upon Edom' (Is. 34:5)."
   C. R. Judah said, "He showed them the building of the house of the sanctuary: 'And it shall come to pass in the end of days that the mountain of the Lord's house shall be established' (Is. 2:2)."

D. Rabbis say, "He came to reveal the time of the end to them, but it was hidden from him."

XCIX:II

1. A. "For the Lord God will do nothing unless he reveals his secret to his servants the prophets" (Amos 3:7).

   B. Jacob linked two of his sons, corresponding to two of the monarchies, and Moses linked two of the tribes, corresponding to two of the monarchies.

   C. Judah corresponds to the kingdom of Babylonia, for this is compared to a lion and that is compared to a lion. This is compared to a lion: "Judah is a lion's whelp" (Gen. 49:9), and so too Babylonia: "The first was like a lion" (Dan. 7:4).

   D. Then by the hand of which of the tribes will the kingdom of Babylonia fall? It will be by the hand of Daniel, who comes from the tribe of Judah.

   E. Benjamin corresponds to the kingdom of Media, for this is compared to a wolf and that is compared to a wolf. This is compared to a wolf: "Benjamin is a ravenous wolf, [in the morning devouring the prey, and at evening dividing the spoil.]" And that is compared to a wolf: "And behold, another beast, a second, like a wolf" (Dan. 7:5).

   H. [Reverting to E:] Then by the hand of which of the tribes will the kingdom of Media fall? It will be by the hand of Mordecai, who comes from the tribe of Benjamin.

   I. Levi corresponds to the kingdom of Greece. This is the third tribe in order, and that is the third kingdom in order. This is written with a word that is made up of three letters, and that is written with a word which consists of three letters. This one sounds the horn and that one sounds the horn, this one wears turbans and that one wears helmets, this one wears pants and that one wears knee-cuts.

   J. To be sure, this one is very populous, while that one is few in numbers. But the many came and fell into the hand of the few.

   K. On account of merit deriving from what source did this take place? It is on account of the blessing that Moses bestowed: "Smiter through the loins of them that rise up against him" (Deut. 33:11).

   L. Then by the hand of which of the tribes will the kingdom of Greece fall? It will be by the hand of sons of the Hasmoneans, who come from the tribe of Levi.

   M. Joseph corresponds to the kingdom of Edom [Rome], for this one has horns and that one has horns. This one has horns: "His firstling bullock, majesty is his, and his horns are the horns of the wild ox" (Deut. 33:17). And that one has horns: "And concerning the ten horns that were on its head" (Dan. 7:20). This one kept away from fornication while that one cleaved to fornication. This one paid respect for the honor owing to his father, while that one despised the honor owing to his father. Concerning this one it is written, "For I fear God" (Gen. 42:18), while in regard to that one it is written, "And he did not fear God" (Deut. 25:18). [So the correspondence in part is one of opposites.]

N. Then by the hand of which of the tribes will the kingdom of Edom fall? It will be by the hand of the anointed for war, who comes from the tribe of Joseph.

O. R. Phineas in the name of R. Samuel b. Nahman: "There is a tradition that Esau will fall only by the hand of the sons of Rachel: 'Surely the least of the flock shall drag them away' (Jer. 49:20). Why the least? Because they are the youngest of the tribes."

We see the ultimate typology: each pagan empire finds representation among the brothers. This impressive theory of Israel's history finds a place here only because of E. Yet the larger relevance—Jacob's predictions of the future—justifies including the composition. What, then, tells sages how to identify the important and avoid the trivial? The answer derives from the fundamental theological conviction that gives life to their search of Scripture. It is that the task of Israel is to hope, and the message of Genesis—there for the sages to uncover and make explicit—is always to hope.

By way of conclusion, if I may state what I conceive to be the sages' fundamental response to the crisis of the day: for a Jew it is a sin to despair. This I think defines the iron law of meaning, telling sages what matters and what does not, guiding their hands to take up those verses that permit expression of hope—that above all. Given the definitive event of their day—the conversion of the great empire of Rome to Christianity—the task of hope proved not an easy assignment.

XCVIII:XIV

4. A. "I hope for your salvation, O Lord" (Gen. 49:18):

    B. Said R. Isaac, "All things depend on hope, suffering depends on hope, the sanctification of God's name depends on hope, the merit attained by the fathers depends on hope, the lust for the age to come depends on hope.

    C. "That is in line with this verse: 'Yes, in the way of your judgments, O Lord, we have hoped for you, to your name, and to your memorial, is the desire of our soul' (Is. 26:8). 'The way of your judgments refers to suffering.

    D. "'. . . to your name:' this refers to the sanctification of the divine name.

E. " '. . . and to your memorial:' this refers to the merit of the fathers.

F. " '. . . is the desire of our soul:' this refers to the lust for the age to come.

G. "Grace depends on hope: 'O Lord, be gracious to us, we have hoped for you' (Is. 33:2).

H. "Forgiveness depends on hope: 'For with you is forgiveness' (Ps. 133:4), then: 'I hope for the Lord' (Ps. 130:5)."

The passage makes explicit the critical importance of hope in the salvific process, and further links the exclamation to the setting in which it occurs. Keeping the faith, sustaining hope—these were all Israel could do. The Jews could control little more than their own attitudes. The world now had passed into the hands of their rivals, their siblings, sharing Scripture, sharing a claim to be "Israel," sharing the same view of history, sharing the same expectation of the Messiah's coming. The typological discourse yields this final lesson: Israel's task is to hope. Under the conditions of the age of Constantine, to be sure, the task proved formidable.

This seems to me to typify the strength of the exegesis at hand, with its twin powers to link all details to a tight narrative and to link the narrative to the history of Israel. What sense, then, did sages in Genesis Rabbah make of the history of Israel? Israel is the extended family of Abraham, Isaac, and Jacob. Whatever happens now works out events in the life of the family long ago. The redemption in the past prefigures what is to come. The merit that protects Israel in the present derives from the heritage of the past. So history is one and seamless, as the life of a family goes on through time. Do people wonder, with the triumph of Christianity in politics, what is to become of Israel? In rereading the story of Israel's beginnings, sifting and resifting the events in the life of the patriarchs and matriarchs, sages found the answer to the question. What will happen is what has happened. History recapitulates the life of the family. And to a family, the politics of empire makes slight difference. Israel therefore will endure in hope.

3

The Talmud of the Land
of Israel and the Messiah:
Christian Triumph, Judaic Response

The Messianic Crisis

Every page of Eusebius's writing bears the message that the conversion of Constantine proves the Christhood of Jesus: his messianic standing. History— the affairs of nations and monarchs—yields laws of society, proves God's will, so that matters now speak for themselves. For Judaism the dramatic shift in the fortunes of the competing biblical faith raised a simple and unpleasant possibility: perhaps Israel had been wrong after all. Since the Jews as a whole, and sages among them, anticipated the coming of the Messiah promised by the prophets, the issue could be fairly joined. If history proves propositions, as the prophets and apocalyptic visionaries had maintained, then how could Jews deny the Christians' claim that the conversion of the emperor, then of the empire, demonstrated the true state of affairs in heaven as much as on earth? And as large numbers of pagans as well as Jews accepted the imperial faith, Christian theologians had also to restate the messianic facts.

Specifically, to former pagans they had to establish the fact that one could worship only Jesus as Christ, no other. To Jews newly entered into the Church, as well as to converts from pagan religions, there was another issue. Since the Church invoked the Israelite Scriptures as warrant for Jesus' messiahship, the standing and status of other statements in those same Scriptures required attention. The messiahship of Jesus—so most of the Church maintained— rendered void the scriptural rules, so that Golgotha did not mark a mere way- station on the road to Sinai. If Jesus was Christ, then Sinai (so to speak) had come to Golgotha, and converts to Christianity were not to adopt the Old Tes- tament rules and regulations, as the Jews kept them, nor were Jewish converts to maintain the old rites. So for the Christian theologians the messianic crisis demanded a clear statement of precisely what Christ demanded—and did not demand—from Christians. Chrysostom, who stands for Christianity in the messianic issue, typifies the Christian theologians' concern that converts not proceed to the synagogue or retain connections with it. For the burden of his case was that, since Christ had now been proved Messiah, Christians no longer could associate themselves with the synagogue. Judaism had lost, Christianity had won, and people had to choose the one and give up the other.

At stake for Chrysostom, whose sermons on Judaism, preached in 386–87, provide for our purpose the statement of Christianity on the Messianic issue, was Christians' participation in synagogue rites and Judaic practices. He invoked the Jews' failure in the fiasco of the proposed rebuilding of the Temple in Jerusalem only a quarter of a century earlier. He drew upon the failure of that project to demonstrate that Judaic rites no longer held any power. He further cited that incident to prove that Israel's salvation lay wholly in the past, in the time of the return to Zion, and never in the future. So the happenings of the day demonstrated proofs of the faith, just as we realized in chapter 2. The struggle between sages and theologians concerned the meaning of important contemporary happenings, and the same happenings, read in light of the same Scripture, provoked discussion of the same issues: a confrontation.

The messianic crisis confronting the Christian theologians hardly matches that facing the Judaic sages. The one dealt with problems of the triumph, the other with despair; the one had to interpret a new day, the other to explain disaster. Scripture explicitly promised that Israel would receive salvation from God's anointed Messiah at the end of time. The teleology of Israelite faith, in the biblical account, focused upon eschatology, and, within eschatology, on the salvific, therefore the messianic, dimension. On the other hand, the Mishnah had for its part taken up a view of its own on the issue of teleology, presenting an ahistorical and essentially nonmessianic teleology. Sages' response to the messianic crisis had to mediate two distinct and, I think, contradictory positions. Sages explained what the messianic hope now entailed, and how to identify the Messiah, who, of course, would be a sage. They further encompassed the messianic issue within their larger historical theory. So we cannot address the question as if the Christians had defined the issue. True, to Israel all they had to say was, "Why not believe in Christ?" But sages responded with a far-reaching doctrine of their own, deeming the question, in its Christian formulation, trivial.

But the issue confronting both Judaic sages and Christian theologians was one and the same: precisely what difference the Messiah makes. To state matters as they would be worked out by both parties: In the light of the events of the day what do I have to do because the Messiah has come (Christian) or because I want the Messiah to come (Judaic)? That question encompasses two sides of a single issue. On the issue of the messiahship of Jesus all other matters depended. It follows that one party believed precisely the opposite of the other on an issue identically defined by both. For Christians, the sole issue—belief or unbelief—carried a clear implication for the audience subject to address. When debate would go forward, it would center upon the wavering of Christians and the unbelief of Jews. Our exemplary figure, Chrysostom, framed matters in those terms, of course drawing upon the events of his own day for ample instantiation of the matter. The Christian formulation thus focused for Chrysostom all matters on the vindication of Jesus as Christ. When Christians found attractive aspects of Judaic rite and belief, the Christian theologians invoked the fundamental issue: Is Jesus the Christ? If so, then Judaism falls. If not, then Christianity falls. No question, therefore, drew the two sets of intellectuals into more direct conflict; none bore such immediate and fundamental consequences. When, therefore, Christians in the Church of Antioch gave evidence of wishing to join in Judaic worship and to practice Judaic rites, with reference to the festivals and the Sabbath, John Chrysostom raised the question of whether Judaic rites yet mattered, and whether Jesus is Christ. So we turn to his framing of matters in our inquiry into the context and circumstances for the Judaic sages' thought on the same topic.

Chrysostom: Jewish Unbelief, Christian Wavering

John "of the golden tongue," Chrysostom, takes pride of place in the confrontation between Judaism, as represented in sages' documents, and Christianity, as represented by substantial theologians, because he addressed the issues head-on. His principal point was that Christians cannot believe in Christ and also worship in synagogues and observe Judaic rites. Judaism is over, offering no salvation, as the fiasco of the rebuilding of the Temple had just proved. In stressing these two points, Chrysostom addressed precisely the issues of the identity of the Messiah and the conditions of his coming—the issues that, as we shall see, sages raised in the Talmud of the Land of Israel. Preacher in Antioch, Chrysostom, who was born in 347 and died in 407, in a set of sermons preached in 386–87 addressed the issue of Judaism by accusing Christians of backsliding. Not concurring on the honorable title "golden-mouthed," some, represented by Ruether, would call John foul-mouthed: "The sermons of John Chrysostom are easily the most violent and tasteless of the anti-Judaic literature of the period" (Ruether 1979, 173). But our point of interest is other than the tradition of anti-Judaism of the fourth-century Church, even though that tradition long outlived its original circumstances. What is important to us, as I have already made clear, is how Christian theologians and Judaic sages confronted the issue of who the Messiah is, whether Jesus or someone else, when he will come (Judaism), or why he will come again (Christianity)—in all, the shape of the Messiah-theme in the discourse of the age of Constantine. The testimony of Chrysostom comes right to the point, because he frames the issue as both sides worked it out. For him the principal issue in Judaic "unbelief" and Christian "backsliding" was whether or not Jesus was Christ. If he was, then the Christians should remain firm in that faith, and the Jews should accept it. If not, then not. The issue for Chrysostom carried concrete and immediate consequences: building solid and permanent foundations for the Christian governance. Christianity by the end of the century hardly enjoyed security as the religion of the empire. Julian called

into doubt the future of the Church in the state, and Judaism remained a vital
faith and force. For political reasons, therefore, the issue proved urgent to
both Christianity and Judaism. For the one, at stake was the future of a Church
resting on the messiahship of Christ; for the other, the future of the holy
people awaiting the Messiah in the future.

But the specific issue framed by Chrysostom was his own—and that of the
Church. For while the messianic question confronted both sides, each framed
the matter in terms of its own situation. Chrysostom's target was "Judaizing"
Christians who attended synagogue worship and observed Judaic rites. Judaism exercised great attraction to Christians who had in mind to observe Jewish festivals. They attended synagogue worship, resorted to Jewish courts, lis-
tened to the reading of the Torah in the synagogue on the Sabbath, and on the
next day came to join in the Eucharist. At issue for John was not "anti-
Semitism," a wholly anachronistic category. What troubled John was the state
of Christian belief. Specifically, John regarded Christian participation in Jewish worship and customs as "Judaizing," backsliding; that is, an act of dis-
belief. The backsliders do not believe that Jesus is Christ, and that is why they
keep the law, that is, the Torah. Clearly at the heart of the matter was the
Messiahship of Jesus. All else depended on that question. There was a common and conventional program of rhetoric: the Jews are guilty of "apostasy,
faithlessness, rejection of God, and hardheartedness." Wilken summarizes
the theological matter.

> Embedded in these passages is to be found a theological argument about the
> status of the Jews after the death of Christ and the destruction of the temple at Jeru-
> salem. Since Christians claimed to be the inheritors of the ancient Jewish tradition,
> the destruction of the temple was taken to be a sign that Jewish law had lost its
> legitimacy. Yet, three hundred years after the destruction of the temple and the loss
> of Jerusalem, the Jews were still observing the ancient laws.

Jesus had predicted the destruction of the Temple. Not a few years back, the
apostate emperor and the Jews had tried to rebuild it. They did not succeed.
That proves that the Temple no longer serves to legitimate Jewish religion. All
of these commonplaces point to a single issue: was, and is, Jesus the Christ?
That is why Chrysostom plays a part in our invention of a common program
of thought for both Judaic and Christian writers in Constantine's age. Since,
as Wilken says, "Much of what John says . . . is commonplace," Chrysostom
admirably serves our purpose as an interesting and representative figure on the
issue of the Messiah, his importance and identity (Wilken 1983, 32–33, 66–
67, 76, 132, xvi).[1]

Chrysostom's eight sermons, *Adversus Judaeos,* given in Antioch probably
in 386 and 387, dealt with Christians soft on Judaism. As a set, the sermons
addressed Christians who observe and defend Jewish rites, keep the Passover,

---

1. On "anti-Semitism," compare Gager: "The very violence of Chrysostom's language dem-
onstrates the potential for a linkage between anti-Jewish beliefs and anti-Semitic feelings"
(1983).

and, in general treat the law of Judaism as valid. The response to these views drew upon the exile of the Jews, the destruction of the Temple as Jesus had predicted, and, it must follow, the divinity of Jesus. Judaism as such was not the issue; the audience comprised backsliding Christians. The preacher referred to festivals of the autumn season, the New Year, Day of Atonement, and Tabernacles, and he evidently did not wish Christians to keep those festivals, or to observe Easter coincident with Passover. What concerned him transcended attendance on Judaic festivals and fasts. Christians were keeping the Sabbath, attending synagogue worship, and did not know the difference between Christian and Judaic worship. Chrysostom claimed that Jews' supposed magical power attracted Christians, who went to synagogues for healing. But the main thrust concerned Christ. Jews do not understand the Hebrew Scriptures. "The Old Testament was shrouded in a veil, which was lifted only with the coming of Christ," and only by reading the Scriptures in light of Christ can anyone understand them.

For their part the Jews did not understand their own Scripture because they did not grasp "the true meaning of the prophecies, because they did not understand the significance of the 'times' the prophets were discussing. They stubbornly refused to apply texts to Christ." Because they had rejected and then murdered Christ, the Jews were "godless and . . . their souls were inhabited by demons." God rejected the worship of Jews, both in the Temple in Jerusalem and in synagogues. God rejected the Jews and Judaism, for the same reason. All of this was because the Jews rejected Christ (Grissom 1978, 191). Because the Jews rejected the Messiah, gentiles took their place. Because of the same error, the Jews were punished with the destruction of Jerusalem and the Temple, which just now had not been rebuilt even though the emperor had planned to restore it. The Jewish law was no longer valid: "Just as the Old Testament was a shadow of the reality fulfilled in the New Testament, so the Jewish law was valid only as a guide to Christ." "Since Christ had come, continuing to observe the law was like going back into the desert from the Promised Land." The present power of the Church, moreover, proved that Christ was the Messiah and that the Church was favored by God. So the issue of Jesus's Messiahship enjoyed priority over all others. The dialogue, such as it was, had therefore to focus on that question alone; nothing else counted. For Chrysostom, the advent of Christ, his death and resurrection, had provided the means of grace for all who believed. The coming of Christ rendered all other religions and religious notions, including Judaism, not only unnecessary but impotent and illegitimate. Grissom makes the matter plain: "Using a Christological exegesis of the Old Testament as well as evidence taken from the New Testament, Chrysostom tried to prove that Jesus was the Messiah predicted by the prophets and that, because of his death, the Jews had been rejected by God and the Gentiles called in their place. Using Old Testament texts, he also argued that the dispersion of the Jews would never end, that the Temple would never be rebuilt, and that no Jewish worship could properly be conducted outside Jerusalem (Grissom 1978, 3).

What is critical to my claim that we deal with a genuine debate on the same issues in the same terms is the argument that the destruction of the Temple and the fiasco of Julian's plan discredit Judaism. In Chrysostom's case the relationship of the destruction of Jerusalem and the divinity of Jesus took pride of place. The longest homily and the most theological-historical, the fifth, is summarized by Wilken as follows:

> The greatest proof that Christ is truly God is that he "predicted the temple would be destroyed, that Jerusalem would be captured, and that the city would no longer be the city of the Jews as it had been in the past." If only ten, twenty, or fifty years had passed since the destruction of the temple, one might understand doubts about Jesus' prophecy, but over three centuries have passed and there is not "a shadow of the change for which you are waiting." . . . If the Jews had never attempted to rebuild the temple during this time, one might say that they could do so only if they made the effort. But the course of events shows the reverse, for the Jews have attempted to rebuild the temple, not once, but three times, and were unsuccessful in every effort. . . . The failure of Julian's effort to rebuilt the temple in Jerusalem, then, is proof that Christ was not an ordinary man among men, but the divine son of God. His word was more powerful than the feeble efforts of men, for by his word alone he defeated the emperor Julian and the "whole Jewish people" . . . The prophecy of Christ is proven true by the historical "facts." . . . the fulfillment of the ancient prophecies and the continued existence of the Church is evidence of the power and divinity of Christ (1983, 155–58)

And from this all the rest followed. So Wilken concludes, "by keeping the Law, by celebrating Jewish festivals, by seeking out Jewish magicians, the Judaizers proclaimed that Judaism was spiritually more potent than Christianity. What greater proof of the truth of Judaism than for the followers of Christ to observe Jewish law?" For Chrysostom, at stake was not Judaism but Christianity: "I ask you to rescue your brothers, to set them free from this error and to bring them back to the truth. There is no benefit in listening to me unless the example of your deeds match my words. What I said was not for your sakes but for the sake of those who are sick. I want them to learn these facts from you and to free themselves from their wicked association with the Jews" (1983, 158, 160).

The upshot is that, as Chrysostom framed the issue, everything depended upon the Messiahship of Jesus, on the one side, and the confirmation of that Messiahship by the events of the age—the power of the Church, the humiliation of the Jerusalem temple—on the other. Everything depended on the Temple, restored or in permanent ruin. Jesus had said no stone would rest another, and none did. Julian had tried to rebuild the Temple and had failed. Chrysostom pointed to the Jews' exile as proof of their defeat: "It is illegitimate to keep their former way of life outside of Jerusalem . . . for the city of Jerusalem is the keystone that supports the Jewish rite" (in Wilken 1983, 149). The argument recurs throughout the homilies on the Judaizers and forms the centerpiece. No wonder then that sages would join the rebuilding of the Temple to the future coming of the Messiah. So the issue framed by Eusebius carried forward in its logical and cogent way. The sages' response transcended the mere affirmation of the messianic hope. They outlined how to recognize the Messiah and what Israel must do to become worthy of his coming.

The Talmud of the Land of Israel and Israel's Messianic Crisis

In my view the Christian challenge is what stimulated sages' thought to focus upon the messiah theme. The Mishnaic system had come to full expression without an elaborated doctrine of the Messiah, or even an eschatological theory of the purpose and goal of matters. The Mishnah had put forth (in tractate Avot) a teleology without any eschatological dimension. By the closing of the Talmud of the Land of Israel, in contrast, the purpose and end of everything centered upon the coming of the Messiah, in sages' terms and definition, to be sure. That is surprising in light of the character of the Mishnah's system, to which the Talmud of the Land of Israel attached itself as a commentary. In order to understand sages' development of the Messiah theme in the Talmud of the Land of Israel, therefore, we have to backtrack and consider how the theme had made its appearance in the Mishnah. Only in comparison to its earlier expression and use, therefore, does the Talmud's formulation of the matter enter the proper context for interpretation. Critical issues of teleology had been worked out through messianic eschatology in other, earlier Judaic systems. Later ones as well would invoke the Messiah theme. These systems, including the Christian one, of course, resorted to the myth of the Messiah as savior and redeemer of Israel, a supernatural figure engaged in political-historical tasks as king of the Jews, even a God-man facing the crucial historical questions of Israel's life and then resolving them—Christ as king of the world, of the ages, even of death itself.

In the Mishnah, ca. A.D. 200, we look in vain for a doctrine of the Messiah. There "messiah" serves as a taxonomic indicator, e.g., distinguishing one type of priest or general from some other. There is no doctrine of the Messiah, coming at the end of time; in the Mishnah's system, matters focus on other issues entirely. Although the figure of a Messiah does appear, when the framers of the Mishnah spoke of "the Messiah," they meant a high priest designated and consecrated to office in a certain way, and not in some other way. The reference to "days of the Messiah" constitutes a conventional division of history at the end of time but before the ultimate end. But that category of time plays no consequential role in the teleological framework established within the Mishnah. Accordingly, the Mishnah's framers constructed a system of Judaism in which the entire teleological dimension reached full exposure while hardly invoking the person or functions of a messianic figure of any kind. Perhaps in the aftermath of Bar Kokhba's debacle, silence on the subject served to express a clarion judgment. I am inclined to think so. But, for the purpose of our inquiry, the main thing is a simple fact, namely, that salvation comes through sanctification. The salvific figure, then, becomes an instrument of consecration and so fits into an ahistorical system quite different from the one built around the Messiah.

In the Talmud of the Land of Israel, ca. A.D. 400, we find a fully exposed doctrine not only of a Messiah but *the* Messiah: who he is, how we will know him, what we must do to bring him. It follows that the Talmud of the Land of Israel presents clear evidence that the Messiah myth had become the larger Torah myth that characterized Judaism in its later formative literature. A clear effort to identify the person of the Messiah and to confront the claim that a specific, named individual had been, or would be, the Messiah—these come to the fore. This means that the issue had reached the center of lively discourse at least in some rabbinic circles. Of course the disposition of the issue proves distinctive to sages: the Messiah will be a sage, the Messiah will come when Israel has attained that condition of sanctification, marked also by profound humility and complete acceptance of God's will, that signify sanctification.

These two conditions say the same thing twice: sages' Judaism will identify the Messiah and teach how to bring him nearer. In these allegations we find no point of intersection with issues important to Chrysostom, even though the Talmud of the Land of Israel reached closure at the same time as Chrysostom's preaching. For Chrysostom dealt with the Messiah theme in terms pertinent to his larger system, and sages did the same. But the issue was fairly joined. In Chrysostom's terms: Jesus is Christ, proved by the events of the recent past. In sages' terms: the Messiah will be a sage, coming when Israel fully accepts, in all humility, God's sole rule. The first stage in the position of each hardly matches that in the outline of the other. But the second does: Jesus is Christ, therefore Israel will have no other Messiah. The Messiah will come, in the form of a sage, and therefore no one who now claims to be the Messiah is in fact the savior. I can hardly claim that sages went out and bought copies of Chrysostom's published sermons and composed replies to them. Issues are joined in a confrontation of ideas, and that is how I see matters here. The reason is the clear fit between one side's framing of the Messiah theme and the other party's framing of the same theme. And, we cannot forget, that larger context in which the theme worked itself out—Messiah joined to the doctrine of history and of Israel, before and after—forms a large and integrated picture. If Jesus is Christ, then history has come to its fulfillment and Israel is no longer God's people. The sages' counterpart system: the Messiah has not yet come, history as the sequence of empires has in store yet one more age, the age of Israel, and, of course, Israel remains the family, the children of Abraham, Isaac, and Jacob. So Christianity, so Judaism: both confronted precisely the same issues defined in exactly the same way.

In the Talmud of the Land of Israel two historical contexts framed discussion of the Messiah: the destruction of the Temple, as with Chrysostom's framing of the issue, and the messianic claim of Bar Kokhba.[2] Rome played a

2. The Talmud of the Land of Israel totally ignores whatever messianic hopes and figures took part in the fiasco of Julian's projected rebuilding of the Temple.

role in both, and the authors of the materials gathered in the Talmud made a place for Rome in the history of Israel. This they did in conformity to their larger theory of who Israel is, specifically by assigning to Rome a place in the family. As to the destruction of the Temple, we find a statement that the Messiah was born on the day that the Temple was destroyed. The Talmud's doctrine of the Messiah therefore finds its place in its encompassing doctrine of history. What is fresh in the Talmud is the perception of Rome as an autonomous actor, as an entity with a point of origin (just as Israel has a point of origin) and a tradition of wisdom (just as Israel has such a tradition). So as Rome is Esau, so Esau is part of the family—a point to which we shall return—and therefore plays a role in history. And—yet another point of considerable importance—since Rome does play a role in history, Rome also finds a position in the eschatological drama. This sense of poised opposites, Israel and Rome, comes to expression in two ways. First, Israel's own history calls into being its counterpoint, the antihistory of Rome. Without Israel, there would be no Rome—a wonderful consolation to the defeated nation. For if Israel's sin created Rome's power, then Israel's repentance would bring Rome's downfall. Here is the way in which the Talmud presents the match:

Y. Avodah Zarah 1:2

[IV E] Saturnalia means "hidden hatred" [*sina'ah temunah*]: The Lord hates, takes vengeance, and punishes.

[F] This is in accord with the following verse: "Now Esau hated Jacob" [Gen. 27:41].

[G] R. Isaac b. R. Eleazar said, "In Rome they call it Esau's Saturnalia."

[H] Kratesis: It is on the day on which the Romans seized power.

[K] Said R. Levi, "It is the day on which Solomon intermarried with the family of Pharaoh Neccho, King of Egypt. On that day Michael came down and thrust a reed into the sea, and pulled up muddy alluvium, and this was turned into a huge pot, and this was the great city of Rome. On the day on which Jeroboam set up the two golden calves, Remus and Romulus came and built two huts in the city of Rome. On the day on which Elijah disappeared, a king was appointed in Rome. "There was no king in Edom; a deputy was king" [1 Kings 22:47].

The important point is that Solomon's sin provoked heaven's founding of Rome. The entire world and what happens in it enter into the framework of meaning established by Israel's Torah. So what the Romans do, their historical actions, can be explained in terms of Israel's conception of the world.

The concept of two histories, balanced opposite one another, comes to particular expression, within the Talmud of the Land of Israel, in the balance of Israelite sage and Roman emperor. Just as Israel and Rome, God and no-gods, compete (with a foreordained conclusion), so do sage and emperor. In this age, it appears that the emperor has the power. God's Temple, by contrast to the great churches of the age, lies in ruins. But just as sages can overcome the emperor through their inherent supernatural power, so too will Israel and Israel's God in the coming age control the course of events. In this doctrine we see the true balance: sage against emperor. In the age of the Christian emperors, the polemic acquires power. The sage, in his small-claims court, weighs in the balance against the emperor in Constantinople—a rather considerable claim. Two stunning innovations appear: first, the notion of emperor and sage in mortal struggle; second, the idea of an age of idolatry and an age beyond idolatry. The world had to move into a new orbit indeed for Rome to enter into the historical context formerly defined wholly by what happened to Israel. How does all this relate to the messianic crisis? The doctrine of sages, directly pertinent to the issue of the coming of the Messiah, holds that Israel can free itself of control by other nations only by humbly agreeing to accept God's rule.

Once the figure of the Messiah has come on stage, there arises discussion on who, among the living, the Messiah might be. The identification of the Messiah begins, of course, with the person of David himself: "If the Messiah-King comes from among the living, his name will be David. If he comes from among the dead, it will be King David himself" (Y. Ber. 2:3 V P). A variety of evidence announced the advent of the Messiah as a figure in the larger system of formative Judaism. The rabbinization of David constitutes one kind of evidence. Serious discussion, within the framework of the accepted document of Mishnaic exegesis and the law, concerning the identification and claim of diverse figures asserted to be messiahs, presents still more telling proof.

Y. Berakhot 2:4
(Translated by T. Zahavy)

[A]   Once a Jew was plowing and his ox snorted once before him. An Arab who was passing and heard the sound said to him, "Jew, loosen your ox and loosen the plow and stop plowing. For today your Temple was destroyed."

[B]   The ox snorted again. He [the Arab] said to him, "Jew, bind your ox and bind your plow, for today the Messiah-King was born."

[C]   He said to him, "What is his name?"

[D]   "Menahem."

[E]   He said him, "And what is his father's name?"

[F]   The Arab said to him, "Hezekiah."

[G]   He said to him, "Where is he from?"

[H]   He said to him, "From the royal capital of Bethlehem in Judea."

[I]   The Jew went and sold his ox and sold his plow. And he became a peddler of infant's felt-cloths [diapers]. And he went from place to place until he came to that very city. All of the women bought from him. But Menahem's mother did not buy from him.

[J] He heard the women saying, "Menahem's mother, Menahem's mother, come buy for your child."

[K] She said, "I want to bring him up to hate Israel. For on the day he was born, the Temple was destroyed."

[L] They said to her, "We are sure that on this day it was destroyed, and on this day of the year it will be rebuilt."

[M] She said to the peddler, "I have no money."

[N] He said to her, "It is of no matter to me. Come and buy for him and pay me when I return."

[O] A while later he returned to that city. He said to her, "How is the infant doing?"

[P] She said to him, "Since the time you saw him a spirit came and carried him away from me."

[Q] Said R. Bun, "Why do we learn this from [a story about] an Arab? Do we not have explicit scriptural evidence for it? 'Lebanon with its majestic trees will fall' [Isa. 10:34]. And what follows this? 'There shall come forth a shoot from the stump of Jesse' [Isa. 11:1]. [Right after an allusion to the destruction of the Temple the prophet speaks of the messianic age.]"

This is a set-piece story, adduced to prove that the Messiah was born on the day the Temple was destroyed. The Messiah was born when the Temple was destroyed; hence, God prepared for Israel a better fate than had appeared.

A more concrete matter—the identification of the Messiah with a known historical personality—was associated with the name of Aqiba. He is said to have claimed that Bar Kokhba, leader of the second-century revolt, was the Messiah. The important aspect of the story, however, is the rejection of Aqiba's view. The discredited messiah figure (if Bar Kokhba actually was such in his own day) finds no apologists in the later rabbinical canon. What is striking in what follows, moreover, is that we really have two stories. At G Aqiba is said to have believed that Bar Kokhba was a disappointment. At H–I, he is said to have identified Bar Kokhba with the King-Messiah. Both cannot be true, so what we have is simply two separate opinions of Aqiba's judgment of Bar Kokhba/Bar Kozebah.

Y. Taanit 4:5

[X G] R. Simeon b. Yohai taught, "Aqiba, my master, would interpret the following verse: 'A star (*kokhab*) shall come forth out of Jacob' [Num. 24:17] "A disappointment (*Kozeba*) shal come forth out of Jacob.'"

[H] R. Aqiba, when he saw Bar Kozeba, said, "This is the King Messiah."

[I]   R. Yohanan ben Toreta said to him, "Aqiba! Grass will grow on your cheeks before the Messiah will come!"

The important point is not only that Aqiba had been proved wrong. It is that the very verse of Scripture adduced in behalf of his viewpoint could be treated more generally and made to refer to righteous people in general, not to the Messiah in particular. And that leads us to the issue of the age, as sages had to face it: what makes a messiah a false messiah? When we know the answer to that question, we also uncover the distinctively rabbinic version of the Messiah theme that the Talmud of the land of Israel contributes.

What matters is not the familiar doctrine of the Messiah's claim to save Israel, but the doctrine that Israel will be saved through total submission, under the Messiah's gentle rule, to God's yoke and service. In the model of the sage, the Messiah will teach Israel the power of submission. So God is not to be manipulated through Israel's humoring heaven in rite and cult. The notion of keeping the commandments so as to please heaven and get God to do what Israel wants is totally incongruent to the text at hand. Keeping the commandments as a mark of submission, loyalty, humility before God is the rabbinic system of salvation. So Israel does not save itself. Israel never controls its own destiny, either on earth or in heaven. The only choice is whether to cast one's fate into the hands of cruel, deceitful men, or to trust the living God of mercy and love. We now understand the stress on the centrality of hope. Hope signifies patient acceptance of God's rule, and as an attitude of mind and heart, it is something that Israel can sustain on its own as well, the ideal action. We shall now see how this critical position that Israel's task is humble acceptance of God's rule is spelled out in the setting of discourse about the Messiah in the Talmud of the Land of Israel. Bar Kokhba weighs in the balance against the sage, much as the Roman emperor weighs in the balance against the sage, and for the same reason. The one represents arrogance, the other humility. Bar Kokhba, above all, exemplified arrogance against God. He lost the war because of that arrogance. In particular, he ignored the authority of sages—a point not to be missed, since it forms the point of critical tension in the tale:

Y. Taanit 4:5

[X J]   Said R. Yohanan, "Upon orders of Caesar Hadrian, they killed eight hundred thousand in Betar."

[K]   Said R. Yohanan, "There were eighty thousand pairs of trumpeteers surrounding Betar. Each one was in charge of a number of troops. Ben Kozeba was there and he had two hundred thousand troops who, as a sign of loyalty, had cut off their little fingers.

[L]   "Sages sent word to him, 'How long are you going to turn Israel into a maimed people?'

[M]   "He said to them, 'How otherwise is it possible to test them?'

[N]   "They replied to him, 'Whoever cannot uproot a cedar of Lebanon while riding on his horse will not be inscribed on your military rolls.'

[O]   "So there were two hundred thousand who qualified in one way, and another two hundred thousand who qualified in another way."

[P]   When he would go forth to battle, he would say, "Lord of the world! Do not help and do not hinder us! 'Hast thou not rejected us, O God? Thou dost not go forth, O God, with our armies'" [Ps. 60:10].

[Q]   Three and a half years did Hadrian besiege Betar.

[R]   R. Eleazar of Modiin would sit on sackcloth and ashes and pray every day, saying "Lord of the ages! Do not judge in accord with strict judgment this day! Do not judge in accord with strict judgment this day!"

[S]   Hadrian wanted to go to him. A Samaritan said to him, "Do not go to him until I see what he is doing, and so hand over the city [of Betar] to you. [Make peace . . . for you.]"

[T]   He got into the city through a drain pipe. He went and found R. Eleazar of Modiin standing and praying. He pretended to whisper something into his ear.

[U]   Th townspeople saw [the Samaritan] do this and brought him to Ben Kozeba. They told him, "We saw this man having dealings with your friend."

[V]   [Bar Kokhba] said to him, "What did you say to him, and what did he say to you?"

[W]   He said to [the Samaritan], "If I tell you, then the king will kill me, and if I do not tell you, then you will kill me. It is better than the king kill me, and not you.

[X]   [Eleazar] said to me, 'I should hand over my city.' ['I shall make peace. . . .']"

[Y]   He turned to R. Eleazar of Modiin. He said to him, "What did this Samaritan say to you?"

[Z]   He replied, "Nothing."

[AA]   He said to him, "What did you say to him?"

[BB]   He said to him, "Nothing."

[CC]   [Ben Kozeba] gave [Eleazar] one good kick and killed him.

[DD]   Forthwith an echo came forth and proclaimed the following verse:

[EE]   "Woe to my worthless shepherd, who deserts the flock! May the sword smite his arm and his right eye! Let his arm be wholly withered, his right eye utterly blinded! [Zech. 11:17].

[FF]   "You have murdered R. Eleazar of Modiin, the right of arm of all Israel, and their right eye. Therefore may the right arm of that man wither, may his right eye be utterly blinded!"

[GG]   Forthwith Betar was taken, and Ben Kozeba was killed.

We notice two complementary themes. First, Bar Kokhba treats heaven with arrogance, asking God merely to keep out of the way. Second, he treats an especially revered sage with a parallel arrogance. The sage had the power to preserve Israel. Bar Kokhba destroyed Israel's one protection. The result was inevitable. Now we may draw together the two related, but distinct themes, the doctrine of history, dealt with in chapter 2, and the theory of the Messiah.

We turn first to history, the point which leads us to the matter of the Messiah. The convictions of Eusebius about how political events prove what God favors finds its counterpart in sages' view here. In the Talmud of the Land of Israel (as much as in Genesis Rabbah) Israel's history works out and expresses Israel's relationship with God. The critical dimension of Israel's life, therefore, is salvation, the definitive trait, a movement in time from now to then. It follows that the paramount and organizing category is history and its lessons. As I suggested at the outset, in the Talmud of the Land of Israel we witness, among the Mishnah's heirs, a striking reversion to biblical convictions about the centrality of history in the definition of Israel's reality. The heavy weight of prophecy, apocalyptic, and biblical historiography, with their emphasis upon salvation and upon history as the indicators of Israel's salvation, stood against the Mishnah's quite separate thesis of what truly mattered. What, from sages' viewpoint, demanded description and analysis and required interpretation? It was the category of sanctification, for eternity. The true issue framed by history and apocalypse was how to move toward the foreordained end of salvation, how to act in time to reach salvation at the end of the time. The Mishnah's teleology beyond time and its capacity to posit an eschatology without a place for a historical Messiah take a position beyond that of the entire antecedent sacred literature of Israel. Only one strand, the priestly one, had ever taken so extreme a position on the centrality of sanctification and the peripheral nature of salvation. Wisdom had stood in between, with its own concerns, drawing attention both to what happened and to what endured. But to Wisdom what finally mattered was not nature or supernature, but rather abiding relationships in historical time.

But we should not conclude that the Talmud has simply moved beyond the Mishnah's orbit. The opposite is the case. What the framers of the document have done is to assemble materials in which the eschatological, therefore messianic, teleology is absorbed within the ahistorical, therefore sagacious, teleology. The Messiah turned into a sage is no longer the Messiah embodied in the figure of the arrogant Bar Kokhba (in the Talmud's representation of the figure). The reversion to the prophetic notion of learning history's lessons carried in its wake a reengagement with the Messiah myth. But the reengagement does not represent a change in the unfolding system. Why not? Because the climax comes in an explicit statement that the conduct required by the Torah will bring the coming Messiah. That explanation of the holy way of life focuses upon the end of time and the advent of the Messiah—both of which therefore depend upon the sanctification of Israel. So sanctification takes priority, salvation depends on it. The framers of the Mishnah had found it possible to construct a complete and encompassing teleology for their system with scarcely a single word about the Messiah's coming at that time when the system would be perfectly achieved.

So with their interest in explaining events and accounting for history, the third- and fourth-century sages represented in these units of discourse invoked what their predecessors had at best found to be of peripheral consequence to their system. The following contains the most striking expression of this viewpoint.

Y. Taanit 1 : 1

[X J]   "The oracle concerning Dumah. One is calling to me from Seir, 'Watchman, what of the night? Watchman, what of the night?' Isa. 21 : 11]."

[K]   The Israelites said to Isaiah, "O our Rabbi, Isaiah, what will come for us out of this night?"

[L]   He said to them, "Wait for me, until I can present the question."

[M]   Once he had asked the question, he came back to them.

[N]   They said to him, "Watchman, what of the night? What did the Guardian of the ages tell you?"

[O]   He said to them, "The watchman says: 'Morning comes; and also the night. If you will inquire, inquire; come back again' [Isa. 21 : 12]."

[P]   They said to him, "Also the night?"

[Q]   He said to them, "It is not what you are thinking. But there will be morning for the righteous, and night for the wicked, morning for Israel, and night for idolaters."

[R]   They said to him, "When?"

[S]   He said to them, "Whenever you want, He too wants [it to be]—if you want it, he wants it."

[T]   They said to him, "What is standing in the way?"

[U]   He said to them, "Repentance: 'Come back again' [Isa. 21 : 12]."

[V]   R. Aha in the name of R. Tanhum b. R. Hiyya, "If Israel repents for one day, forthwith the son of David will come.

[W]   "What is the scriptural basis? 'O that today you would hearken to his voice!' [Ps. 95 : 7]."

[X]   Said R. Levi, If Israel would keep a single sabbath in the proper way, forthwith the son of David will come.

[Y]   "What is the scriptural basis for this view? 'Moses said, "Eat it today, for today is a sabbath to the Lord; today you will not find it in the field"' [Exod. 16 : 25].

[Z]   "And it said, 'For thus said the Lord God, the Holy One of Israel, "In returning and rest you shall be saved; in quietness and in trust shall be your strength." And you would not' [Isa. 30 : 15]."

A discussion of the power of repentance would hardly have surprised a Mishnah sage. What is new is at V–Z, the explicit linkage of keeping the law which achieving the end of time and the coming of the Messiah. That motif stands separate from the notions of righteousness and repentance, which surely did not require it. We must not lose sight of the importance of this passage, with its emphasis on repentance on the one side, and the power of Israel to reform itself on the other. The Messiah will come any day that Israel makes it possible. Let me underline the most important statement of this large conception:

If all Israel will keep a single sabbath in the proper (rabbinic) way, the Messiah will come. If all Israel will repent for one day, the Messiah will come. "Whenever you want . . . ," the Messiah will come.

Two things are happening here. First, the system of religious observance, including study of Torah, is explicitly invoked as having salvific power. Second, the persistent hope of the people for the coming of the Messiah is linked to the system of rabbinic observance and belief. In this way, the austere program of the Mishnah develops in a different direction, with no trace of a promise that the Messiah will come if and when the system is fully realized. Here a teleology lacking all eschatological dimension gives way to an explicitly messianic statement that the purpose of the law is to attain Israel's salvation: "If you want it, God wants it too." The one thing Israel commands is its own heart; the power it yet exercises is the power to repent. These suffice. The entire history of humanity will respond to Israel's will, to what happens in Israel's heart and soul. With the Temple in ruins, repentance can take place only within the heart and mind.

We should note, also, a corollary to this doctrine, which carries to the second point of interest, the Messiah. Israel may contribute to its own salvation by the right attitude and the right deed. But Israel bears responsibility for its present condition. So what Israel does makes history. Any account of the Messiah doctrine of the Talmud of the Land of Israel must lay appropriate stress on that conviction: Israel makes its own history, therefore shapes its own destiny. This lesson, sages maintained, derives from the very condition of Israel even then, its suffering and its despair. How so? History taught moral lessons. Historical events entered into the construction of a teleology for the Talmud of the Land of Israel's system of Judaism as a whole. What the law demanded reflected the consequences of wrongful action on the part of Israel. So, again, Israel's own deeds defined the events of history. Rome's role, like Assyria's and Babylonia's, depended upon Israel's provoking divine wrath. This mode of thought comes to simple expression in what follows.

Y. Erubin 3:9

[IV B]   R. Ba, R. Hiyya in the name of R. Yohanan: " 'Do not gaze at me because I am swarthy, because the sun has scorched me. My mother's sons were angry with me, they made me keeper of the vineyards, but, my one vineyard, I have not kept!' What made me guard the vineyards? It is because of not keeping my own vineyard.

[C]   "What made me keep two festival days in Syria? It is because I did not keep the proper festival day in the Holy Land.

[D]   "I imagined that I would receive a reward for the two days, but I received a reward only for one of them.

[E]   "Who made it necessary that I should have to separate two pieces of dough-offering from grain grown in Syria? It is because I did not separate a single piece of dough-offering in the Land of Israel."

Israel had to learn the lesson of its history to also take command of its own destiny. But this notion of determining one's own destiny should not be misunderstood. The framers of the Talmud of the Land of Israel were not telling the Jews to please God by doing commandments in order that they should thereby gain control of their own destiny. God was not there to be humored and manipulated.

To the contrary, the paradox of the Talmud of the Land of Israel's system of history and Messiah lies in the fact that Israel can free itself of control by other nations only by humbly agreeing to accept God's rule. The nations—Rome, in the present instance—rest on one side of the balance, while God rests on the other. Israel must choose between them. There is no such thing for Israel as freedom from both God and the nations, total autonomy and independence. There is only a choice of masters, a ruler on earth or a ruler in heaven. In the Talmud's theory of salvation, therefore, the framers provided Israel with an account of how to overcome the unsatisfactory circumstances of an unredeemed present, so as to accomplish the movement from here to the much-desired future. When the Talmud's authorities present statements on the promise of the law for those who keep it, therefore, they provide glimpses of the goal of the system as a whole. These invoked the primacy of the rabbi and the legitimating power of the Torah, and in those two components of the system we find the principles of the messianic doctrine. And these bring us back to the argument with Christ triumphant, as the Christians perceived him.

Looking backward from the end of the fourth century to the end of the first, the framers of the Talmud surely perceived what two hundred years earlier, with the closure of the Mishnah, need not have appeared obvious and unavoidable, namely, the definitive end, for here and now at any rate, of the old order of cultic sanctification. After a hundred years there may have been some doubt. After two centuries more, with the fiasco of Julian near at hand, there can have been little hope left. The Mishnah had designed a world in which the Temple stood at the center, a society in which the priests presided at the top, and a way of life in which the dominant issue was the sanctification of Israelite life. Whether the full realization of that world, society, and way of life was thought to come sooner or later, the system had been meant only initially as a utopia, but in the end as a plan and constitution for a material society here in the Land of Israel.

Two hundred years now had passed from the closure of the Mishnah to the completion of the Talmud of the Land of Israel. Much had changed. Roman power had receded from part of the world. Pagan rule had given way to the sovereignty of Christian emperors. The old order was cracking; the new order was not yet established. But, from the perspective of Israel, the waiting went on. The interim from Temple to Temple was not differentiated. Whether conditions were less favorable or more favorable hardly made a difference. History stretched backward, to a point of disaster, and forward, to an unseen and incalculable time beyond the near horizon. Short of supernatural events, salvation was not in sight. Israel for its part lived under its own government, framed within the rules of sanctification, and constituted a holy society. But when would salvation come, and how could people even now hasten its day? These issues, in the nature of things, proved more pressing as the decades rolled by, becoming first one century, then another, while none knew how many more, and how much more, must still be endured. So the unredeemed state of Israel and the world, the uncertain fate of the individual—these concerns framed and defined the context in which all forms of Judaism necessarily took shape. The question of salvation presented each of these forms with a single ineluctable task. But it is not merely an axiom generated by our hindsight that makes it necessary to interpret all of a system's answers in the light of the single question of salvation. In the case of the Judaism to which the Talmud of the Land of Israel attests, the matter is explicitly stated.

For the important fact is that Talmud of the Land of Israel expressly links salvation to keeping the law. And, in the opposite way, so did Chrysostom. We recall that he held that not keeping the law showed that the Messiah had come and Israel's hope had finally been defeated. Sages maintained that keeping the law now signified keeping the faith: the act of hope. This means that the issues of the law were drawn upward into the highest realm of Israelite consciousness. Keeping the law in the right way is represented as not merely right or expedient. It is the way to bring the Messiah, the son of David. This—to review—is stated by Levi, as follows:

Y. Taanit 1:1.IX

X. Said R. Levi, "If Israel would keep a single Sabbath in the proper way, forthwith the son of David would come.

Y. "What is the Scriptural basis for this view? 'Moses said, Eat it today, for today is a sabbath to the Lord; today you will not find it in the field' (Ex. 16:25)."

Z. And it says, "For thus said the Lord God, the Holy One of Israel, 'In returning and rest you shall be saved; in quietness and in trust shall be your strength. And you would not' (Is. 30:15)."

Here, in a single saying, we find the entire Talmudic doctrine set forth. How like, yet how different from, the Mishnah's view. Keeping the law of the Torah represented the visible form of love of God.

The Mishnah's system, whole and complete, had remained reticent on the entire Messiah theme. By contrast, our Talmud finds ample place for a rich collection of statements on the messianic theme. What this means is that, between the conclusion of the Mishnah and the closure of the Talmud, room had been found for the messianic hope, expressed in images not revised to conform to the definitive and distinctive traits of the Talmud itself. We do not have to argue that the stunning success of Christ (in the Christians' view) made the issue urgent for Jews. My judgment is that the issue had never lost its urgency, except in the tiny circle of philosophers who, in the system of the Mishnah, reduced the matter to a minor detail of taxonomy. And yet, in that exercise, the Mishnah's sages confronted a considerable social problem, one that faced the fourth-century authorities as well.

The messianic hope in concrete political terms also required neutralization, so that peoples' hopes would not be raised prematurely, with consequent incalculable damage to the defeated nation. That was true in the second century, in the aftermath of Bar Kokhba's war, and in the fourth century, for obvious reasons, as well. This "rabbinization" of the Messiah theme meant, first of all, that rabbis insisted the Messiah would come in a process extending over a long period time, thus not imposing a caesura upon the existence of the nation and disrupting its ordinary life. Accordingly, the Talmud of the Land of Israel treats the messianic hope as something gradual, to be worked toward, not a sudden cataclysmic event. That conception was fully in accord with the notion that the everyday deeds of people formed a pattern continuous with the salvific history of Israel.

Y. Yoma 3:2.III

A. One time R. Hiyya the Elder and R. Simeon b. Halapta were walking in the valley of Arabel at daybreak. They saw that the light of the morning star was breaking forth. Said R. Hiyya the Elder to R. Simeon b. Halapta, "Son of my master, this is what the redemption of Israel is like—at first, little by little, but in the end it will go along and burst into light.

B. "What is the Scriptural basis for this view? 'Rejoice not over me, O my enemy; when I fall, I shall rise; when I sit in darkness, the Lord will be a light to me' (Mic. 7:8).

C. "So, in the beginning, 'When the virgins were gathered together the second time, Mordecai was sitting at the king's gate' (Est. 2:19).

D. "But afterward: 'So Haman took the robes and the horse, and he arrayed Mordecai and made him ride through the open square of the city, proclaiming, Thus shall it be done to the man whom the king delights to honor' (Est. 6:11).

E. "And in the end: 'Then Mordecai went out from the presence of the king in royal robes of blue and white, with a great golden crown and a mantle of fine linen and purple, while the city of Susa shouted and rejoiced" [Est. 8:15].

F. "And finally: 'The Jews had light and gladness and joy and honor' (Est. 8:16)."

The pattern laid out here obviously does not conform to the actualities of the Christianization of the Roman Empire. From the viewpoint of Eusebius and Chrysostom alike, the matter had come suddenly, miraculously. Sages saw things differently. We may regard the emphasis upon the slow but steady advent of the Messiah's day as entirely consonant with the notion that the Messiah will come when Israel's condition warrants it. The improvement in standards of observing the Torah, therefore, to be effected by the nation's obedience to the clerks, will serve as a guidepost on the road to redemption. The moral condition of the nation ultimately guarantees salvation. God will respond to Israel's regeneration, planning all the while to save the saved, that is, those who save themselves.

What is most interesting in the Talmud of the Land of Israel's picture is that the hope for the Messiah's coming is further joined to the moral condition of each individual Israelite. Hence the messianic fulfillment was made to depend on the repentance of Israel. The entire drama, envisioned by others in earlier types of Judaism as a world-historical event, was reworked in context into a moment in the life of the individual and the people of Israel collectively. The coming of the Messiah depended not on historical action but on moral regeneration. So from a force that moved Israelites to take up weapons on the battlefield, the messianic hope and yearning were transformed into motives for spiritual regeneration and ethical behavior. The energies released in the messianic fervor were then linked to rabbinical government, through which Israel would form the godly society. When we reflect that the message, "If you want it, He too wants it to be," comes in a generation confronting a dreadful disappointment, its full weight and meaning become clear.

The advent of the Messiah will not be heralded by the actions of a pagan or of a Christian king. Whoever relies upon the salvation by a gentile is going to be disappointed. Israel's salvation depends wholly upon Israel itself. Two things follow. First, as we saw, the Jews were made to take up the burden of guilt for their own sorry situation. But, second, they also gained not only responsibility for, but also power over, their fate. They could do something about salvation, just as their sins had brought about their tragedy. This old, familiar message, in no way particular to the Talmud's bureaucrats, took on specificity and concreteness in the context of the Talmud, which offered a rather detailed program for reform and regeneration. The message to a disappointed generation, attracted to the kin-faith, with its now-triumphant messianic fulfillment, and fearful of its own fate in an age of violent attacks upon the synagogue buildings and faithful alike, was stern. But it also promised strength to the weak and hope to the despairing. No one could be asked to believe that the Messiah would come very soon. The events of the day testified otherwise. So the counsel of the Talmud's sages was patience and consequential deeds. People could not hasten things, but they could do something. The duty of Israel, in the meantime, was to accept the sovereignty of heavenly government.

Y. Sanhedrin 6:9.III

A. R. Abbahu was bereaved. One of his children had passed away from him. R. Jonah and R. Yose went up [to confront him]. When they called on him, out of reverence for him, they did not express to him a word of Torah. He said to them, "May the rabbis express a word of Torah."

B. They said to him, "Let our master teach us."

C. He said to them, "Now if in regard to the government below, in which there is no reliability, [but only] lying, deceit, favoritism, and bribe taking—

D. "which is here today and gone tomorrow—

E. "if concerning that government, it is said, **And the relatives of the felon come and inquire after the welfare of the judges and of the witnesses, as if to say, 'We have nothing against you, for you judged honestly'** [M. San. 6:9],

F. "in regard to the government above, in which there is reliability, but no lying, deceit, favoritism, or bribe taking—

G. "and which endures forever and to all eternity—

H. "all the more so are we obligated to accept upon ourselves the just decree [of that heavenly government]."

I. And it says, "That the Lord . . . may show you mercy, and have compassion on you . . ." (Deut. 13:17).

The heavenly government, revealed in the Torah, was embodied in this world by the figure of the sage. The meaning of the salvific doctrine just outlined becomes fully clear when we uncover the simple fact that the rule of heaven and the learning and authority of the rabbi on earth turned out to be identified with one another. It follows that salvation for Israel depended upon adherence to the sage and acceptance of his discipline. God's will in heaven and the sage's words on earth—both constituted Torah. And Israel would be saved through Torah, so the sage was the savior.

To conclude, let us ask Chrysostom and the framers of the Talmud of the Land of Israel to take up the same issue.

Will there be a Messiah for Israel?

Sages: Yes.

Chrysostom: No.

Will the Messiah save the world, including Israel?

Sages: Yes, in the future.

Chrysostom: He already has.

And if we ask whether or not the parties to the dispute invoke the same facts, in the form of a shared corpus of texts, the answer is affirmative. The messianic texts of Isaiah and other passages, important to Christians, gain a distinctive reading on the part of sages as well. So the issue is shared, the probative facts a point of agreement. True, Chrysostom and the authors and framers of the Yerushalmi in no way confront the viewpoints of one another. But they do argue about the same matter and invoke the same considerations: Is the Messiah coming or has he come? Do we have now to keep the law or not? The linking of the Messiah to the keeping of the Torah joins the two sides in a single debate. To be sure, Chrysostom's framing of the messianic issue responds to concerns of the Church and the young presbyter's worry for its future. That is why the matter of the keeping of the law forms the centerpiece of his framing of the messianic question. But the issue of keeping the laws of the Torah then joins his version of the Messiah theme with that of sages. Again, everything we hear from sages turns inward, upon Israel. There is no explicit confrontation with the outside world: with the Christian emperor, with the figure of Christ enthroned. It is as if nothing has happened to demand attention. Yet the stress for sages is on the centrality of the keeping of the laws of the Torah in the messianic process. Keep the law and the Messiah will come. This forms an exact reply to Chrysostom's doctrine: do not keep the law, for the Messiah has come.

What follows is a simple fact. The formation by both Christian theologians and Judaic sages of their respective Messiah doctrines, their points of stress and concern, turn out to form a remarkably apt and appropriate response to precisely what has happened. Has Israel lost out in the messianic drama?

Chrysostom: Indeed so.

Sages: Not at all, Israel remains in command.

Do the events in Rome make a difference?

Chrysostom: All the difference in the world.

Sages: Not at all, Rome (merely) forms the counterpart to Israel, so that what happens now will play out the next to last act in the history of humanity.

Israel will take the heroic part in that final act by becoming, in all humility and submission to the Torah, all together and all at once, a society in the model of the sages' community even now: like God, in accord with the image of the Torah. The figure of Christ in the icons in the churches and the figure of the Torah in the persons of the sages in the streets truly formed mirror-images of one another, and each, in the eyes of the respective communities, really was in the image and after the likeness of God. So the argument was fairly joined.

4

Leviticus Rabbah, Genesis Rabbah, and the Identification of Israel

Who Is Israel?

The legacy of ancient Israel consisted not only of Scriptures but also of a paramount social category: Israel, God's people and first love. The Church from its origins in the first century confronted the task of situating itself in relationship to "Israel," and Paul's profound reflections in Romans constitute only one among many exercises in responding to that question. For the society of the Church, like the society of the Jews, required a metaphor by which to account for itself. And revering the Scriptures, each group found in "Israel" the metaphor to account for its existence as a distinct social entity. It follows that within the issue Who is Israel? we discern how two competing groups each framed theories, of itself and also of the other. We therefore confront issues of the identity of a given corporate society as these were spelled out in debates about salvation. The salvific framing of the issue of social definition—Who is Israel today (for Judaism)? What sort of social group is the Church (for Christianity)?—served both parties.

We deal with a debate on a single issue. It finds its cogency in the common premise of the debate on who is Israel. The shared supposition concerned God's favor and choice of a given entity, one that was sui generis, among the social groups of humanity. Specifically, both parties concurred that God did favor and therefore make use of one group and not another. So they could undertake a meaningful debate on the identity of that group. The debate gained intensity because of a further peculiarity of the discourse between these two groups but no others of the day. Both concurred that the group chosen by God will bear the name Israel. God's choice among human societies would settle the question of which nation God loves and favors. Jews saw themselves as the Israel today joined in the flesh to the Israel of the scriptural record. Christians explained themselves as the Israel formed just now, in recent memory, even in the personal experience of the living, among those saved by faith in God's salvation afforded by the resurrection of Jesus Christ.

We therefore must not miss the powerful social and political message conveyed by what appear to be statements of a narrowly theological character about salvation and society. In these statements on who is Israel, each party to the debate chose to affirm its unique legitimacy and to deny the other's right to endure at all as a social and national entity.

But both parties shared common premises as to definitions of issues and facts to settle the question. They could mount a sustained argument between themselves because they talked about the same thing, invoked principles of logic in common, shared the definition of the pertinent facts. They differed only as to the outcome. Let us turn to the articulation of the question at hand. The issue of who is Israel articulated in theological, not political, terms covers several topics: Are the Jews today "Israel" of ancient times? Was, and is, Jesus the Christ? If so, who are the Christians, both on their own and also in relationship to ancient Israel? These question scarcely can be kept distinct from one another. And all of them cover the ground we have already traversed concerning the meaning of history and the identity of the Messiah. Was, and is, Jesus the Christ? If so, then the Jews who reject him enjoy no share in the salvation at hand. If not, then they do. The Christian challenge comes first. If Jesus was and is Christ, then Israel "after the flesh" no longer enjoys the status of the people who bear salvation. Salvation has come, and Israel "after the flesh" has denied it. If he is Christ, then what is the status of those—whether Jews or gentiles—who accept him? They have received the promises of salvation and their fulfillment. The promises to Israel have been kept for them. Then there is a new Israel, one that is formed of the saved, as the prophets had said in ancient times that Israel would be saved. A further issue that flowed from the first—the rejection of Jesus as Christ—concerns the status of Israel, the Jewish people, now and in time to come. Israel after the flesh, represented from the Gospels forward as the people that rejected Jesus as Christ and participated in his crucifixion, claims—as we saw in chapter 2—to be the family of Abraham, Isaac, Jacob. Then further questions arise. First, does Israel today continue the Israel of ancient times? Israel maintains that Israel now continues in a physical and spiritual way the life of Israel then. Second, will the promises of the prophets to Israel afford salvation for Israel in time to come? Israel "after the flesh" awaits the fulfillment of the prophetic promise of salvation. Clearly, a broad range of questions demanded sorting out. But the questions flow together into a single issue, faced in common. The Christian position on all these questions came to expression in a single negative: no, Israel today does not continue the Israel of old; no, the ancient promises will not again bear salvation, because they have already been kept; no, the Israel that declines to accept Jesus' claim to be the Christ is a no-people.

The response of Israel's sages to these same questions proves equally unequivocal. Yes, the Messiah will come in time to come, and yes, he will come to Israel of today, which indeed continues the Israel of old. So the issue is squarely and fairly joined. Who is Israel raises a question that stands second in line to the messianic one, with which we have already dealt. And, it must follow, the further question of who are the Christians requires close attention to that same messianic question. So, as is clear, the initial confrontation generated a genuine argument on the status and standing, before God, of Israel "after the flesh," the Jewish people. And that argument took on urgency because of the worldly, political triumph of Christianity in Rome, joined, as the fourth century wore on, by the worldly, political decline in the rights and standing of Israel, the Jewish people.

Before Christianity had addressed the issue of who the Christians were, Paul had already asked what the Jews were not. Christians formed the true people of God. So the old and lasting Israel, the Jewish people, did not. Paul had called into question "Israel's status as God's chosen people," because (in Ruether's words) "Israel had failed in its pursuit of righteousness based on the Torah . . . [and] had been disobedient . . . [so that] the privileged relation to God provided by the Mosaic covenant has been permanently revoked." So from its origins, Christianity had called into question Israel's former status, and, as Gager says, held that "Israel's disobedience is not only not accidental to God's plan of salvation, it has become an essential part of its fulfillment." The Christian position on one side of the matter of who is Israel, namely, who is not Israel, had reached a conclusion before the other aspect of the matter— the Christians' status as a New Israel—came to full expression (Ruether 1979, 64ff.; Gager 1983, 256–58).

That matter of status closely follows the issue of salvation, as we have already noted. As soon as Christians coalesced into groups, they asked themselves what *sort* of groups they formed. They in fact maintained several positions. First, they held that they were a people, enjoying the status of the Jewish people, and that attitude, as Harnack says, "furnished adherents of the new faith with a political and historical self-consciousness." So they were part of Israel and continued the Israel of ancient times; not a new group but a very old one. They further defined themselves as not only a new people but a new *type* of group, recognizing no taxonomic counterpart in the existing spectrum of human societies, peoples, or nations. The claims of the Christians varied according to circumstance, so Harnack summarizes matters in a passage of stunning acuity:

> Was the cry raised, "You are renegade Jews"—the answer came, "We are the community of the Messiah, and therefore the true Israelites." If people said, "You are simply Jews," the reply was, "We are a new creation and a new people." If again they were taxed with their recent origin and told that they were but of yesterday, they retorted, "We only seem to be the younger People; from the beginning we have been latent; we have always existed, previous to any other people; we are the original people of God." If they were told, "You do not deserve to live" the answer ran, "We would die to live, for we are citizens of the world to come, and sure that we shall rise again" (1972, 241, 244)

These reflections on the classification of the new group—superior to the old, sui generis, and whatever the occasion of polemic requires the group to be— fill the early Christian writings. In general there were three such classifications: Greeks or gentiles, Jews, and the Christians as the new People.

When Christians asked themselves what sort of group they formed, they answered that they constituted a new group, one of a new type altogether. They identified with the succession to Israel after the flesh, with Israel after the spirit, with a group lacking all parallel or precedent, with God-fearers and law-keepers who existed before Judaism was given at Sinai. The dilemma comes to expression in Eusebius:

> In the oracles directed to Abraham, Moses himself writes prophetically how in the times to come the descendants of Abraham, not only his Jewish seed but all the tribes and all the nations of the earth, will be deemed worthy of divine praise because of a common manner of worship like that of Abraham. . . . How could all the nations and tribes of the earth be blessed in Abraham if no relationship of either a spiritual or a physical nature existed between them? . . . How therefore could men reared amid an animal existence . . . be able to share in the blessings of the godly, unless they abandoned their savage ways and sought to participate in a life of piety like that of Abraham? . . . Now Moses lived after Abraham, and he gave the Jewish race a certain corporate status which was based upon the laws provided by him. If the laws he established were the same as those by which godly men were guided before his time, if they were capable of being adopted by all peoples so that all the tribes and nations of the earth could worship God in accordance with the Mosaic enactments, one could say that the oracles had foretold that because of Mosaic laws men of every nation would worship God and live according to Judaism. . . . However since the Mosaic enactments did not apply to other peoples but to the Jews alone . . . a different way, a way distinct from the law of Moses, needed to be established, one by which the nations of all the earth might live as Abraham had so that they could receive an equal share of blessing with him. (In Luibheid 1966, 41)

Since, with the advent of Constantine, a political dimension served to take the measure of the Christian polity, we have to ask about the political consciousness of the Church in its original formulation. In this matter Harnack points out that the political consciousness of the Church rests on three premises: first, the political element in the Jewish apocalyptic, second, the movement of the gospel to the Greeks, and third, the ruin of Jerusalem and the end of the Jewish state. He says, "The first of these elements stood in antithesis to the others, so that in this way the political consciousness of the church came to be defined in opposite directions and had to work itself out of initial contradictions (1972, 256–57). From early times, Harnack says, the Christians saw Christianity as "the central point of humanity as the field of political history as well as its determining factor." That had been the Jews' view of themselves. With Constantine the corresponding Christian conception matched reality.

Now the Christians formed a new people, a third race. When the change came, with the Christianization of the empire at the highest level of government, the new people, the third race, had to frame a position and policy about the old people, the enduring Israel "after the flesh." And, for its part, the Jewish people, faced with the Christian *défi*, found the necessity to reaffirm its enduring view of itself, now, however, in response to a pressure without precedent in its long past. The claim of the no-people that the now and enduring Israel is the no-people, knew no prior equivalent. The age of Constantine marked the turning of the world: all things were upside down. How to deal with a world that (from the perspective of Israel, the Jewish people) had gone mad? Israel's answer, which we shall reach in due course, proves stunningly apropos: right to the issue, in precisely the terms of the issue. But first let us see how a substantial Christian theologian phrases the matter.

Aphrahat and the People Which Is No People

To see how a fourth-century Christian theologian addressed the question of who is Israel in the light of the salvation of Jesus Christ, we turn to Aphrahat, a Christian monk in the western satrapy of the Iranian empire we know as Mesopotamia, ca. 300–350, who wrote, in Syriac, a sustained treatise on the relationship of Christianity and Judaism. His demonstrations, written in 337–44, take up issues facing the Syriac-speaking Church in the Iranian empire, enemy of Christian Rome. The relevance of Aphrahat, who lived not in Rome but in Iran, requires explanation. The world he faced placed him squarely in confrontation with the political change effected by the recognition of Christianity as Rome's religion. True, it was not a favorable change, since the now-Christian government of Rome made it clear to the Iranian government that Christians within Iran formed the object of special concern of the Christian emperor. That fact formed a datum of politics that dictated conditions of theological reflection as much for Aphrahat as for his counterparts in the West. For Iran's government had long tolerated Christian evangelism, and the Church in Mesopotamia and Babylonia was nearly a century and a half old by the time Aphrahat became a bishop. With the recognition of Christianity on the other side of the frontier, Aphrahat's Church came under suspicion, and so the political shift affected him as much as it affected Eusebius, beforehand, and Chrysostom, later on. The issue of who are the Christians and what is the Church, moreover, demanded attention for a second, equally political, consideration. The Israel of Iran, that is, the Jews, pointed toward the sorry condition of the Church as evidence that they, Jewry, and not Christianity's monks and nuns, constituted the true and only Israel of God. The political issue therefore joined with the theological one to require from Aphrahat a systematic restatement of the Church's position, now fully and elegantly argued for three hundred years, on who is Israel.[1]

---

1. On this point Rosemary Ruether comments, "There might be a word here of further discussion of the way the Constantinian establishment affected Christians outside its borders. Political success for Christians adds further 'proofs' that God is on their side, but it is not decisive for their

The Church then—ca. 337–45—was suffering severe persecution by the government, for the monks and nuns, maintaining they had no property, could not pay taxes. Since at that time Jews enjoyed stable and peaceful relationships with the Iranian government while Christians did not, the contrast between weak Christianity and secure Judaism required attention as well. Aphrahat presents his case on the basis of historical facts shared in common by both parties to the debate, Judaism and Christianity, that is, facts of Scripture. He rarely cites the New Testament in his demonstrations on Judaism. Moreover, when he cites the Hebrew Scriptures, he ordinarily refrains from fanciful or allegoristic reading of them, but, like the rabbis with whom Jerome dealt, stressed that his interpretation rested solely on the plain and obvious factual meaning. His arguments thus invoked rational arguments and historical facts: this is what happened, this is what it means. Scriptures therefore present facts, on which all parties concur. Then the argument goes forward on a common ground of shared reason and mutually agreed-upon facts. Still more important, the program of argument—whether Israel, the Jewish people, is going to be saved in the future, along with the issue of the standing and status of the Christian people—likewise follows points important to both parties.

Here, as I claimed at the outset, we find Judaic and Christian thinkers disagreeing on a common set of propositions: Who is Israel? Will Israel be saved in the future, or have the prophetic promises already been kept? We take up Aphrahat's explanation of "the people which is of the peoples," the people "which is no people," and then proceed to his address to Israel after the flesh. The two issues complement one another. Once the new people formed out of the peoples enters the status of Israel, then the old Israel loses that status. And how to express that judgment? By denying the premise of the life of Israel after the flesh, that salvation for the people of God would come in future time. If enduring Israel would never enjoy salvation, then Israel had no reason to exist: that is the premise of the argument framed on behalf of the people that had found its reason to exist (from its perspective) solely in its salvation by Jesus Christ. So what explained to the Christian community how that community had come into being also accounted, for that same community, for the (anticipated) disappearance of the nation that had rejected that very same nation-creating event.

Let me first summarize Aphrahat's *Demonstration Sixteen, "On the Peoples which are in the Place of the People."* [2] Aphrahat's message is this: "The

---

basic belief that the Christian 'new Israel' has superseded the 'old Israel' in God's favor. When persecuted, Christians adopt a martyr theology that looks forward to eschatological vindication. Thus political disfavor of persecution does not falsify the Christian belief in their divinely elected status, any more than it falsifies Jewish belief in their elected status. Thus Jews and Christians had parallel ways of interpreting lack of political success" (1979).

2. I provide in Appendix 2 a complete translation of the demonstrations summarized and paraphrased here.

people Israel was rejected, and the peoples took their place. Israel repeatedly was warned by the prophets, but to no avail, so God abandoned them and replaced them with the gentiles. Scripture frequently referred to the gentiles as 'Israel.' The vocation of the peoples was prior to that of the people of Israel, and from of old, whoever from among the people was pleasing to God was more justified than Israel: Jethro, the Gibeonites, Rahab, Ebedmelech the Ethiopian, Uriah the Hittite. By means of the gentiles God provoked Israel." The entire demonstration, in my translation, is given in the appendix to this chapter. It suffices to point to a few important components of the argument.

First, Aphrahat maintains, "The peoples which were of all languages were called first, before Israel, to the inheritance of the Most High, as God said to Abraham, 'I have made you the father of a multitude of peoples' (Gen. 17:5). Moses proclaimed, saying, 'The peoples will call to the mountain, and there will they offer sacrifices of righteousness' (Deut. 33:19)." Not only so, but God further rejected Israel: "To his people Jeremiah preached, saying to them, 'Stand by the ways and ask the wayfarers, and see which is the good way. Walk in it.' But they in their stubbornness answered, saying to him, 'We shall not go.' Again he said to them, 'I established over you watchmen, that you might listen for the sound of the trumpet.' But they said to him again, 'We shall not hearken.' And this openly, publicly did they do in the days of Jeremiah when he preached to them the word of the Lord, and they answered him, saying, 'To the word which you have spoken to us in the name of the Lord we shall not hearken. But we shall do our own will and every word which goes out of our mouths, to offer up incense-offerings to other gods'" (Jer. 44:16–17). That is why God turned to the peoples: "When he saw that they would not listen to him, he turned to the peoples, saying to them, 'Hear O peoples, and know, O church which is among them, and hearken, O land, in its fullness' (Jer. 6:18–19)." So who is now Israel? It is the peoples, no longer the old Israel: "By the name of Jacob [now] are called the people which is of the peoples." That is the key to Aphrahat's case. The people that was a no people, that people that had assembled out of the people, has now replaced Israel.

Like Eusebius, Aphrahat maintained that the peoples had been called to God before the people of Israel: "See, my beloved, that the vocation of the peoples was recorded before the vocation of the people. But because the time of the peoples had not come, and another was [to be] their redeemer, Moses was not persuaded that a redeemer and a teacher would come for the people which was of the peoples, which was greater and more worthy than the people of Israel." The people that was a no-people should not regard itself as alien to God: "If they should say, 'Us has he called alien children,' they have not been called alien children, but sons and heirs. . . . But the peoples are those who hearken to God and were lamed and kept back from the ways of their sins." Indeed, the peoples produced believers who were superior in every respect to Israel: "Even from the old, whoever from among the peoples was pleasing to God was more greatly justified than Israel. Jethro the priest who was of the peoples and his seed were blessed: 'Enduring in his dwelling place, and his nest is set on a rock' (Num 24:21)." Aphrahat here refers to the Gibeonites, Rahab, and various other gentiles mentioned in the scriptural narrative.

Addressing his Christian hearers, Aphrahat then concludes, "By us they are provoked. On our account they do not worship idols, so that they will not be shamed by us, for we have abandoned idols and call lies the thing which our fathers left us. They are angry, their hearts are broken, for we have entered and have become heirs in their place. For theirs was this covenant which they had, not to worship other gods, but they did not accept it. By means of us he provoked them, and ours was the light and the life, as he preached, saying when he taught, 'I am the light of the world' (John 8:12)." So he concludes, "This brief memorial I have written to you concerning the peoples, because the Jews take pride and say, 'We are the people of God and the children of Abraham. 'But we shall listen to John [the Baptist] who, when they took pride [saying], 'We are the children of Abraham,' then said to them, 'You should not boast and say, Abraham is father unto us, for from these very rocks can God raise up children for Abraham' (Matthew 3:9)."

In *Demonstration Nineteen, "Against the Jews, on account of their saying that they are destined to be gathered together,"* Aphrahat proceeds to the corollary argument, that the Israel after the flesh has lost its reason to endure as a nation. Why? Because no salvation awaits them in the future. The prophetic promises of salvation have all come to fulfillment in the past, and the climactic salvation for Israel, through the act of Jesus Christ, brought the salvific drama to its conclusion. Hence the Jews' not having a hope of "joining together" at the end of their exile forms a critical part of the entire picture. Here is a summary of the argument: "The Jews expect to be gathered together by the Messiah, but this expectation is in vain. God was never reconciled to them but has rejected them. The prophetic promises of restoration were all fulfilled in the return from Babylonia. Daniel's prayer was answered, and his vision was realized in the time of Jesus and in the destruction of Jerusalem. It will never be rebuilt."

Aphrahat thus stresses that the Jews' sins caused their own condition, a position which sages accepted: "On account of their sins, which were many, he uprooted and scattered them among every nation, for they did not listen to his prophets, whom he had sent to them." The Jews now maintain that they will see salvation in the future, but they are wrong: "I have written this to you because even today they hope an empty hope, saying, 'It is still certain for Israel to be gathered together,' for the prophet thus spoke, 'I shall leave none of them among the nations' (Ex. 39:28). But if all of our people is to be gathered together, why are we today scattered among every people?" But, Aphrahat states, "Israel never is going to be gathered together." The reason is that God has never reconciled to Israel: "I shall write and show you that never did God accept their repentance [through] either Moses or all of the prophets. . . . Further, Jeremiah said, 'They are called rejected silver, for the Lord has rejected them' (Jer. 6:30). . . . See, then, they have never accepted correction in their lives." Let us turn directly to the reply of Leviticus Rabbah's authorship.

II:IV

I. A. Returning to the matter (GWPH): "Speak to the children of Israel" (Lev. 1:2).

B. R. Yudan in the name of R. Samuel b. R. Nehemiah: "The matter may be compared to the case of a king who had an undergarment, concerning which he instructed his servant, saying to him, 'Fold it, shake it out, and be careful about it!'

C. "He said to him, 'My lord, O king, among all the undergarments that you have, [why] do you give me such instructions only about this one?'

D. "He said to him, 'It is because this is the one that I keep closest to my body.'

E. "So too did Moses say before the Holy One, blessed be he, Lord of the Universe: 'Among the seventy distinct nations that you have in your world, [why] do you give me instructions only concerning Israel? [For instance,] "Command the children of Israel" [Num. 28:2], "Say to the children of Israel" [Ex. 33:5], "Speak to the children of Israel"' [Lev. 1:2].

F. "He said to him, 'The reason is that they stick close to me, in line with the following verse of Scripture: "For as the undergarment cleaves to the loins of a man, so have I caused to cleave unto me the whole house of Israel"'" (Jer. 13:11).

G. Said R. Abin, "[The matter may be compared] to a king who had a purple cloak, concerning which he instructed his servant, saying, 'Fold it, shake it out, and be careful about it.'

H. "He said to him, 'My Lord, O king, among all the purple cloaks that you have, [why] do you give me such instructions only about this one?'

I. "He said to him, 'That is the one that I wore on my coronation day.'

J. "So too did Moses say before the Holy One, blessed be he, Lord of the Universe: 'Among the seventy distinct nations that you have in your world, [why] do you give instructions to me only concerning Israel? [For instance,] "Say to the children of Israel," "Command the children of Israel," "Speak to the children of Israel."

K. "He said to him, 'They are the ones who at the [Red] Sea declared me to be king, saying, "The Lord will be king"'" (Ex. 15:18).

The point of the passage has to do with Israel's particular relationship to God: Israel cleaves to God, declares God to be king, and accepts God's dominion. Further evidence of God's love for Israel derives from the commandments themselves. God watches over every little thing that Jews do, even caring what they eat for breakfast. The familiar stress on the keeping of the laws of the Torah as a mark of hope finds fulfillment here: the laws testify to God's deep concern for Israel. So there is sound reason for his hope, expressed in particular in keeping the laws of the Torah. Making the matter explicit, Simeon b. Yohai (Lev. R. II:V.1.A–B) translates this fact into a sign of divine favor.

II:V

1. A.   Said R. Simeon b. Yohai, "[The matter may be compared] to a king who had an only son. Every day he would give instructions to his steward, saying to him, 'Make sure my son eats, make sure my son drinks, make sure my son goes to school, make sure my son comes home from school.'

    B.   "So every day the Holy One, blessed be he, gave instructions to Moses, saying, 'Command the children of Israel,' 'Say to the children of Israel,' 'Speak to the children of Israel.'"

We now come to the statement of how Israel wins and retains God's favor. The issue concerns Israel's relationship to the nations before God, which is corollary to what has gone before. It is in two parts. First of all, Israel knows how to serve God in the right way. Second, the nations, though they do what Israel does, do things wrong.

V:VIII

1. A.   R. Simeon b. Yohai taught, "How masterful are the Israelites, for they know how to find favor with their creator."

    E.   Said R. Hunia [in Aramaic:], "There is a tenant farmer who knows how to borrow things, and there is a tenant farmer who does not know how to borrow. The one who knows how to borrow combs his hair, brushes off his clothes, puts on a good face, and then goes over to the overseer of his work to borrow from him. [The overseer] says to him, 'How's the land doing?' He says to him, 'May you have the merit of being fully satisfied with its [wonderful] produce.' 'How are the oxen doing?' He says to him, 'May you have the merit of being fully satisfied with their fat.' 'How are the goats doing?' 'May you have the merit of being fully satisfied with their young.' 'And what would you like?' Then he says, 'Now if you might have an extra ten denars, would you give them to me?' The overseer replies, 'If you want, take twenty.'

    F.   "But the one who does not know how to borrow leaves his hair a mess, his clothes filthy, his face gloomy. He too goes over to the overseer to borrow from him. The overseer says to him, 'How's the land doing?' He replies, 'I hope it will produce at least what [in

seed] we put into it.' 'How are the oxen doing?' 'They're scrawny.'
'How are the goats doing?' 'They're scrawny too.' 'And what do you
want?' 'Now if you might have an extra ten denars, would you give
them to me?' The overseer replies, 'Go, pay me back what you already owe me!' "

If Aphrahat had demanded a direct answer, he could not have received a more
explicit one. He claims Israel does nothing right. Sages counter, speaking in
their own setting, of course, that they do everything right. Sages then turn the
tables on the position of Aphrahat—again addressing it head-on. While the
nations may do everything Israel does, they do it wrong.

The testimony of language itself proves that fact, for the same word, applied to Israel, brings credit, and applied to gentiles, brings derision:

2. A. Said R. Eleazar, "The nations of the world are called a congregation, and Israel is called a congregation.

   B. "The nations of the world are called a congregation: 'For the congregation of the godless shall be desolate' [Job 15:34]. . . .

   J. "The nations of the world are called sages, and Israel is called sages.

   K. "The nations of the world are called sages: 'And I shall wipe out
   sages from Edom' [Ob. 1:8].

   L. "And Israel is called sages: 'Sages store up knowledge' [Prov.
   10:14].

   M. "The nations of the world are called unblemished, and Israel is
   called unblemished.

   N. "The nations of the world are called unblemished: 'Unblemished as
   are those that go down to the pit' [Prov. 1:12].

   O. "And Israel is called unblemished: 'The unblemished will inherit
   goodness' [Prov. 28:10].

   S. "The nations of the world are called righteous, and Israel is called
   righteous.

   T. "The nations of the world are called righteous: 'And righteous men
   shall judge them' [Ez. 23:45].

   U. "And Israel is called righteous: 'And your people—all of them are
   righteous' [Is. 60:21].

   V. "The nations of the world are called mighty, and Israel is called
   mighty.

   W. "The nations of the world are called mighty: 'Why do you boast of
   evil, O mighty man' [Ps. 52:3].

   X. "And Israel is called mighty: 'Mighty in power, those who do his
   word' " [Ps. 103:20].

The concluding element is the striking one. "Might" now takes on a meaning
of its own, one that is comfortable for the subordinated party to the dispute.
At each point Israel stands in the balance against the nations of the world, the

one weighed against the other. We cannot identify the passage with the age at hand. "Rome" is hardly "the nations of the world." Even though the nations of the world are subject to the same language as is applied to Israel, they still do not fall into the same classification. For language is dual. When a word applies to Israel, it serves to praise, and when the same word applies to the nations, it underlines their negative character. Both are called "congregation," but the nations' congregation is desolate, and so throughout, as the context of the passage cited concerning the nations repeatedly indicates. The nations' sages are wiped out; the unblemished nations go down to the pit; the nations, called men, only work iniquity. Now that is precisely the contrast drawn in Isaac's saying, so, as I said, the whole should be deemed a masterpiece of unitary composition. Then the two types of exegesis—direct and peripheral—turn out to complement one another, each making its own point.

We turn to yet a third response to the same question, does God yet love Israel? This one goes still further than the preceding, since it credits Israel with nothing less than the creation of the world!

XXXVI:IV

1. A. "But now thus says the Lord, he who created you is Jacob, and he who formed you is Israel" (Is. 43:1).

   B. R. Phineas in the name of R. Reuben said, "[Said] the Holy One, blessed be he, to his world, 'O my world, my world! Shall I tell you who created you, Israel is the one who formed you,' as it is written, 'He who created you is Jacob, and he who formed you is Israel'" (Is. 43:1).

   D. R. Joshua b. Nehemiah in the name of R. Haninah bar Isaac: "The heaven and the earth were created only on account of the merit of Jacob.

   E. "What is the proof text? 'For he established a testimony on account of Jacob' [Ps. 78:5], and 'testimony' can mean only heaven and earth, as it is written, 'I call heaven and earth to testify against you this day'" (Deut. 4:26).

   H. Said R. Benaiah, "The heaven and earth were created only on account of the merit of Moses.

   I. "For it is written, 'And he chose a beginning part [namely Moses] for himself'" (Deut. 33:21).

   J. Said R. Abbahu, "Everything was created only on account of the merit of Jacob."

In the contrast to Aphrahat's statements we find these allegations provocative indeed. And this brings us back, in the setting of the affirmation of Israel, to the allegation of Aphrahat that Israel enjoys no future. Within their theory of Israel as an extended family, sages laid heavy emphasis on the legacy of merit bequeathed by the patriarchs and matriarchs. And that merit is what saves

Israel, as at Lev. R. XXXVI:V.1.B: "if the deeds of Jacob are insufficient, there are the deeds of Isaac, and if the deeds of Isaac are insufficient, there are the deeds of Abraham." Each component of the system plays its role, even the land itself possessing merit:

Aphrahat presents an array of prophetic proof-texts for the same proposition. Then he turns to the peoples and declares that they have taken the place of the people: "Concerning the vocation of the peoples Isaiah said, 'It shall come to be in the last days that the mountain of the House of the Lord will be established at the head of the mountains and high above the heights. Peoples will come together to it, and many peoples will go and say, Come, let us go up to the mountain of the Lord, to the House of the God of Jacob. He will teach us his ways, and we shall walk in his paths. For from Zion the law will go forth, and the word of the Lord from Jerusalem' (Is. 2:2, 3)." Does Israel not hope for redemption in the future? Indeed so, but they are wrong: "Two times only did God save Israel: Once from Egypt, the second time from Babylonia; from Egypt by Moses, and from Babylonia by Ezra and by the prophecy of Haggai and Zechariah. Haggai said, 'Build this house, and I shall have pleasure in it, and in it I shall be glorified, says the Lord' (Hag. 1:8). . . . All of these things were said in the days of Zerubbabel, Haggai, and Zechariah. They were exhorting concerning the building of the house." The house was built—and then destroyed, and it will not be rebuilt (Aphrahat wrote before Julian's proposed rebuilding of the Temple, so he could not have derived further proof from that disaster).

So much for the challenge of those who held such views as Aphrahat expresses. The case is complete: the people which is no-people, the people which is of the peoples, have taken the place of the people which claims to carry forward the salvific history of ancient Israel. The reason is in two complementary parts. First, Israel has rejected salvation, so lost its reason to exist, and, second, the no-people have accepted salvation, so gained its reason to exist. The threads of the dispute link into a tight fabric: The shift in the character of politics, marked by the epochal triumph of Christianity in the state, bears profound meaning for the messianic mission of the Church, and, further, imparts a final judgment on the salvific claim of the competing nations of God—the Church and Israel. What possible answer can sages have proposed to this indictment? Since at the heart of the matter lies the claim that Israel persists in the salvific heritage that has passed to the Christians, sages reaffirm that Israel persists—just as Paul had framed matters—after the flesh, an unconditional and permanent status. For one never ceases to be the son of his mother and his father, and the daughter is always the daughter of her father and her mother. So Israel after the flesh constitutes the family, in the most physical form, of Abraham, Isaac, and Jacob. And, moreover, as that family, Israel inherits the heritage of salvation handed on by the patriarchs and matriarchs. The spiritualization of "Israel" here finds its opposite and counterpart: the utter and complete "genealogization" of Israel.

Leviticus Rabbah and Israel's National Crisis

Israel remains Israel, the Jewish people, after the flesh, because Israel today continues the family begun by Abraham, Isaac, Jacob, Joseph, and the other tribal founders, and bears the heritage bequeathed by them. That conviction they were Israel never required articulation. The contrary possibility fell wholly outside of sages' (and all Jews') imagination. To state matters negatively, the people could no more conceive that they were not the daughters and sons of their fathers and mothers than that they were not one large family, that is, the family of Abraham, Isaac, and Jacob: Israel after the flesh. That is what "after the flesh" meant. The powerful stress on the enduring merit of the patriarchs and matriarchs, the social theory that treated Israel as one large extended family, the actual children of Abraham, Isaac, and Jacob—these metaphors for the fleshly continuity surely met head-on the contrary position framed by Paul and restated by Christian theologians from his time onward. In this respect, while Aphrahat did not deny the Israel-ness of Israel, the Jewish people, he did underline the futility of enduring as Israel. Maintaining that Israel would see no future salvation amounted to declaring that Israel, the Jewish people, pursued no worthwhile purpose in continuing to endure. Still, the argument is direct and concrete: "Who is Israel? Who enjoys salvation? To sages, as we shall see, the nations of the world serve God's purpose in ruling Israel, just as the prophets had said, and Israel, for its part, looks forward to a certain salvation.

The position of the framers of Leviticus Rabbah emerges in both positive and negative formulations. On the positive side, Israel, the Jewish people, the people of whom Scriptures spoke and to whom, today, sages now speak, is God's first love. That position presents no surprises and could have been stated with equal relevance in any circumstances. We in no way can imagine that the authors of Leviticus Rabbah stress the points that they do because Christians have called them into question. When we survey the verses important to Aphrahat's case and ask what, in the counterpart writings of sages in all of late antiquity, people say about those same verses, we find remarkably little attention to the florilegium of proof-texts adduced by Aphrahat (see Neusner 1971, 150–95). While the argument over who is Israel did not take shape on the foundation of a shared program of verses, on which each party entered its position, the issue was one and the same. And the occasion—the political crisis of the fourth century—faced both parties.

Sages delivered a message particular to their system. The political context imparted to that message urgency for Israel beyond their small circle. As to confronting the other side, no sage would concede what to us is self-evident. This was the urgency of the issue. For the definition of what was at issue derived from the common argument of the age: Who is the Messiah? Christ or someone else? Here too, while the argument between Christian theologians and Judaic sages on the present status of Israel, the Jewish people, went forward on the same basic issues, it ran along parallel lines. Lines of argument never intersected at all, just as, in our review of sage's doctrine of the Messiah, we could not find a point of intersection with the Christian position on the Christhood of Jesus. The issue in both topics, however, is the same, even though the exposition of arguments on one side's proposition in no way intersected with the other side's.

When Aphrahat denied that God loves Israel any more, and contemporary sages affirmed that God yet loves Israel and always will, we come to a clear-cut exchange of views on a common topic. Parallel to Aphrahat's sustained demonstrations on a given theme, the framers of Leviticus Rabbah laid forth thematic exercises, each one serving in a cumulative way to make a given point on a single theme. To describe the sages' position, therefore, we do well to follow their ideas in their own chosen medium of expression. I can find no more suitable way of recapitulating their reply to the question, Who is Israel? than by a brief survey of one of the sustained essays they present on the subject in Leviticus Rabbah.[3] We proceed to the unfolding, in Leviticus Rabbah Parashah Two, of the theme: Israel is precious. At Lev. R. II:III.2.B, we find an invocation of the genealogical justification for the election of Israel: "He said to him, 'Ephraim, head of the tribe, head of the session, one who is beautiful and exalted above all of my sons will be called by your name: [Samuel, the son of Elkanah, the son of Jeroham,] the son of Tohu, the son of Zuph, an Ephraimite' [1 Sam. 1:1]: 'Jerobaom son of Nabat, an Ephraimite' [1 Sam. 11:26]. 'And David was an Ephraimite, of Bethlehem in Judah'" (1 Sam. 17:12). Since Ephraim, that is Israel, had been exiled, the deeper message cannot escape our attention. Whatever happens, God loves Ephrain. However Israel suffers, God's love endures, and God cares. In context, that message brings powerful reassurance. Facing a Rome gone Christian, sages had to state the obvious, which no longer seemed self-evident at all. What follows spells out this very point: God is especially concerned with Israel.

C. "So the Holy One, blessed be he, makes mention of the merit of the fathers and alongside he makes mention of the merit of the land: 'Then I will remember my covenant with Jacob, [and I will remember my covenant with Isaac and my covenant with Abraham,] and I will remember the land" (Lev. 26:42).

Then has the merit of the patriarchs and matriarchs exhausted itself? That question demands a response, and, at XXXVI:VI.1ff., we find the one that people must have hoped to hear:

J. R. Yudan bar Hanan in the name of R. Berekiah said, "If you see that the merit of the patriarchs is slipping away, and the merit of the ma-

3. The complete texts are in the Appendix to this chapter.

triarchs is trembling, then go and cleave to the performance of deeds of
loving kindness.

K.   "That is in line with the following verse of Scripture: 'For the mountains
      will melt (YMWSW), and the hills will tremble, [but my love will not
      depart from you]' [Is. 54:10].

L.   " 'Mountains' refer to the patriarchs, and 'hills' to the matriarchs.

M.   "Henceforward: 'But my love will not (YMWS) depart from you' " (Is.
      54:10).

N.   Said R. Aha, "The merit of the patriarchs endures forever. Forever do
      people call it to mind, saying, 'For the Lord your God is a merciful God.
      He will not fail you nor destroy you nor forget the covenant he made
      with your fathers' " (Deut. 4:31).

The theme of the patriarchs, occuring at Lev. 26:42, accounts for the inclusion of this elegant exercise.

Sages recognized in the world only one counterpart to Israel, and that was
Rome. Rome's history formed the counterweight to Israel's. So Rome as a social entity weighed in the balance against Israel. That is why we return to the
corollary question: who is Rome? For we can know who is Israel only if we
can also explain who is Rome. And, I should maintain, explaining who is
Rome takes on urgency at the moment when Rome presents to Israel problems
of an unprecedented character. This matter belongs in any picture of who is
Israel. Sages' doctrine of Rome forms the counterpart to Christian theologians' theory on who is Israel. Just as Aphrahat explains who are the Christians and also who is Israel today, so sages in Leviticus Rabbah develop an
important theory on who is Rome. They too propose to account for the way
things are, and that means they have to explain who is this counterpart to
Israel. And sages' theory does respond directly to the question raised by the
triumph of Christianity in the Roman Empire. For, as we shall see, the characterization of Rome in Leviticus Rabbah bears the burden of their judgment on
the definition of the Christian people, as much as the sages' characterization
of Rome in Genesis Rabbah expressed their judgment of the place of Rome in
the history of Israel.

To understand that position on the character of Rome, we have first of all to
see that it constitutes a radical shift in the characterization of Rome in the
unfolding canon of the sages' Judaism. Rome in the prior writings, the Mishnah
(ca. A.D. 200) and the Tosefta (ca. A.D. 300–400), stood for a particular
place. We begin, once more, with the view of the Mishnah. Had matters remained much the same from the earlier writings, in the late second century, to
the later ones, in the fourth and fifth centuries, we could not maintain that
what is said in the fourth-century documents testifies in particular to intellectual events of the fourth century. We should have to hold that, overall, the
doctrine was set and endured in its original version. What happened later on
would then have no bearing upon the doctrine at hand, and my claim of a

confrontation on a vivid issue would not find validation. But the doctrine of Rome does shift from the Mishnah to the fourth-century sages' writings, Leviticus Rabbah, Genesis Rabbah, and the Talmud of the Land of Israel. That fact proves the consequence, in the interpretation of ideas held in the fourth century, of the venue of documents in that time.

In chapter 2 we saw the adumbration of the position that, in Leviticus Rabbah, would come to remarkably rich expression. Rome now stood for much more than merely a place among other places. Rome took up a position in the unfolding of the empires—Babylonia, Media, Greece, then Rome. Still more important, Rome is the penultimate empire on earth. Israel will constitute the ultimate one. That message, which puts the shifts in world history in a pattern and places at the apex of the shift Israel itself, directly and precisely takes up the issue made urgent just now: the advent of the Christian emperors. Why do I maintain, as I do, that in the characterization of Rome as the fourth and penultimate empire/animal, sages address issues of their own day? Because Rome, among the successive empires, bears special traits, most of which derive from the distinctively Christian character of Rome. Let me spell this out.

We start with the symbolization of Rome in the books that reached closure before the conversion of Constantine—the Mishnah, Pirqé Avot, and the Tosefta, and only then we turn to Leviticus Rabbah (and, for yet another exercise in symbolization of Christian Rome, Genesis Rabbah). If we ask the Mishnah, ca. A.D. 200, its chief view of the world beyond, it answers with a simple principle: the framers of the document insist that the world beyond was essentially undifferentiated. The important fact is that Rome was in no way singled out; it formed part of an undifferentiated world, not a way-station on the road to Israel's redemption. Rome, to the authors of the Mishnah, proved no more, and no less, important than any other place in that undifferentiated world; so far as the epochs of human history were concerned, these emerged solely from within Israel, and, in particular, from the history of Israel's cult, as M. Zeb. 14:4–9 lays matters out in terms of the cult's location, and M. R.H. 4:1–4 in terms of the before and after of the destruction. The undifferentiation of the outside world may be conveyed in a simple fact. In the Mishnah's law the entire earth outside of the Land of Israel was held to suffer from contamination by corpses. Hence the earth was unclean with a severe mode of uncleanness, inaccessible to the holy and life-sustaining processes of the cult. If an Israelite artist were asked to paint a wall-portrait of the world beyond the Land, he would paint the entire wall white, the color of death. The outside world, in the imagination of the Mishnah's law, was the realm of death. Among corpses, how are we to make distinctions? We turn then to how the Mishnah and the tractate Abot treat Rome, both directly and in the symbolic form of Esau and Edom. Since the system treats all gentiles as essentially the same, Rome, for its part, will not present a theme of special interest. If my description of the Mishnah's basic mode of differentiation among outsiders proves sound, then Rome should not vastly differ from other outsiders.

As a matter of fact, if we turn to H. Y. Kasovsky (1956, vols. 1, 2, 4) and look for Edom, Esau, Ishmael, and Rome, we come away disappointed. "Edom" and "Esau" in the sense of Rome do not occur. "Edom," stands for the Edomites of biblical times (M. Yeb. 8:3) and the territory of Edom (M. Ket. 5:8). "Ishmael," who like Edom later stands for Rome, supplies the name of a sage, nothing more. As to Rome itself, the picture is not notably different. There is a "Roman hyssop," (M. Par. 11:7, M. Neg. 14:6), and Rome occurs as a place-name (M. A.Z. 4:7). Otherwise I do not see a single passage indicated by Kasovsky in which Rome serves as a topic of interest, and, it goes without saying, in no place does "Rome" stand for an age in human history, let alone the counterpart to and opposite of Israel. Rome is part of the undifferentiated other, the outside world of death beyond. That fact takes on considerable meaning when we turn to the later fourth- and fifth-century compilations of scriptural exegeses. But first, we turn to the Mishnah's closest companion, the Tosefta.

In the Tosefta, a document containing systematic and extensive supplements to the sayings of the Mishnah, we find ourselves entirely within the Mishnah's circle of meanings and values. When, therefore, we ask how the Tosefta's authors incorporate and treat apocalyptic verses of Scripture, as they do, we find that they reduce to astonishingly trivial and local dimensions materials bearing for others world-historical meaning—including symbols later invoked by sages themselves to express the movement and meaning of history. No nation, including Rome, plays a role in the Tosefta's interpretation of biblical passages presenting historical apocalypse, as we now see in the Tosefta's treatment of the apocalyptic vision of Daniel. That fact matters, because in Leviticus Rabbah the resort to animals to symbolize empires and so express an apocalyptic view of history does center on the identification of the animals of Scripture with the great pagan empires, including Rome. But here we find that history happens in what takes place in the sages' debates—there alone!

T. Miqvaot 7:11

A.   A cow which drank purification-water, and which one slaughtered within twenty-four hours—

B.   This was a case, and R. Yose the Galilean did declare it clean, and R. Aqiba did declare it unclean.

C.   R. Tarfon supported R. Yose the Galilean. R. Simeon ben Nanos supported R. Aqiba.

D.   R. Simeon b. Nanos dismissed [the arguments of] R. Tarfon. R. Yose the Galilean dismissed [the arguments of] R. Simeon b. Nanos.

E.   R. Aqiba dismissed [the arguments of] R. Yose the Galilean.

F.   After a time, he [Yose] found an answer for him [Aqiba].

G.   He said to him, "Am I able to reverse myself?"

H.   He said to him, "Not anyone [may reverse himself], but you [may do so], for you are Yose the Galilean."

I.   [He said to him,] "I shall say to you: Lo, Scripture states, 'And they shall be kept for the congregation of the people of Israel for the water for impurity' (Num. 19:9).

J.   "Just so long as they are kept, lo, they are water for impurity—but not after a cow has drunk them."

K.   This was a case, and thirty-two elders voted in Lud and declared it clean.

L.   At that time R. Tarfon recited this verse:

M.   'I saw the ram goring westward and northward and southward, and all the animals were unable to stand against it, and none afforded protection from its power, and it did just as it liked and grew great' (Dan. 8:4)—

N.   "[This is] R. Aqiba.

O.   " 'As I was considering, behold, a he-goat came from the west across the face of the whole earth, without touching the ground; and the goat had a conspicuous horn between his eyes.

P.   " 'He came to the ram with the two horns, which I had seen standing on the bank of the river, and he ran at him in his mighty wrath. I saw him come close to the ram, and he was enraged against him and struck the ram and broke his two horns'—this is R. Aqiba and R. Simeon b. Nanos.

Q.   " 'And the ram had no power to stand before him'—this is R. Aqiba.

R.   " 'But he cast him down to the ground and trampled upon him'—this is R. Yose the Galilean.

S.   " 'And there was no one who could rescue the ram from his power'— these are the thirty-two elders who voted in Lud and declared it clean.' "

I cite the passage here only to underline the contrast between the usage at hand and the one we shall find in the late fourth- or early fifth-century composition. Without seeing the foregoing treatment of the vision at hand, we shall hardly realize how vast a shift is about to take place.

Since, in a moment, we shall take up later fourth- or early fifth-century writings, when Rome had turned definitively Christian, we do well to ask the Tosefta to tell us how it chooses to speak of Christianity. The contrast to Christians' view of themselves as the new Israel proves striking. Here too the topic (if it is present at all) turns out to deal with a trivial heresy, and not with a world-historical social entity, a fact that in a moment will strike us as significant. We have no firm date for the Tosefta, so we do not know for whom the document speaks. Still, we note that to the first-century authority, Tarfon is attributed the angry observation that there were people around who knew the truth of the Torah but rejected it:

Tosefta Shabbat 13:5

A.   The books of the Evangelists and the books of the minim they do not save from a fire [on the Sabbath]. They are allowed to burn up where they are, they and [even] the references to the Divine Name that are in them. . . .

B.   Said R. Tarfon, "May I bury my sons if such things come into my hands
     and I do not burn them, and even the references to the Divine Name
     which are in them. And if someone was running after me, I should es-
     cape into a temple of idolatry, but I should not go into their houses of
     worship.
C.   "For idolaters do not recognize the Divinity in denying him, but these
     recognize the Divinity and deny him. About them Scripture states, 'Be-
     hind the door and the doorpost you have set your symbol for deserting
     me, you have uncovered your bed' (Is. 57:8)."

In this passage, to be sure, the Christians are a variety of Israel, but they form
merely a heretical group. They know the truth but deny it—a kind of exasper-
ated judgment Christians would later lay on Israel. But a view of this kind
hardly generates a cosmic theory of who the Christians are in the setting of
Israel. Christians play no role in history, because they do not form a social
group, an entity demanding attention, the way Israel does—and, as we shall
see, the way Rome does.

Sages make history through the thoughts they think and the rules they lay
down. In such a context, we find no interest either in the outsiders and their
powers, or in the history of the empires of the world, or even less, in redemption and the messianic fulfillment of time. The statement has long persuaded
scholars that the rabbinic authority recognized the difference between pagans
and those *minim* under discussion, reasonably assumed to be Christian. I see
no reason to differ from the established consensus. The upshot is simple:
when Christians come under discussion, they appear as a source of exasperation, not as "Rome," that is, Israel's counterpart and opposite, let alone as
ruler of the world and precursor to Israel's final triumph in history. We stand a
considerable distance from deep thought about Israel and Rome, Jacob and
Esau, this age and the coming one. What we witness is a trivial dispute within
the community about heretics who should, but do not, know better. And when
we hear that mode of thought, we look back with genuine disappointment
upon the materials at hand. They in no way consider the world-historical
issues that would face Israel, and the reason, I maintain, is that, at the point at
which the document in which the passage occurs was brought to closure, no
one imagined what would ultimately take place: the conversion of the empire
to Christianity, the triumph of Christianity on the stage of history.

We turn, finally, to the usage in the Tosefta of the words Esau, Edom, Ishmael, and Rome, which in just a moment will come to center stage. Relying
on H. Y. Kasovsky (1932–61, vols. 1, 3, 6), we find pretty much the same
sort of usages, in the same proportions, as the Mishnah has already shown us.
Specifically, Edom is a biblical people, T. Yeb. 8:1, Niddah 6:1, Qid. 5:4.
Ishmael is a proper name for several sages. More important, Ishmael never
stands for Rome. And Rome itself? We have Todor of Rome (T. Bes. 2:15),
Rome as a place where people live, e.g., "I saw it in Rome" (T. Yoma 3:8), "I

taught this law in Rome" (T. Nid. 7:1, T. Miq. 4:7). And that is all. Rome undergoes no process of symbolization, plays no role in an apocalyptic conception of history. Rome is like any other place, only more important; a mere metropolis, not the counterweight to Israel in the history of the world from creation to salvation.

If we were to propose a thesis on the social theory of "Rome" and of "Christianity," or of the people that was a no-people or of the people that is made up of the peoples, in the Talmud and Midrash, based on the evidence at hand, it would not produce many propositions. Sages in the documents we have rapidly reviewed do not theorize on such matters; we detect not the slightest effort to symbolize these closely related figures. That fact takes on importance when, in Leviticus Rabbah, we do see a substantial effort to characterize, through symbolization, the Rome that has become Christian. But for the present writings Rome is a place, and no biblical figures or places prefigure the place of Rome in the history of Israel. That is so even though the authors of the Mishnah and the Tosefta knew full well who had destroyed the Temple and closed of Jerusalem and what these events had meant. Christianity plays no role of consequence; no one takes the matter very seriously. Christians are people who know the truth but deny it. To state the negative: Rome does not stand for Israel's nemesis and counterpart, Rome did not mark an epoch in the history of the world, Israel did not encompass Rome in Israel's history of humanity, and Rome did not represent one of the four monarchies—the last and the worst, prior to Israel's rule. To invoke a modern category, Rome stood for a perfectly secular matter: a place where things happened. Rome in no way symbolized anything beyond itself. And Israel's sages did not find they had to take seriously the presence or claims of Christianity. So much for books brought to closure, in the case of the Mishnah, at ca. A.D. 200, and, in the case of the Tosefta perhaps a hundred years later (no one knows). We come now to the year 400 or so, to documents produced in the century after such momentous events as the conversion of Constantine to Christianity, the catastrophe of Julian's failure in attempting to rebuild the Temple, the repression of paganism and its affect on Judaism, the Christianization of the Holy Land, and, it appears, the conversion of sizable numbers of Jews in the Land of Israel to Christianity and the consequent Christianization of Palestine (no longer, in context, the Land of Israel at all).

What is the alternative to the sages' use, in the Mishnah and the Tosefta, of the sort of symbols just now examined? Let us briefly place into context the apocalyptic treatment of history we are about to examine in Leviticus Rabbah. We do so by seeing how Jerome, great exegete of the Bible and contemporary of the framers of our documents, dealt with the symbols of the animals of Leviticus 11. When we turn to Jerome's comment on Leviticus 11:3, we find a preparation for the treatment of the same matter in Leviticus Rabbah, namely, the apocalyptic reading of the humble matters of the beasts Israel may and may not eat:

> The Jew is single-hoofed and therefore he is unclean. The Manichean is single-hoofed and therefore he is unclean. And since he is single-hoofed he does not chew what he eats, and what has once gone into his stomach he does not bring up again and chew and make fine, so that what had been coarse would return to the stomach fine. This is indeed a matter of divine mystery. The Jew is single-hoofed, for he believes in only one Testament and does not ruminate; he only reads the letter and things over nothing, nor does he seek anything deeper. The Christian, however, is cloven-hoofed and ruminates. That is, he believes in both Testaments and he often ponders each Testament, and whatever lies hidden in the letter he brings forth in the spirit. (In Ramsay 1985, 25–26)

This kind of writing is hardly history at all, or so it would seem. But apocalyptic bears a judgment of history as well, and the writing of this kind of reflection serves a deep purpose indeed, even within the historical realm.

What we are about to examine is a statement in which Rome is represented as only Christian Rome can have been represented: it looks kosher but it is unkosher. Pagan Rome cannot ever have looked kosher, but Christian Rome, with its appeal to ancient Israel, could and did and moreover claimed to. It bore some traits that validate, but lacked others that validate—just as Jerome said of Israel. It would be difficult to find a more direct confrontation between two parties to an argument. Now the issue is the same—who is the true Israel?—and the proof-texts are the same; moreover, the proof-texts are read in precisely the same way. Only the conclusions differ.

The polemic represented in Leviticus Rabbah by the symbolization of Christian Rome makes the simple point that, first, Christians are no different from, and no better than, pagans; they are essentially the same. The Christians' claim to form part of Israel, then, requires no serious attention. Since Christians came to Jews with precisely that claim, the sages' response—they are another Babylonia—bears a powerful polemic charge. But that is not the whole story, as we see. Second, just as Israel had survived Babylonia, Media, Greece, so would it endure to see the end of Rome (whether pagan, whether Christian). But there is a third point. Rome really does differ from the earlier, pagan empires, and that polemic shifts the entire discourse, once we hear its symbolic vocabulary properly. Christianity was not merely part of a succession of undifferentiated modes of paganism. The symbols assigned to Rome attributed worse, more dangerous traits than those assigned to the earlier empires. The pig pretends to be clean, just as the Christians give the signs of adherence to the God of Abraham, Isaac, and Jacob. That much the passage concedes. For the pig is not clean, exhibiting some, but not all, of the required indications, and Rome is not Israel, even though it shares Israel's Scripture. That position, denying to Rome in its Christian form a place in the family of Israel, forms the counterpart to the view of Aphrahat that Israel today is no longer Israel—again, a confrontation on issues. Since the complete passage is given in the appendix to this chapter, I present only the critical point at which the animals that are invoked include one that identifies Rome as partly kosher, partly not, therefore more dangerous than anyone else.

XIII:V

9. A. Moses foresaw what the evil kingdoms would do [to Israel].

    B. "The camel, rock badger, and hare" (Deut. 14:7). [Compare: "Nevertheless, among those that chew the cud or part the hoof, you shall not eat these: the camel, because it chews the cud but does not part the hoof, is unclean to you. And the hare, because it chews the cud but does not part the hoof, is unclean to you, and the pig, because it parts the hoof and is cloven-footed, but does not chew the cud, is unclean to you" (Lev. 11:4–8).]

    C. The camel (GML) refers to Babylonia, [in line with the following verse of Scripture: "O daughter of Babylonia, you who are to be devastated!] Happy will be he who requites (GML) you, with what you have done to us" (Ps. 147:8).

    D. "The rock badger" (Deut. 14:7)—this refers to Media.

    E. Rabbis and R. Judah b. R. Simon.

    F. Rabbis say, "Just as the rock badger exhibits traits of uncleanness and traits of cleanness, so the kingdom of Media produced both a righteous man and a wicked one."

    G. Said R. Judah b. R. Simon, "The last Darius was Esther's son. He was clean on his mother's side and unclean on his father's side."

    H. "The hare" (Deut 14:7)—this refers to Greece. The mother of King Ptolemy was named "Hare" [in Greek: lagos].

    I. "The pig" (Deut. 14:7)—this refers to Edom [Rome].

    J. Moses made mention of the first three in a single verse and the final one in a verse by itself [Deut. 14:7, 8)]. Why so?

    K. R. Yohanan and R. Simeon b. Laqish.

    L. R. Yohanan said, "It is because [the pig] is equivalent to the other three."

    M. And R. Simeon b. Laqish said, "It is because it outweighs them."

    N. R. Yohanan objected to R. Simeon b. Laqish, "Prophesy, therefore, son of man, clap your hands [and let the sword come down twice, yea thrice]' (Ez. 21:14)."

    O. And how does R. Simeon b. Laqish interpret the same passage? He notes that [the threefold sword] is doubled (Ez. 21:14).

10. A. [Gen. R. 65:1:] R. Phineas and R. Hilqiah in the name of R. Simon: "Among all the prophets, only two of them revealed [the true evil of Rome], Assaf and Moses.

    B. "Assaf said, 'The pig out of the wood ravages it' (Ps. 80:14).

    C. "Moses said, 'And the pig, [because it parts the hoof and is cloven-footed but does not chew the cud]' (Lev. 11:7).

    D. "Why is [Rome] compared to a pig?

    E. "It is to teach you the following: Just as, when a pig crouches and produces its hooves, it is as if to say, 'See how I am clean [since I have a cloven hoof],' so this evil kingdom takes pride, seizes by violence, and steals, and then gives the appearance of establishing a tribunal for justice."

11. A. Another interpretation: "The camel" (Lev. 11:4).

B. This refers to Babylonia.

C. "Because it chews the cud [but does not part the hoof]" (Lev. 11:4).

D. For it brings forth praises [with its throat] of the Holy One, blessed be he. [The Hebrew words for "chew the cud"—bring up cud—are now understood to mean "give praise." GRH is connected with GRWN, throat, hence, "bring forth [sounds of praise through] the throat."

N. "The rock badger" (Lev. 11:5)—this refers to Media.

O. "For it chews the cud"—for it gives praise to the Holy One, blessed be he: "Thus says Cyrus, king of Persia, 'All the kingdoms of the earth has the Lord, the God of the heaven, given me'" (Ezra 1:2).

P. "The hare"—this refers to Greece.

Q. "For it chews the cud"—for it gives praise to the Holy One, blessed be he.

S. "The pig" (Lev. 11:7)—this refers to Edom.

T. "For it does not chew the cud"—for it does not give praise to the Holy One, blessed be he.

U. And it is not enough that it does not give praise, but it blasphemes and swears violently, saying, "Whom do I have in heaven, and with you I want nothing on earth" (Ps. 73:25).

We first review the message of the construction as a whole, only part of which is before us. This comes in two parts, first the explicit, then the implicit. As to the former, the first claim is that God had told the prophets what would happen to Israel at the hands of the pagan kingdoms, Babylonia, Media, Greece, Rome. These are further represented by Nebuchadnezzar, Haman, Alexander for Greece, Edom or Esau, interchangeably, for Rome. The same vision came from Adam, Abraham, Daniel, and Moses. The same policy toward Israel—oppression, destruction, enslavement, alienation from the true God—emerged from all four. How does Rome stand out? First, it was made fruitful through the prayer of Isaac in behalf of Esau. Second, Edom is represented by the fourth and final beast. Rome is related through Esau, as Babylonia, Media, and Greece are not. The fourth beast was seen in a vision separate from the first three. It was worst of all and outweighed the rest. In the apocalypticizing of the animals of Lev. 11:4–8/Deut. 14:7—the camel, rock badger, hare, and pig—the pig, standing for Rome, again emerges as different from the others and more threatening than the rest. Just as the pig pretends to be a clean beast by showing the cloven hoof, but in fact is an unclean one, so Rome pretends to be just but in fact governs by thuggery. Edom does not pretend to praise God but only blasphemes. It does not exalt the righteous but kills them.

These symbols concede nothing to Christian monotheism and veneration of the Torah of Moses (in its written medium). Of greatest importance, while all the other beasts bring further beasts in their wake, the pig does not: "It does not bring another kingdom after it." It will restore the crown to the one who will truly deserve it, Israel. Esau will be judged by Zion, so Obadiah 1:21. Now how has the symbolization delivered an implicit message? It is in the treatment of Rome as distinct but essentially equivalent to the former kingdoms. This seems to me a stunning way of saying that the now Christian empire in no way requires differentiation from its pagan predecessors. Nothing has changed, except that matters have gotten worse. Beyond Rome, standing in a straight line with the others, lies the true shift in history, the rule of Israel and the cessation of the dominion of the (pagan) nations.

Leviticus Rabbah came to closure, it is generally agreed, around A.D. 400, that is, approximately a century after the Roman Empire in the east had begun to become Christian, and a half-century after the last attempt to rebuilt the Temple in Jerusalem had failed—a tumultuous age indeed. Accordingly, we have had the chance to see how distinctive and striking are the ways in which, in the text at hand, the symbols of animals that stand for the four successive empires of humanity and point towards the messianic time serve for the framers' message. When the sages of the Mishnah and the Tosefta spoke of Edom and Edomites, they meant biblical Edom, a people in the vicinity of the land of Israel. By Rome they mean the city—that alone. That fact bears meaning when we turn to documents produced two centuries later, and one hundred years beyond the triumph of Christianity. When the sage of Genesis Rabbah spoke of Rome, it was not a political Rome but a messianic Rome that was at issue: Rome as surrogate for Israel, Rome as obstacle to Israel. Why? It is because Rome now confronts Israel with a crisis, and, I argue, Genesis Rabbah constitutes a response to that crisis. Rome in the fourth century became Christian. Sages responded by facing that fact quite squarely and saying, "Indeed, it is as you say, a kind of Israel, an heir of Abraham as your texts explicitly claim. But we remain the sole legitimate Israel, the bearer of the birthright—we and not you. So you are our brother: Esau, Ishmael, Edom." And the rest follows.

By rereading the story of the beginnings, sages discovered the answer and the secret of the end. Rome claimed to be Israel, and, indeed, sages conceded, Rome shared the patrimony of Israel. That claim took the form of the Christians' appropriation of the Torah as "the Old Testament," so sages acknowledged a simple fact in acceding to the notion that, in some way, Rome too formed part of Israel. But it was the rejected part, the Ishmael, the Esau, not the Isaac, not the Jacob. The advent of Christian Rome precipitated the sustained, polemical, and, I think, rigorous and well-argued rereading of beginnings in light of the end. Rome marked the conclusion of human history as Israel had known it. And beyond? The coming of the true Messiah, the redemption of Israel, the salvation of the world, the end of time. So the issues were not inconsiderable, and when the sages spoke of Esau/Rome, as they did so often, they confronted the life-or-death decision of the day. That in the age of Constantine a direct confrontaton, on a shared agenda of issues, between Judaic and Christian thinkers, took place hardly demands further proof.

Genesis Rabbah: The Claim of the Siblings

Having emphasized the genealogical theory of Israel, we have now to return to Genesis Rabbah and its account of the matter. For the framers of that document present a viewpoint that we do not find in Leviticus Rabbah, one important in outlining sages' view of Israel. Sages' mode of thought, as we know, reqired them to treat as personal matters of family relationships the history of Israel. It followed from this policy of the personalization of social entities—tribes as brothers, sons of one father—that if sages wished to absorb into their view of the world other components of the world community as they saw it, they would have to place into genealogical relationship with Israel these originally alien elements. So it is quite natural that sages found a genealogical tie to Rome. In that way they fit Rome into the history of Israel. The biblical account of Israel's history in Genesis showed the way. The time and urgency of the enterprise—the *genealogization* of Rome—derived of course from the crisis of the fourth century. Prior to that time, as we have noted, the documents of the canon reveal no such consideration. Afterward it became a commonplace.

We recall (chapter 2) that sages read the book of Genesis as a typology, as if at important points in the narrative it portrayed the history of Israel and Rome. Rome, as we shall now see, found representation in Esau, Edom, Ishmael, but, in Genesis Rabbah, mainly in Esau. It seems to me that the choice of Esau represents as powerful a judgment as the choice of the pig in Leviticus Rabbah. The message is the same. Rome is the brother—the genealogical connection—but the rejected brother. History thus has expanded to take account of what demanded explanation, what insisted upon categorization within the family theory of history. But at what cost for the larger apologetic! For that symbolization of Rome as brother concedes much, specifically recognizing—if only for the purpose of rejection—the claim of Christian Rome along with the family of Israel to inherit biblical Israel.

Why Rome in the form it takes in Genesis Rabbah? And why the obsessive character of the sages' disposition of the theme of Rome? Were their picture merely of Rome as tyrant and destroyer of the Temple, we should have no reason to link the text to the problems of the age of redaction and closure, namely the late fourth or early fifth century. But, as we have repeatedly observed, now it is Rome as Israel's brother, counterpart, and nemesis, Rome as the one thing standing in the way of Israel's, and the world's, ultimate salvation. So the stakes are different, and much higher. It is not a political Rome but a messianic Rome that is at issue: Rome as surrogate for Israel, Rome as obstacle to Israel. Rome now confronts Israel with a crisis, and, I argue, Genesis Rabbah like Leviticus Rabbah constitutes a response to that crisis. My argument is simple: Rome in the fourth century became Christian. Sages responded by facing that fact quite squarely and saying, "Indeed, it is as you say, a *kind* of Israel, an heir of Abraham as your texts explicitly claim. But we remain the sole legitimate Israel, the bearer of the birthright—we and not you. So you are our brother: Esau, Ishmael, Edom." And the rest follows. Accordingly, we should not find surprising sages' recurrent references, in the reading of Genesis, to the struggle of two equal powers, Rome and Israel, Esau and Jacob, Ishmael and Isaac. The world-historical change, marking the confirmation in politics and power of the Christians' claim that Christ was king over all humanity, demanded from sages an appropriate, and, to Israel, persuasive response.

By rereading the story of the beginnings, sages discovered the answer and the secret of the end. Rome claimed to be Israel, and, indeed, sages conceded, Rome shared the patrimony of Israel. That claim took the form of the Christians' appropriation of the Torah as "the Old Testament," so sages acknowledged a simple fact in acceding to the notion that, in some way, Rome too formed part of Israel. But, as I said, it was the rejected part, the Ishmael, the Esau; not the Isaac, not the Jacob. The advent of Christian Rome precipitated the sustained, polemical, and, I think, rigorous and well-argued rereading of beginnings in light of the end.

Let us begin our survey of the position of Genesis Rabbah with a simple example of how ubiquitous is the shadow of Ishmael/Esau/Edom/Rome. Wherever in Genesis Rabbah sages reflect on future history, their minds turn to their own day. They found the hour difficult, because Rome, now Christian, claimed that very birthright and blessing that they understood to be theirs alone. Christian Rome posed a threat without precedent. Now another dominion, besides Israel's, claimed the rights and blessings that sustained Israel. Sages found comfort in the iteration that the birthright, the blessing, the Torah, and the hope—all belonged to them and to none other. As the several antagonists of Israel stand for Rome in particular, so the traits of Rome, as sages perceived them, characterized the biblical heroes. Esau provided a favorite target. From the womb, Israel and Rome contended.

LXIII:VI

11. A. "And the childen struggled together [within her, and she said, 'If it is thus, why do I live?' So she went to inquire of the Lord. And the Lord said to her, 'Two nations are in your womb, and two peoples, born of you, shall be divided; the one shall be stronger than the other, and the elder shall serve the younger']" (Gen. 25:22–23):

3. A. "And the children struggled together within her:"

B. [Once more referring to the letters of the word "struggled," with special attention to the ones that mean "run,"] they wanted to run within her.

C. When she went by houses of idolatry, Esau would kick, trying to get out: "The wicked are estranged from the womb" (Ps. 58:4).

D. When she went by synagogues and study-houses, Jacob would kick, trying to get out: "Before I formed you in the womb, I knew you" (Jer. 1:5)."

LXIII:VII

2. A. "Two nations are in your womb, [and two peoples, born of you, shall be divided; the one shall be stronger than the other, and the elder shall serve the younger]" (Gen. 25:23).:

B. There are two proud nations in your womb, this one takes pride in his world, and that one takes pride in his world.

C. This one takes pride in his monarchy, and that one takes pride in his monarchy.

D. There are two proud nations in your womb.

E. Hadrian represents the nations, Solomon, Israel.

F. There are two who are hated by the nations in your womb. All the nations hate Esau, and all the nations hate Israel.

4. A. ". . . the one shall be stronger than the other, [and the elder shall serve the younger]" (Gen. 25:23):

B. R. Helbo in the name of the house of R. Shila: "Up to this point there were Sabteca and Raamah, but from you will come Jews and Romans." [Freedman, *Genesis Rabbah,* p. 561, n. 8: "Hitherto even the small nations such as Sabteca and Raamah counted; but henceforth all these will pale into insignificance before the two who will rise from you.]

5. A. ". . . and the elder shall serve the younger" (Gen. 25:23):

B. Said R. Huna, "If he has merit, he will be served, and if not, he will serve."

The verse underlines the point that there is natural enmity between Israel and Rome. Esau hated Israel even while he was still in the womb. Jacob, for his part, revealed from the womb those virtues that would characterize him later on, eager to serve God as Esau was eager to worship idols. The following is already familiar, but bears review because it links the two distinct symbolizations of Rome, the pig and Esau:

LXV:I

1. C.   R. Phineas and R. Hilqiah in the name of R. Simon: "Among all of the prophets, only two of them spelled out in public [the true character of Rome, represented by the swine], Asaf and Moses.

    D.   "Asaf: 'The swine out of the wood ravages it.'

    E.   "Moses: 'And the swine, because he parts the hoof' (Deut. 14:8).

    F.   "Why does Moses compare Rome to the swine? Just as the swine, when it crouches, puts forth its hoofs as if to say, 'I am clean,' so the wicked kingdom steals and grabs, while pretending to be setting up courts of justice.

    G.   "So Esau, for all forty years, hunted married women, ravished them, and when he reached the age of forty, he presented himself to his father, saying, 'Just as father got married at the age of forty, so I shall marry a wife at the age of forty.'

    H.   " 'When Esau was forty years old, he took to wife Judith, the daughter of Beeri, the Hittite, and Basemath, the daughter of Elon the Hittite.' "

The exegesis of course once more identifies Esau with Rome. The roundabout route linking the fact at hand, Esau's taking a wife, passes through the territory of Roman duplicity. Whatever the government does, it claims to do in the general interest. But it really has no public interest at all. Esau for his part spent forty years ravishing women and then, at the age of forty, pretended, to his father, to be upright. That, at any rate, is the parallel clearly intended by this obviously unitary composition. The issue of the selection of the intersecting verse does not present an obvious solution to me; it seems that only the identification of Rome with the swine accounts for the choice. The contrast between Israel and Esau produced an anguished observation. But here the Rome is not yet Christian, so far as the clear reference is concerned. More compelling evidence that the radical change in the character of Rome lies behind the exegetical polemic derives from Genesis Rabbah LXXV:IV, which follows.

The theories of the meaning of history and the identification of Israel cannot be sorted out. The one imparts its character to the other, and together the two theories take up the pressing issue of the turning of the age, the meaning of the new era. That the whole bears a profoundly eschatological meaning emerges at the end. For, if we follow sages' thought to its logical conclusion, they express the expectation that after Rome will come Israel, so they have reframed history into an eschatological drama—in the here and now. The sequence of empires—Babylonia, Media, Greece, Rome—does not end the story. There will then come Israel, the conclusion and climax of human history. So Rome bears a close relationship to Israel in yet another respect, and the genealogical definition of who is Israel—and who is Rome—bears consequences in a world-historical framework. Here Roman rule comes prior to Israel's:

LXXV:IV

2. A. "And Jacob sent messengers before him:"
   B. To this one [Esau] whose time to take hold of sovereignty would come before him [namely, before Jacob, since Esau would rule, then Jacob would govern].
   C. R. Joshua b. Levi said, "Jacob took off the purple robe and threw it before Esau, as if to say to him, 'Two flocks of starlings are not going to sleep on a single branch [so we cannot rule at the same time.'"
3. A. ". . . to Esau his brother:"
   B. Even though he was Esau, he was still his brother.

Numbers 2 and 3 make a stunning point. It is that Esau remains Jacob's brother, and that Esau rules before Jacob will. The application to contemporary affairs cannot be missed, both in the recognition of the true character of Esau—a brother!—and in the interpretation of the future of history. Rome claims now to serve the Messiah. But Esau, meaning Rome, will fall by the hand of the Messiah. The polemic is of course unmistakable. Not only is Rome not the messianic kingdom, but Rome will fall before the messianic kingdom that is coming.

LXXXIII:I

1. A. "These are the kings who reigned in the land of Edom before any king reigned over the Israelites: Bela the son of Beor reigned in Edom, the name of his city being Dinhabah" (Gen. 36:31–32):
   B. R. Isaac commenced discourse by citing this verse: "Of the oaks of Bashan they have made your oars" (Ez. 27:6).
   C. Said R. Isaac, "The nations of the world are to be compared to a ship. Just as a ship has its mast made in one place and its anchor somewhere else, so their kings: 'Samlah of Masrekah' (Gen. 36:36), 'Shaul of Rehobot by the river' (Gen. 36:27), and: 'These are the kings who reigned in the land of Edom before any king reigned over the Israelites.'"
2. A. ["An estate may be gotten hastily at the beginning, but the end thereof shall not be blessed" (Prov. 20:21)]: "An estate may be gotten hastily at the beginning:" "These are the kings who reigned in the land of Edom before any king reigned over the Israelites."
   B. ". . . but the end thereof shall not be blessed:" "And saviors shall come up on mount Zion to judge the mount of Esau" (Ob. 1:21).

Number 1 contrasts the diverse origin of Roman rulers with the uniform origin of Israel's king in the house of David. Number 2 makes the same point still more forcefully. Freedman makes sense of number 2 as follows: Though Esau was the first to have kings, his land will eventually be overthrown (Freedman, p. 766, n. 3). So the point is that Israel will have kings after Esau no longer does, and the verse at hand is made to point to the end or Rome, a striking revision to express the importance in Israel's history of events in the lives of the patriarchs. The same point is made in what follows, but the expectation proves acute and immediate.

LXXXIII:IV

3. A. "Magdiel and Iram: these are the chiefs of Edom, that is Esau, the father of Edom, according to their dwelling places in the land of their possession" (Gen. 36:42):

   B. On the day on which Litrinus came to the throne, there appeared to R. Ammi in a dream this message: "Today Magdiel has come to the throne."

   C. He said, "One more king is required for Edom [and then Israel's turn will come]."

We should not regard the eschatological drama in sages' theory as something in the far-distant future: "one more king" is coming. That is a stunning statement. Number 3 presents once more the theme that Rome's rule will extend only for a foreordained and limited time, at which point the Messiah will come. Israel's saints even now make possible whatever wise decisions Rome's rulers make. That forms an appropriate conclusion to the matter. Ending in the everyday world of the here and now, sages attribute to Israel's influence anything good that happens to Israel's brother, Rome.

Genealogy and the Political Crisis

Sages framed their political ideas within the metaphor of genealogy, because to begin with they appealed to the fleshly connection, the family, as the rationale for Israel's social existence. A family beginning with Abraham, Isaac, and Jacob, Israel could best sort out its relationships by drawing into the family other social entities with which it found it had to relate. So Rome became the brother. That affinity came to light only when Rome had turned Christian, and that point marked the need for the extension of the genealogical net. But the conversion to Christianity also justified sages' extending membership in the family to Rome, for Christian Rome shared with Israel the common patrimony of Scripture—and said so. The two facts, the one of the social and political metaphor by which sages interpreted events, the other of the very character of Christianity, account for the striking shift in the treatment of

Rome that does appear to have taken place in the formative century represented by work on Genesis Rabbah and Leviticus Rabbah.

In documents closed in earlier times, the Mishnah and the Tosefta, Rome symbolized little beyond itself, and Edom, Esau (absent in the Mishnah, a singleton in Tosefta), and Ishmael were concrete figures in the biblical narrative; they did not stand for nations in relationship to Israel. In later times these figures bore traits congruent with the facts of Christian rule. So we note the correspondence between the modes of symbolization—the pig, the sibling—and the facts of the Christian challenge to Judaism. That correspondence turns out to be remarkable when we compare the earlier writings, the Mishnah and the Tosefta, to the later ones, the two Rabbah-compilations. The substance of the matter is that Israel remains what it always was, and so too Esau. Esau now rules, Israel is next. In response to Aphrahat's program, we may compose out of Leviticus Rabbah and Genesis Rabbah an entirely appropriate reply: Israel "after the flesh" will enjoy salvation in time to come. And there is no other Israel. So to conclude where we began: does Israel today continue the Israel of ancient times? Indeed so. Israel now continues in a physical and spiritual way the life of Israel then. Second, will the promises of the prophets to Israel afford salvation for Israel in time to come? Yes, Israel "after the flesh" awaits the fulfillment of the prophetic promise of salvation. The issue is joined, fully, completely, head-on.

And well it was. Because the stakes, for both sides, were very high. Aphrahat alerts us to the Christians' human problem. They saw themselves as a people without a past, a no-people, a people gathered from the peoples. Who they can claim to be hardly derives from who they have been. Identifying with ancient Israel—a perfectly natural and correct initiative—admirably accounted for the Christian presence in humanity, provided a past, explained to diverse people what they had in common. One problem from Christian theologians' perspective demanded solution: the existing Israel, the Jewish people, which revered the same Scriptures and claimed descent, after the flesh, from ancient Israel. These—the Jews—traced their connection to ancient Israel, seeing it as natural and, also, supernatural. The family tie, through Abraham, Isaac, Jacob, formed a powerful apologetic indeed. The Jews furthermore pointed to their family record, the Scriptures, to explain whence they came and who they are.

So long as the two parties to the debate shared the same subordinated political circumstance, Jewry could quite nicely hold its own; the pleading tone of Aphrahat's writing opens a window onto the heart of the historical newcomers to salvation, as Christians saw themselves. But with the shift in the politics of the Empire, the terms of debate changed. The parvenu became paramount, the Christian party to the debate invoked its familiar position now with the power of the state in support.

For Israel, what was there to say, but what, in Israel's view, God had said to Israel in the Torah's record of the very beginnings of the world? What now makes that old message matter is simple: the specific context to which, at just this moment, the old words were spoken. That milieu is what imparts meaning to the message: the rise to state recognition and favor of one of the two parties to the dispute of the godly genealogy. And what gives that fact weight for us is the further, equally simple fact that, in the unfolding of the canon of the sages' Judaism, the documents before us contain the first explicit and emphatic statement of the age-old genealogy of God's people. So while the framers of Leviticus Rabbah may have stated in their own medium a familiar and routine message, and those of Genesis Rabbah may have contributed merely the recognition of suitable images for symbolizing a long-standing conception, still, the setting turns out to supply the catalyst of significance. Content, out of political context, is mere theology. But in political context, the theological issues, fully understood in all their urgency, focus on matters of social life or death. The doctrines of history and merit, of Israel's identity, selection, and grace, turn out to deal with the very life and identity of a people and their society.

5

Politics and Proof-Texts: Exegesis and Canon

A Test of Falsification

To show that two parties share a common debate presents more problems than to demonstrate the opposite. We have now accomplished the more difficult of the two tasks and turn to the easier but equally important one: to locate points at which no debate took place. Let me explain. A catastrophic political event imposed upon both sides a single agendum, and that is why each party defined issues in the same way. The same reason explains why each side appealed to a set of facts conceded as accurate by the other. That is, the requirements of discourse about a crisis shared in common demanded appeal to arguments that the one side imagined the other would find intelligible.[1] The categories of history, Messiah, and Israel presented the same principles of cogency and logic to both. A single historical imperative constituted by political change bearing religious implications impressed all sides, so we should hardly be surprised that one argument joined the two in a single prickly discourse. To test this theory, spelled out in the preceding chapters, we have to compose a test of falsification. Specifically, we ask whether the *absence* of a matter of public policy characterizes a case in which Judaic sages and Christian theologians do *not* undertake a debate on the same terms. The test must address a matter on which both parties formed opinions, that is, an issue of theological consequence. But discourse on such a matter, far from involving the same definition of what is at issue and invoking the same evidence, should show each party talking essentially to itself. Then we may discern the consequence to be imputed to the cases in which the two sides really do debate the same matters in

1. In this respect Aphrahat is our model. In all his arguments addressed to (imaginary) Jewish counterparts, he appeals only to verses cited from the Israelite prophets and writings. When he turns to Christian hearers, he cites New Testament writings. Overall, his mode of argument is historical, in that he appeals to historical facts he believes all parties concede, and then he adduces from those facts propositions that sustain his case and demolish that of his opponent. None of this is directed (in his mind) only to Church interests.

the same terms. For, as we have seen, the fourth century really did produce debate between Judaic and Christian intellectuals in a way in which the first, second, and third centuries did not.

The matter of the political consequences of debate therefore proves critical. Without them no confrontation on the same matters will have taken place— just as, for the rest of the history of the West, none did. I have argued that the reason for the shift in the fourth century derives from political events, which determined what we should today call public policy. My explanation is that what happened in the government of the Roman Empire imposed on all parties that uniform program of debate. We have now reviewed three cases in which, talking among themselves to be sure, each side in fact addressed an issue the other also took up. More significantly, each introduced into evidence arguments and evidence the other conceded to be valid. In each case, moreover, I was able to point to the political foundation of the issue: the consequences, for public policy, of the debate. So within a single framework of interpretation I have read Eusebius, Chrysostom, Aphrahat, and the sages who put together Genesis Rabbah, the Talmud of the Land of Israel, Leviticus Rabbah, and, again, Genesis Rabbah. I have asked an essentially political question and shown that each party answered that essentially political question.

The matter of public policy in these cases may be easily discerned. The interpretation of the historical turning, the identification of the facts of a shared systemic teleology, the definition of the social entity—all three formed at their foundations distinctively political issues. The reason is that conclusions people would reach on such matters would determine how each group would relate to, and treat, the other. In the case of the Christian government, public policy based on the theology at hand (in secular terms, the Christian ideology of state and government) would dictate the treatment of the Jews; for example, differentiating Jews from pagans as to matters of law and policy. The legislation of Theodosius on what Jews could and could not do constitutes an act of public policy; and that legislation expresses in political terms judgments on the Jews as a group, on the nature of the Christian state, on the identity of the Messiah and the salvation brought by him, and on the definition of Israel.

In the case of the Judaic sages, of course, the public policy entailed matters of attitude and viewpoint more than of immediate legislation. Christians ran the state and Jews governed, at best, some aspects of their collective life as a community. But Jewry too constituted a political entity, in that it did act collectively, and as an entity it did impose its will upon its members. So if Jews determined that, as a family, they carried forward the salvific history of Genesis, yet awaited redemption in the future, and truly constituted the children of Abraham, Isaac, and Jacob, then they would follow one set of policies rather than another. If, as was the case, they reached such conclusions, then as a group they would pursue one course of action rather than some other. They would persist in their hope, and therefore in their distinctive group life (these things seem nearly too obvious to say). They would not collectively convert to Christianity—surely a decision bearing important consequences, within the Jewish polity, for public, not merely social, policy.

To spell out the terms of the present exercise of falsification, I must exclude as well as include, explaining what is not, as well as what *is,* subject to description. For I maintain that the three categories we have treated are not exemplary of a general capacity for argument between Judaic and Christian intellectuals. I have then to explain why these categories—*and no others*—defined the condition for a genuine exchange of conflicting views on a single point, such as I have demonstrated took place, to be sure in a theoretical framework, if not in a concrete face-to-face disputation. My thesis concerning the centrality of political change in affecting theological discourse explains omissions: they bore no political consequences recognized by participants to the confrontation. In insisting on the political dimension of the three theological issues, I have now to construct a test of falsification of my theory. That is to say, I must now ask whether other issues, confronting groups but *not* of a political character, may present themselves. If they do, then I have further to find out whether, in disposing of such issues, a single shared program—a common definition of what is at hand, a common designation of probative arguments—turns up as well.

If in an essentially nonpolitical setting we find the two sides arguing about the same thing on the basis of shared evidence and modes of thought, then the political dimension is *not* what explains the fact that different people, talking to different people, argued about the same things. Some other explanation then will demand attention, not the political one. Then my argument as to the essentially political character of the theological debates on history, teleology, and theory of the social group fails. If, on the other hand, I can point to a topic of inquiry important to both sets of intellectuals, in which each side frames matters in a way distinctive to its own setting and draws on evidence not utilized by the other, then I may ask what differentiates that shared topic from the ones before us. If it should turn out that what characterizes that topic differs from what characterizes the ones we have treated, in that the latter topics entail decisions on public policy and the former topic does not, my test of falsification will have been passed. So the issue is whether, in the aggregate, *any* sort of issues may prove to undergo much the same analysis along nearly identical lines of definition, fact, and argument. How then shall I show that it is the political dimension of the three important categories we have surveyed that differentiates those categories from others? The answer derives from Scripture.

The one thing that drew the two groups together is Scripture, and that in two aspects: exegesis, on the inner dimension, and identification and definition of the canon of Scripture, on the outer. Let me now specify the test of falsification: when they address the most important shared heritage, one prized by each, do the two parties take up the same issues and invoke the same evidence as they did in their discussions of the matters treated earlier? And do they pursue the same lines of thought as I think their discussions examined in prior chapters showed they did? If the answer to these questions proved to be affirmative and if, as I said, *no* issues of public policy find a place at the end of the argument, then everything I have proposed is false.

Now as to the positive side of the same test of falsification: if, in talking about the same thing, the two sides in no way and at no point compose intersecting agenda, then we must ask what differentiates the topic at hand from the topics considered in chapters 2, 3, and 4. If the trait that differentiates the topic before us from the topics treated earlier is that the former set bear political implications in a direct way, so that the results of argument affect public policy, while the present topic bears no outward-facing implications but focuses upon internal issues, particular to each of the two groups respectively, then my basic thesis will have passed the test. So what lies before is what will tell us whether, to this point, we have been right or wrong. The nub of the matter is simple: on the topics at hand are the two groups talking about the same thing at all? And if not, why not?

Same Topic, Different Program: No Encounter

When they read the shared Scriptures—the Old Testament/Written Torah—the two sides in fact worked different agenda. The twin agenda cover two matters: the hermeneutical issues that would generate meanings of verses, and the canonical theory that would identify the character of the whole corpus ("Scripture," "Torah"). To say the whole thing in one sentence, When God revealed God's will to humanity, precisely what did God mean—and where did that will come to writing, where not? I begin with a simple question: Why was Rome a pig? Sages' answer is that Rome showed some kosher traits, some not kosher. The kosher trait of the pig is the cloven hoof. And what (speaking all the time out of homely analogy of Leviticus Rabbah, because Jerome understood it and turned it on Israel) is the cloven hoof of Christianity? In sages' view, it is the Scriptures of ancient Israel, the Old Testament. From Jerome's perspective, Israel too showed the cloven hoof, but it did not ruminate on the Scriptures and therefore did not gain their full nourishment.

So the agreement—the confrontation—is exact. On that point, the compilers of Leviticus Rabbah and Christian exegetes such as Jerome came to explicit agreement: each saw in what the other cherished something that, for their side, they too cherished. And for both it was the same thing, Scripture. In identifying the principal, the fundamental point in common, therefore, looking backward, we do not have to impose our own judgment. Both parties to the debate in the age of Constantine, in thinking about the other, said precisely the same thing, in referring to precisely the same passage of Scripture. On the face of it, the little test of falsification proves positive: we really do have two sides talking about the same thing, in the same way, producing the same arguments about the same facts. So, it would appear, an entirely non-political topic yields the debate that I held takes place solely on matters of public policy, theologically expressed. But, happily for my larger case, the exercise must encompass more ground than a single verse in common.

To frame our specific inquiry we wonder whether with reference to Scripture the two parties asked the same questions, adduced the same facts in evidence, worked out the same logic, or whether they asked different questions, dealt with different evidence, and thought in differing logical patterns. If the answer is negative, then we must further ask why Scripture did not provoke a confrontation in the way in which the categories of history, Messiah, and Israel clearly produced a conflict over those categories. For, after all, the Judaic sages and Christian theologians did resort to the same Scriptures. The two parties certainly shared the same premises about God's role in the making of the Scriptures, by which the Israelite Scriptures assumed authority for both parties.

I take up two distinct issues concerning Scripture, one exegetical, the other canonical. How to read Scripture? How to identify scriptures as canon, as Scripture? These are distinct, if related, questions.

Exegesis. When the Christian exegetes planned a systematic program for the exegesis of Scripture, did they present matters in terms that Judaic exegetes understood? Did the two groups intersect and carry on the sort of confrontation as to issues that we have seen in other settings? Or did each set of exegetes pursue issues generated within the internal logic of its own setting, so that, as to the exegesis of Scripture, different people found themselves talking about different things to different people? The cogency of the question on exegesis hardly requires explanation. When exegetes of each party proposed to read and explain the sense of Scripture, they assuredly dealt with the same topic, namely, the meaning of Scripture, and they certainly did so in the same way, namely, through commentaries on that meaning. The form of confrontation self-evidently coheres between the two groups. The intersection at Leviticus 11 has shown us that possibility of a genuine argument: reading the same texts in the same way, coming up with diametrically opposed answers would add up to a confrontation as clearcut as whether or not Jesus was and is Christ, and whether or not Israel will be saved in the future. So the possibility of debate about the same texts and modes of thought, assuredly existed. But did debate on exegesis take place, or did the exegetes talk about different things to different people?

Canon. When the Christian theologians worked out the idea of "the Bible," consisting of "the Old Testament and the New Testament," and when the Judaic theologians worked out the idea of "the dual Torah," consisting of "the Written Torah and the Oral Torah," did each group propose to answer a question confronting the other group as well? Or did each party pursue a problem particular to the internal logic and life of its own group? The question on the canon does not enjoy the same self-evident pertinence to each party. Why should we imagine that when the one party asked the question of the canon, it considered the same issue that the other did? The answer derives from the character of the canonical issue. Each party had to designate within the larger corpus of scriptures deriving from ancient Israel those writings that it regarded as authoritative, therefore divinely revealed. But did the one side do so for the same reasons, and within the same sort of theological logic, that the other did? Each party had further to explain to itself the end-result, that is, the revealed words as a whole. What are they all together, all at once? The one party characterized the whole as a single Bible, book, piece of writing, and the other party characterized the whole as a single Torah, revelation, in two media, writing and memory. Do these characterizations of the result of revelation, that is, of the canon, constitute intersecting statements? Or are the issues essentially defined by considerations internal to the respective groups?

Jerome and the Christian Exegetical Tradition

Hard-working, prolific, and remarkably intelligent, Jerome produced prefaces to various biblical books, a vast corpus of letters, lives of Paul, Hilarion, and others, dialogues, and on and on. Our interest in Jerome as an exegete transcends specific remarks about passages of Scripture, since agreement on a minor detail—e.g., how to explain the symbolism of the pig in Leviticus 11— may obscure disagreement on the task at hand. We ask a more general question. It is whether, as exegetes, Jerome and the authorship of Sifré to Numbers [2] found themselves guided by Scripture to ask one set of questions rather than some other. With Jerome we have a case in which a Christian theologian did enter into interchange with Judaic counterparts. Jerome testifies that discourse among Judaic and Christian intellectuals on the meaning of Scripture took place. "The only person from whom he could learn Hebrew was a Jew; the only copies of the Hebrew text available to him came from the Jews; and, when he met with difficultues in his translation, he turned to a learned Jew from Tiberias for assistance" (Wilken 1983, 83). But Jerome's interest, as we shall see, brought to the text a less theological and a more philological program than did the authorship of Sifré to Numbers. As a translator, he will have found himself more at home with the Targumists, who translated Scripture into Aramaic. But we do not know that the Targumists found a place in the larger rabbinic circles under discussion (except, of course, for the authorship of Onquelos), so we cannot venture such a comparison. In fact, even though at

---

2. Sifré to Numbers reached closure after the time of the Mishnah, to which it makes reference, but a terminus ante quem is not entirely evident to me. So we assign, for convenience, a date of somewhere between 200 and 400. It is not an ideal choice, but it brings us closer to the kind of exegesis of a verse-by-verse character that was carried on by Christian exegetes than do Genesis Rabbah or Leviticus Rabbah. There I find the comparison not possible, there being no shared foundation at all.

particular points Jerome and sages may have produced something like an intersecting comment, Jerome's interest in the matter—determining the correct text of Scripture, the correct meaning of the Hebrew words—did not produce an exegetical program that at any point corresponded to one we can identify with Judaic exegetes, e.g., those whose work we have examined in Genesis Rabbah and Leviticus Rabbah.[3] Jerome pursued a powerful interest in the translation of the text in terms of its simplest layer of meaning, much like the authors of some of the Targumim. Sages, for their part, followed a program of typology, such as we saw in Genesis Rabbah and Leviticus Rabbah, or a program of polemic directed toward issues particular to their own circle. In sages' compilations we find no sustained interest in the level of a simple statement of the plain sense of a given passage.

Born in 331 in Dalmatia, Jerome spent much of his life, from 372, in the Near East, in Antioch, Constantinople, the Syrian desert, and, from 386, in Bethlehem. Even before reaching there, he had begun to study Hebrew as well as Syriac. Earlier Jerome had translated Eusebius from Greek into Latin, so supplying the Christian West with a universal history of its own. From 383–84 he began his labor of translating the Bible into Latin, working from the Hebrew rather than from the Greek or earlier Latin version(s). The work went on for twenty-two years. Jerome made extensive use of contemporary Jewish biblical exegesis, avoided mystical or allegorical exegesis, and, in general, strove to say in Latin what the text said in Hebrew (Kelly 1975, 73–74, 156–57).[4] Jerome's program and that of the framers of the Judaic sages' treatments of books of Scripture, exemplified by Genesis Rabbah and Leviticus Rabbah, simply are not the same. The Judaic sages, as we shall see in the case of Sifré to Numbers, brought to Scripture their own questions, generated by issues internal to their movement, and answered them in their own way. Their questions were not Jerome's, and his interests were not theirs. In fact Jerome's translation bore directly on the confrontation with the Jews. What interested him were questions of no pertinence to the Judaic exegetes of Scripture, who undertook no explicit confrontation with Christian exegesis. Jerome had in mind a translation that would permit a confrontation with Israel and Judaism on the question of conversion. Nothing could have been further from the minds of the authors of Genesis Rabbah and Leviticus Rabbah than the con-

---

3. But the exegetical program we shall compare to Jerome's does not derive from documents already examined for a different purpose. The reason is that neither Genesis Rabbah nor Leviticus Rabbah forms a counterpart, as exegesis, to the kind of word-by-word and phrase-by-phrase commentary characteristic of such exegetes as Jerome, for whom, after all, the principal exegesis constituted a translation.

4. In this regard, as I said, we should have to compare Jerome to the framers of the Aramaic translations of Scripture, the Targumim. But the policy of translation of the Targumim favored paraphrase and insertion into a "translation" of extensive materials not found in the original. I cannot point to a Targum into Aramaic so closely tied to the received Hebrew text as Jerome's translations into Latin were.

frontation with Rome and Christianity on the question of conversion. Their issues and Jerome's did not intersect at the exegetical level.

In 390 Jerome undertook a completely fresh translation of the Hebrew Scriptures directly from the Hebrew into Latin. The motive, as Kelly explains it, is instructive:

> It became translucently clear to himself and certain close friends that their only hope of demolishing the arguments of Jewish critics was to take their stand on a text of the Old Testament which both parties agreed was authentic. . . . He wished to deprive them of their present vantage-point for deriding Christians and to refute them on their own ground by appealing, when controversy arose, to a version which they had to acknowledge as indisputably accurate and which nevertheless spoke unmistakably of the coming of Christ. (1975, 160)

If, then, we ask about Jerome's larger hermeneutical program, we see that it derived from the argument with Judaism.

The work lasted until 405–6. His commentaries distinguished the factual or historical level from the allegorical or spiritual. But he held open the door to contemporary meaning of the ancient Scriptures, as when he dealt with Zephaniah's warning on the day of the Lord as a day of wrath:

> Zephaniah's horrifying imagery finds its fulfillment in the wretched plight of the Jews of Jerome's own day, virtually excluded from the city that was once their pride and admitted once a year, on the anniversary of its capture and destruction, and then only for a fee, to gaze, weeping and wailing, under the watchful eyes of Roman guards, at the ruined Temple site with its shattered altar. For them this is the prophesied day of calamity and misery, of darkness and gloom. But in the midst of their shame the Church of the Resurrection shines resplendent, and the cross rises triumphant on the Mount of Olives. (Kelly 1975, 166–67)

His selection of biblical books for his prefaces provides a clue as to his purpose. Here, while he worked on Joshua, Samuel and Kings, Chronicles, Esther, Job, Psalms, and so on, his more important prefaces address Isaiah, Jeremiah, Ezekiel, and the other prophetic books. These prefaces are like those we expect today: descriptive, factual, focused on problems of text, language, and plain meaning. His emphasis lay upon the accuracy of his translations, his selection of manuscripts, the perfidy and ignorance of his critics: "I beg you to confront with the shields of your prayers the mad dogs who bark and rage against me and go about the city and think themselves learned if they disparage others" (Fremantle et al. 1961, 490). Introducing his translation of Job, he says, "My detractors must therefore learn either to receive altogether what they have in part admitted, or they must erase my translation." His preface to Jeremiah states, "I pay little heed to the ravings of disparaging critics who revile not only my words but the very syllables of my words." In short, Jerome writes like a scholar, with a keen interest in problems of learning and in proving his claim to say what the text really means. One looks in vain for a statement of a theological agenda, such as we shall shortly address in Sifré to Numbers.

This is not to suggest that in other aspects of the task Jerome ignored theological issues. Within the Church, he confronted Origenism and Pelagianism, and his letters and treatises take up issues involving both theological movements. Addressing himself to the Jews, he advanced the established and conventional polemic against the Jews' unbelief (as he would put it). These debates in no way intersected with Jews' interests in the exegesis of Scripture, the inner-facing issues, by definition. Where Jerome argued with Jews, the shaping of the question derived from issues particular to his side. We look in vain for sages' confrontation with that same set of issues. Let me give one example. Part of Jerome's task was to determine which books were canonical. Here too the dialogue with Judaism proved determinative, as Kelly says: "What chiefly moved him was the embarrassment he felt at having to argue with Jews on the basis of books which they rejected or even . . . found frankly ridiculous" (1975, 161). But I know of not a single passage in the fourth-century Jewish writings that addresses the issue of a canon with reference to acceptance or rejection of a given book of the Hebrew Scriptures. Jerome's polemic in the translation emerges in his emphasis on the messianic or otherwise Christian implication of passages in which the Hebrew did not require or sustain that theme (Kelly 1975, 162). Obviously, no comment of a sage addressed that matter in a direct way.

Jerome persisted because the program served the Church, and what he found critical were issues important within the life of the Church. While Judaic and Christian exegetes may have met in confrontation on a given verse, as we have already noticed, each group of biblical exegetes took up its task in its own way. True enough, we find numerous indications of Jerome's knowledge of Judaic exegesis. For example, he knew that the Jews identified Rome with the Edom that Obadiah predicted would be destroyed. That identification is wrong, according to Jerome. Edom stood for the Jews themselves or for heretics. He refers in particular to "the pride of the Jews." But he drew heavily on rabbinic exegesis, especially for what he called his "historical exposition." But, Kelly says, "He was quick to reject, to give one obvious example, specifically Jewish hopes of a splendidly restored Jerusalem dominating the rest of the world." Again, when he read the book of Daniel, Jerome had to confront the Jews' view that the author predicted the destruction in 70 but also the Messiah in time to come. Christians read the book as a manifest prophecy of Christ. These matters had to be addressed. Jerome in general accuses the Jews of blindness, immorality, greed, and "exulting in their present humiliation, which . . . would last until the world's end." None of this, in spirit but also in actual wording, is necessarily original to Jerome; he borrowed heavily from many, especially Origen (Kelly 1975, 222, 292, 300, 301).

A falsification test for the theory of this book now presents itself. Do the Judaic counterparts, writing large-scale and systematic commentaries on biblical books, frame the issues they wish to discuss in order to confront their Christian critics? That is to ask, first, do we find answers to Christian uses of biblical verses? An answer to that question does not derive from my survey of the florilegium of verses used by Aphrahat in his argument with Judaic sages. Judaic sources of the same period do not take up those same verses and counter what Aphrahat says. On the basis of the materials I reviewed in connection with verses adduced in evidence by Aphrahat, I could hardly locate evidence, based on comments on the same verses from different perspectives, of either a rabbinic dialogue with Christianity or a Christian dialogue with rabbis known to us. In the main, neither side confronted the other's scriptural testimonies. The rabbis scarcely paid attention to the verses of Scripture Aphrahat was certain proved Christian belief. Aphrahat found nothing interesting in verses that sages, in the Talmud of Babylonia for example, thought exemplary. The most striking result of my survey is the discovery that the rabbis simply did not interest themselves in the Scriptures that most interested Aphrahat (Neusner 1971, 168).

The second question—do sages frame their large-scale program in response to issues important to the large-scale program of their counterparts?—brings us to an examination of the generative tension of Sifré to Numbers. There, as we shall see, what is on the minds of the framers of the document bears no point of contact with the argument over Scripture with Christianity.[5] To restate my particular point of concern, it is whether or not the same people are talking about the same things, each to his own group; whether the issues are shared, whether the modes of thought unfold in common. Jerome's exegesis, in part, concerned how Scripture can be shown to prove that Jesus was predicted by the prophets, and that, as the Christ, be legitimately fulfilled those promises that the prophets had made. We know that this issue occupied Christian theologians. But, in the exegetical context, did it occupy Judaic ones?[6] If it did, then the program is the same, the confrontation real, the dispute parallel to the ones we considered in chapters 2, 3, and 4. If the Judaic sages, when they composed an exegesis of Scripture, found provocative a set of issues internal to their own life, then, on the surface, we can discern no parallel between Jerome as exegete and a sample of Judaic sages as exegetes.

5. That is not to suggest that the issues of the age do not inform the minds of the Judaic exegetes when they turn to Scripture. The challenge of Constantine's conversion and its effects surely accounts in large part for the intense interest of the framers of Genesis Rabbah in the meaning of the history of Israel. But that concern does not derive from a specific dispute about the exegesis of the verse of Genesis or from a general argument (all the more so) about the canonicity of Genesis. So it is not the same thing as finding that the same people cited the same verses in an argument on the same issue, and that is what we presently seek.

6. I refer once more to my survey, in *Aphrahat and Judaism,* of the proof-texts adduced by Aphrahat in the argument on the Christhood of Jesus. There I showed that the verses important to Aphrahat scarcely elicited comment from Judaic sages represented in the Talmudic canon. So, on the face of it, the exegetical programs of the two groups did not coincide. But I have in mind a deeper issue, namely, did the large-scale exegetical work of the one party bear any resemblance to those of the other. For that purpose, we proceed not to the comparison of whether each group talked about the texts important to the other, but whether the larger exegetical issue concerning the one defined issues interesting to the other. For that purpose I take up Sifré to Numbers.

Sifré to Numbers and the Judaic Exegetical Tradition

The intellectual program of the exegetes of Sifré to Numbers, so far as I can define it whole, just as, with Kelly's help, I have briefly defined Jerome's intellectual program whole, emerges from the confluence of form and meaning, structure and sustained polemic. Here I find myself on firmer ground (see Neusner 1968b, 1:1–43). On the face of it, the framers of Sifré to Numbers proposed to write a sustained commentary on passages from the book of Numbers. For that is precisely what they did provide. We know only that they had the Mishnah in hand. So the document derives from redactors who worked at some point after 200 but, it is generally assumed, before the closure of the Talmud of Babylonia in 600. Whether the work was done before 400, no one up to now has demonstrated. The comparison with Jerome, who lived in the fourth century, would prove more apt if we knew that the document reached closure in the time in which Jerome flourished. But since the work on Numbers falls into the same classification as Jerome's work on diverse books of the Hebrew Scriptures, a characterization of the program of exegesis proves not entirely inappropriate for the exercise of comparison. For both works constitute commentaries, and both commentaries are of the same kind, namely, sustained, not episodic; focused on phrases and words, not on large-scale compositions or cogent theological propositions. With that much in common, the two writings may be compared, even though, admittedly, the comparison proves inexact.

The description of the exegetical program of Sifré to Numbers will require somewhat of a detour, since we shall concentrate on that book and the problem of stating its fundamental hermeneutical program, and only at the end recover the focus of comparison. I characterize the program of this document not by summarizing its many individual messages but by treating the recurrent formal-exegetical traits and modes of the document as a whole. These are few, characteristic, and intellectually, as much as formally, definitive. My purpose is to describe the incremental message, the cumulative effect, as to the points of exegetical interest and concern, of the formal traits of speech and thought revealed in the uniform rhetoric and syntax of the document. That characterization will permit us to ask what, if anything, the sages' document has in common with the writings of Jerome as these have been described here. So I ask this question: What do the formal structures of our document emphasize, and what (as in the case of stories about sages) do they ignore? Let me rapidly review these structures, highlighting their main traits.

1. Extrinsic exegetical form. The form consists of the citation of an opening verse, followed by an issue stated in terms extrinsic to the cited verse. The formal traits: [1] citation of a base verse from Numbers, [2] a generalization ignoring clauses or words in the base verse, [3] a further observation without clear interest in the verse at hand. The form yields a syllogism proved by a list of facts beyond all doubt.

2. Intrinsic exegetical form. The verse itself is clarified. The focus is on the base verse and not on a broader issue. There are diverse versions of this exercise, some consisting only of a verse or a clause and a statement articulating the sense of the matter, others rather elaborate.

3. Dialectical Exegesis: Intrinsic. A sequence of arguments about the meaning of a passage, in which the focus is upon the meaning of the base verse. This is the internal exegetical counterpart to the on-going argument on the efficacy of logic. Logic pursues the sense of a verse, but the results of logic are tested, forthwith and one by one, against the language at hand, e.g.: Why is this stated? Or, you say it means X but why not Y? Of, if X, then what about Y? If Y, then what about Z? All of these rather nicely articulated exegetical programs impose a scriptural test upon the proposals of logic.

4. Dialectical Exegesis: Extrinsic. The Fallacy of Logic Uncorrected by Exegesis of Scripture. The formal indicator is the presence of the question, in one of several versions: Is it not a matter of logic? The exegesis of the verse at hand plays no substantial role.

5. Scriptural Basis for a Passage of the Mishnah. What we have is simply a citation of the verse plus a law in prior writing (Mishnah, Tosefta) which the verse is supposed to sustain. The Mishnah's or the Tosefta's rule then cannot stand as originally set forth, that is, without any exegetical foundation. On the contrary, the rule, verbatim, rests on a verse of Scripture, given with slight secondary articulation: verse, then Mishnah-sentence. That suffices, the point is made.

Let us now characterize the formal traits of Sifré to Numbers as a commentary. These we may reduce to two classifications, based on the point of origin of the verses that are catalogued or subjected to exegesis: exegesis of a verse in the book of Numbers in terms of the theme or problems of that verse, hence, *intrinsic* exegesis; exegesis of a verse in Numbers in terms of a theme or polemic not particular to that verse, hence, *extrinsic* exegesis. The forms of extrinsic exegesis are easy to characterize. The implicit message of the external category proves simple to define, since the several extrinsic classifications turn out to form a cogent polemic.

1. The Syllogistic Composition. Scripture supplies hard facts, which, properly classified, generate syllogisms. By collecting and classifying facts of Scripture, therefore, we may produce firm laws of history, society, and Israel's everyday life. The diverse compositions in which verses from various books of the Scriptures are compiled in a list of evidence for a given proposition— whatever the character or purpose of that proposition—make that one point. And given their power and cogency, they make the point stick.

2. The Fallibility of Reason Unguided by Scriptural Exegesis. Scripture alone supplies reliable basis for speculation. Laws cannot be generated by reason or logic unguided by Scripture. Efforts at classification and contrastive-analogical exegesis, in which Scripture does not supply the solution to all problems, prove few and far between (and always in Ishmael's name, for whatever that is worth). This polemic forms the obverse of the point above.

So when extrinsic issues intervene in the exegetical process, they coalesce to make a single point. Let me state that point with appropriate emphasis the recurrent and implicit message of the forms of external exegesis:

Scripture stands paramount; logic, reason, analytical processes of classifi-cation and differentiation, are secondary. Reason not built on scriptural foun-dations yields uncertain results. The Mishnah itself demands scriptural bases.

The forms of intrinsic exegesis present problems when we come to attempt an equivalent characterization. At least three intrinsic exegetical exercises focus on the use of logic, specifically, the logic of classification, comparison and contrast of species of a genus, the explanation of the meaning of verses from the book of Numbers. The internal dialectical mode, moving from point to point as logic dictates, underlines the main point already stated: logic produces possibilities, Scripture chooses among them. Again, the question, why is this passage stated? commonly produces an answer generated by fur-ther verses of Scripture, e.g., this matter is stated here to clarify what other-wise would be confusion left in the wake of other verses. So Scripture pro-duces problems of confusion and duplication, and Scripture—not logic, not differentiation, not classification—solves those problems. To state matters simply: Scripture is complete, harmonious, perfect. Logic not only does not generate truth beyond the limits of Scripture but also plays no important role in the harmonization of difficulties yielded by what appear to be duplications or disharmonies. These forms of internal exegesis, then, make the same point that the extrinsic ones do.

In so stating the basic exegetical polemic that animates Sifré to Numbers, of course, we cover all but the single most common category of exegesis, which we have treated as simple and undifferentiated: (1) verse of Scripture or a clause, followed by (2) a brief statement of the meaning at hand. Here I see no unifying polemic in favor of, or against, a given proposition. The most common form also proves the least pointed: X bears this meaning, Y bears that meaning, or citation of verse X, followed by, [what this means is]. . . . Whether simple or elaborate, the outcome is the same. What can be at issue when no polemic expressed in the formal traits of syntax and logic finds its way to the surface? What do I do when I merely clarify a phrase? Or, to frame the question more logically: what premises must validate my *intervention,* that is, my willingness to undertake to explain the meaning of a verse of Scrip-ture? These seem to me propositions that must serve to justify the labor of intrinsic exegesis as we have seen its results here:

1. My independent judgment bears weight and produces meaning. I—that is, my mind—therefore may join in the process.

2. God's revelation to Moses at Sinai requires my intervention. I have the role, and the right, to say what that revelation means.

3. What validates my entry into the process of revelation is the correspon-dence between the logic of my mind and the logic of the document.

Only if I think in accord with the logic of the revealed Torah can my thought processes help to clarify what is at hand: the unfolding of God's will in the

Torah. To state matters more accessibly: if the Torah does not make statements in accord with a syntax and a grammar that I know, I cannot so understand the Torah as to explain its meaning. But if I can join in the discourse of the Torah, it is because I speak the same language of thought: syntax and grammar at the deepest levels of my intellect. Then to state matters affirmatively and finally: Since a shared logic of syntax and grammar joins my mind to the mind of God as revealed in the Torah, I can say what a sentence of the Torah means. So I too can amplify, clarify, expand, revise, rework: that is to say, create a commentary. It follows that the intrinsic exegetical forms stand for a single proposition:

While Scripture stands paramount, and logic, reason, analytical processes of classification and differentiation are secondary, nonetheless man's mind joins God's mind when man receives and sets forth the Torah.

In few words and in simple language what do the formal rules of the document tell us about the purpose of Sifré to Numbers? Beyond all concrete propositions, the document as a whole, through its fixed and recurrent formal preferences or literary structures, makes two complementary points.

1. Reason unaided by Scripture produces uncertain propositions.

2. Reason operating within the limits of Scripture produces truth.

To whom do these moderate and balanced propositions matter? Sages in particular, I think. The polemic addresses arguments internal to their circles. How do we know, and how may we be certain? If we contrast the polemic of our document about the balance between revelation and reason, Torah and logic, with the polemic of another canonical document about some other topic altogether, the contrast will tell. Then and only then shall we see the choices people faced. In that way we shall appreciate the particular choice the authorship at hand has made. With the perspective provided by an exercise of comparison, we shall see how truly remarkable a document we have in Sifré to Numbers. By itself the book supplies facts. Seen in context, the book makes points. So we require a context of comparison. But, it seems scarcely to require saying, Jerome does not define that context. He follows a different program, because the issues that interest him in no way coincide with the issues that are paramount for the framers of Sifré to Numbers.

So we return, via this rather circuitous route through familiar territory, to the (to me) unfamiliar ground of Jerome. Having seen how a Judaic work of sustained exegesis, Sifré to Numbers, makes large points through repeated resort to a given theme, we realize that the character of an exegetical program does dictate the substance of the exegesis of a given verse. Then we ask whether or not the character of the program of Jerome, so far as we have lightly touched on it, bears any resemblance to that of the Judaic exegetes of (for Sifré to Numbers) an indeterminate period? The answer, for Sifré to Numbers, is no, there is no point in common between the issues important to Jerome and those important to the Judaic exegetes, nothing whatsoever in common, let alone a point of intersection. Why not? Because what troubles the framers of the work on Numbers is an issue deeply internal to the rabbis who received the Mishnah and worked on it. Since the authors of the Mishnah rarely cited proof-texts of Scripture in support of their statements, the framers of Sifré to Numbers[7] ask whether the laws of the Mishnah, and others like them, may stand unsupported by verses of Scripture. The authors wonder, further, whether on the basis of logic alone, without resort to exegesis, people may come to a correct and reliable definition of the law. And they answer, no, people may not do so. Who wants the answer to that question? Obviously sages, obviously not Christians. So the exegetes of the sages' group worked on an issue deeply particular to the unfolding of the canon in their hands, and the exegetes of the Christian theologians' circle pursued issues equally distinctive to the problems of discourse—whether internal to the Church or otherwise—of their own setting.

As to exegesis, we find nothing in common between the program of Jerome and the program of the authors of Sifré to Numbers. They studied the same Hebrew Scriptures, and they pursued the same sort of inquiry, namely, the exegetical past. But they rarely worked on the same texts of those Scriptures, and such formal points as they had in common mask essentially independent exercises on the part of the respective groups of intellectuals. The one authorship answered its question, the other dealt with its issues, and neither party pretended to take up a program shared with the other (despite Jerome's interest in arguing with Jews). In fact, we have a case of different people, while reading the same Scripture, talking about different things to different people. As to exegesis, the Christian theologians and the Judaic sages did not compose and carry through a common argument. Now we proceed to a second exercise of falsification, the matter of a canon.

The Christian Canon in the Fourth Century: Old and New Testaments

First, we want to know if Christian theologians and Judaic sages understood the same thing when they engaged in the task of identifying authoritative writings and rejecting spurious ones? And, second, we ask whether the result of the work of the one group in any way runs parallel to the result of the work of the other. We raise the question of whether, by "canon," the two groups even meant the same thing at all, and whether "the Bible" of Christianity and "the one whole Torah" of Judaism constitute counterpart documents. If so, then we have an argument about the same issue conducted in the same terms. We therefore ask, in the present setting, whether the category of canon served both Judaic sages and Christian theologians, and, if it did, whether, when they discussed that category, they composed a single argument, involving the same definitions, the same facts, and the same modes of argument and thought. Let me explain this problem, since it is somewhat complicated.

---

7. Also of Sifra, which serves Leviticus. That document also pursues the same polemic, in an equally systematic, way; see Neusner (1976).

We realize that, in the centuries after the Gospels were written, the Church had to come to a decision on whether, in addition to the Scriptures of ancient Israel, there would be a further corpus of authoritative writing. The Church affirmed that there would be, and the New Testament as counterpart to the Old Testiment evolved. In the centuries from the publication of the Mishnah, the standing and status of that document required an explanation. Gradually a number of theories evolved, defining the sense of the category "Torah," encompassing both the Hebrew Scriptures, now called the Written Torah, as well as other authoritative teachings. These teachings came to be deemed of the same status as the Written Torah, hence they too constituted statements of the authority and status of the Torah. They then were called Torah—without the definite article, meaning, of that same standing as the Written Torah. When we speak of the canon of Judaism, we refer to the Torah, meaning both media in which the Torah reached Israel, the written and the oral. The two categories—the Old and New Testaments as the Christian canon, the Torah of two media as the Judaic canon—really do not address the same issues and exhibit no important points of correspondence. Hence we cannot maintain that, as to the issue of the canon, an argument or a debate of any kind proceeded. Quite to the contrary, I know not a single indication, other than the passage in which Tarfon in the Tosefta is supposed to have referred to Christian Scriptures, that sages took account of the Christians' claim that their Scriptures constituted writings that found a relationship to the Written Torah. That concept, it seems to me, found no comprehension at all among sages.

Let me expand on this matter of the development of the theory of the dual Torah, with special attention to how the theory got under way. For only in seeing what was at stake shall we grasp how little connection there was between sages' thought on the dual Torah and the Christian theologians' work on the Bible. At issue for sages was not the status of a diverse corpus of available writings, but the ongoing process of reception and analysis of a single document. In the age under consideration, the Judaic sages developed an answer to the question of the standing and authority of the Mishnah. As I said, that answer involved the conception that at Sinai God had revealed the Torah through two media, one in writing, the other in memory. Through the medium of writing, what is called the Written Torah was handed on, and that is now the Hebrew Scriptures shared, more or less in the same terms, with Christianity. Through the medium of memory, the other Torah, called "the Torah that is memorized," or "the Oral Torah," was handed on. In the first apologetic for the Mishnah, Pirqé Abot, the conception came to expression that what sages teach falls into the category of Torah, that is, God's revelation at Sinai.

The reader may wonder why this information prefaces a discussion of the canon of Christianity, the Bible. The reason is that the process by which the myth being considered here reached public expression in the Talmud of the Land of Israel involved the identification of books that fell into the category of Torah—hence, on the surface, a labor of canonical inquiry. For, the same theory proceeded to posit, one principal component of that Oral Torah comprised the teachings now assembled in the Mishnah. So we may claim that the age of Constantine marked the point at which the Mishnah entered the status of Oral Torah.[8] That is why the issue of canon comes to the fore, presenting a category of more than routine interest. When we contemplate the process which culminated in the development of the notion of the single Torah in two media, we realize that, in mythic terms, we trace the formation of the canon of Judaism: the identification of the books that fall into "the one whole Torah of Moses, our rabbi," as God revealed that Torah to Moses at Sinai.

But we wonder about the New Testament. Would that not constitute the counterpart to the oral sector of "the one whole Torah"? And, more germane to our inquiry, does not the joining of the New Testament to the Old Testament in the formation of the canon, the Bible, mirror the recognition of "one whole Torah" in two parts, written and oral? I think not. In both cases, the closer we come to the Christian side, the less alike do Torah and Bible appear. The issues for Christianity in the identification of the canon and in the explanation of the status of the canon as "the Bible" flow from a different set of politics. It was a politics internal to the life of the Church, the unfolding of Church order and doctrine, with no bearing that I can see on the argument with Judaism.

In the third and fourth centuries, when the canon of Judaism attained mythic expression of a decisive and enduring order, important steps were taken toward the conclusion of the canon of Christianity, that is, in the recognition of "the Bible," as "the Old Testament and the New Testament." So we turn to the canon of Christianity. When we speak of canon, we refer, in Childs' words, to "the process of theological interpretation by a faith community [that] left its mark on a literary text which did not continue to evolve and which became the normative interpretation of the events to which it bore witness for those identifying with that religious community." When did the Christian Bible, that is, the Old Testament and the New Testament, come into being? Christians from the very beginning revered the Hebrew Scriptures as "the Old Testament," regarding it as their sacred book. They denied the Jews any claim to the book, accusing them of misinterpreting it. The Old Testament served, in Harnack's words, to prove "that the appearance and the entire history of Jesus had been predicted hundreds and even thousands of years ago; and further, that the founding of the New People which was to be fashioned out of all the nations upon earth had from the very beginning been prophesied and prepared for" (Childs 1985, 26; Harnack 1972, 283). The text of the Hebrew Scriptures supplied proofs for various propositions of theology, law, and liturgy. It served as a source of precedents: "if God had praised or punished this or that in the past, how much more . . . are we to look for similar treatment from him, we who are now living in the last days and who have received 'the calling of promise.'" Even after the rise of the New Testament, much of

8. I expand on this point in the next section. It rests on the research in Neusner (1984b).

the Old Testament held its own. And, Harnack concludes, "The New Testament as a whole did not generally play the same role as the Old Testament in the mission and practice of the church."

In the beginning the Church did not expect the canon—the Hebrew Scriptures—to grow through Christian additions. As Cross says, "In the new covenant the sole complement to the Word in the Torah was the Word made flesh in Christ." So it would be some time before a Christian canon encompassing not only the received writings but the writings of the new age would come into being. Before Marcion the Bible of the Church was the Hebrew Scriptures, pure and simple. While Filson assigns to the years between 160 and 175 the crystallization of the concept of the canon, the process came to an end by the end of the fourth century. Filson states, "There was no longer any wide dispute over the right of any of our twenty-seven books to a place in the New Testament canon." What was not a settled question for Eusebius, in 330, had been worked out in the next span of time. So, in general, when we take up the issue of the canon of Christianity, we find ourselves in the third and fourth centuries (Cross 1960, 60; von Campenhausen 1972, 147; Filson 1957, 121). The bulk of the work was complete by 200, with details under debate for another two hundred years (Childs 1985, 18). The orthodoxy in which "the canon of an Old and a New Testament was firmly laid down," did not come into being overnight. From the time of Irenaeus the Church affirmed the bipartite Christian Bible, containing the Old Testament, and, parallel with this and controlling it, the New Testament (von Campenhausen 1972, 209). But what was to be the New Testament, and when were the limits of the canon decided? Von Campenhausen concludes the description for us:

> [The Muratorian fragment] displays for the first time the concept of a collection of New Testament scriptures, which has deliberately been closed, and the individual books of which are regarded as "accepted" and ecclesiastically "sanctified," that is to say . . . they have been "incorporated" into the valid corpus. We have thus arrived at the end of the long journey which leads to a New Testament thought of as "canonical" in the strict sense. Only one thing is still lacking: the precise name for this collection, which will make it possible to refer to the new Scripture as a unity and thus at one and the same time both to distinguish it from the old Scriptures and combine it with them in a new totality. . . . This is the last feature still wanting to the accomplishment of the bipartite Christian Bible. (1972, 261–62)

This last matter proves vital for what is to follow on the Judaic side, so we had best pursue it to the conclusion. When does the Old Testament join the New as the Bible? Von Campenhausen makes a striking point. "There was no need to look for a single name for the entire document. There was no such thing as an Old Testament or a New Testament as a single physical entity. To the eye the whole canon was still fragmented into a series of separate rolls or volumes." Von Campenhausen makes a still more relevant point: "There was no reason why in themselves the two parts of the Bible should not have different names. In the early period one possibility suggested itself almost automatically: if one had the New and the Old Testament in mind, one could speak of the 'Gospel' and the 'Law'" (1972, 262; cf. also 261–62). The use of "Old" and "New" Testament represents a particular theology. It was from the beginning of the third century that Scripture for orthodox Christianity consisted of an Old and a New Testament. So, we conclude, "Both the Old and the New Testaments had in essence already reached their final form and significance around the year 200." The authority of the Bible, for Christianity, rested on the reliability of the biblical record of the predictions of Christ in the prophets and the testimony to Christ of the apostles (von Campenhausen 1972, 327, 330). The biblical component of the "canon of truth" proved contingent, not absolute and dominant. The issues important to the Judaism of the sages were in no way consubstantial, let alone comparable, with these issues. None of the cited theological precipitants for the canonical process played any role in a Judaic formulation I can discern in the theory of the Torah in two media. It follows that asking about the "canonization" of the dual Torah confuses language-categories and produces a senseless statement in Judaic parlance. The myth of the dual Torah, which functioned as a canonical process, validating as it did the writings of sages as part of Torah from Sinai, derives neither from the analogy to the Old Testament process nor—to begin with—from the narrow issue of finding a place for the specific writings of rabbis within the larger Bible of Judaism.[9] Both clauses of that sentence constitute gibberish in the context of the Judaism of sages. But what is at issue in the doctrine of the dual Torah of Sinai? To that doctrine and its unfolding we now turn.

9. To state the simple fact, first comes the explanation of the place and role of the sage and his teachings, then comes the explanation of the place of the books that contain those teachings. I do not mean to ignore interesting debates on the canonization of the Christian Bible, i.e., the Old and the New Testaments. Childs alerts us to issues that require further study: "an important and highly debatable issue turns on determining the direction from which the New Testament canonical process proceeded. Did the canonization of the New Testament develop in analogy to an Old Testament process which had largely reached its goal of stabilization before the New Testament period, or rather did the major canonical force stem from the side of the Christian church, which resulted in the definition of the Jewish Scriptures as an Old Testament within the larger Christian Bible?" (1985, 19).

The answer to that question self-evidently does not affect our study of the doctrine of the dual Torah of Sinai. The reason is that, from the viewpoint of that doctrine, the question is meaningless. So Childs' quite proper question addresses the wrong category. The category is not the place of the teaching but of the teacher. In many ways the Montanist crisis turns on its head in Judaism. That is to say, sages held that they had every authority to teach Torah, then produced books that contained Torah from Sinai (beginning of course with the Mishnah). That is the message of Pirqé Abot. But by that theory Montanism is "right" and Orthodoxy wrong, so far as Montanism validates contemporary prophecy, hence, revelation by living persons—such as, within Judaism, sages. I hasten to apologize for venturing beyond my limits. These comments rely on the little I learned about Montanism in the secondary sources cited above, and I do not mean to offer a theory of the matter, only a contrast that seems suggestive. But I do mean to suggest that the process of canonization of the persons and authority of sages comes about through the myth of the dual Torah, and that process only later on also validates sages' principal documents—so showing us what the process of Christian canonization would have looked like had Montanism won.

The Judaic Canon in the Fourth Century:
The Written and Oral Torah

The reason that the issue of the canon places us squarely into the age of Constantine is very simple. That issue addressed to the Mishnah, joined by the doctrine of the dual media of revelation, first surfaces in the writings of the late fourth century. Specifically, it was in the Talmud of the Land of Israel that the conception of the dual Torah, one in writing, the other preserved in memory and handed on orally, first served to explain the status of the Mishnah. Documents that reached closure earlier than that Talmud know nothing of the Mishnah as part of the Torah or as enjoying the status of Torah (a distinction I shall explain in a moment). Only in passages of the Talmud of the Land of Israel does the Mishnah clearly enter the status of part of the Torah of Moses—namely, the oral part. One might, therefore, find appealing the theory that the conception of the dual Torah, specifically encompassing the Mishnah, served to counter the position of Christian critics of the Judaism of the sages that the Mishnah is nothing more than a human and late mode of revelation, not part of the Scriptures of Israel.[10] Christians, including Jerome, so regarded the Mishnah (Simon 1964, 116–17). But, as we shall now see, the conception of the dual Torah, explaining, specifically, the standing and the status of the Mishnah, took shape along lines dictated by the internal problems facing the sages in the unfolding of their own canon. The issues proved particular to that canon and distinctive to their task of accounting for the source of their own doctrines and writings. Just as we found that the critical tension of the compilers of Sifré to Numbers, generated by the issue of the conflicting roles of logic and exegesis in making laws, took up a concern rather private to sages, so the framing of the problem of the Judaic canon and the solution to that problem concentrated on issues quite remote from the confrontation with Christian thinkers or with issues shared with them.

Indeed, the very conception of "canon" when I use the word for the unfolding of the writings of sages, and the sense of the word when Childs and von Campenhausen use it for the identification of the authoritative Scriptures of the Church, are hardly the same. As we have noted, when scholars of the formation of the canon of Christianity use the word "canon," they mean, first, the recognition of Sacred Scripture, over and beyond the (received) Hebrew Scriptures; second, the identification of writings revered within the Church as canonical, hence authoritative; third, the recognition of these accepted writings as forming a Scripture; fourth, the role of this Scripture as the counterpart to the Hebrew Scriptures; and hence, fifth, the formation of the Bible as the Old and New Testaments. Now, as a matter of fact, none of these categories, stage by stage, corresponds in any way to the processes in the unfolding of the holy books of the sages, which I shall now describe in terms of Torah.

---

10. I would be disingenuous if I denied entertaining that theory. But it does not work, for reasons I shall explain.

But the word "Torah" in the context of the writings of the sages in no way forms that counterpart to the word "canon" as used (quite correctly) by Childs, von Campenhausen, and others; moreover the word "Bible" and the word "Torah" in no way speak of the same thing, that is, they do not refer to the same category or classification.

The Judaism of the sages, as portrayed in the fourth-century documents, is not a canonical system at all. For revelation does not close or reach conclusion. God speaks all the time, through the sages. Torah speaks of God's revelation of God's will to Moses, our rabbi. The Scriptures fall into the category of Torah, but they do not fill that category up. Other writings, and, more important, other things besides books, fall into that same category. This usage of Torah as an essentially taxonomic category exhibits no traits parallel to the conception of canon as the authoritative collection of holy books. Canon and Torah, in the present setting, simply have nothing in common. Canon refers to particular books that enjoy a distinctive standing; Torah refers to various things that fall into a particular classification. So as we follow the story of the unfolding of the Torah, from the Mishnah forward, and, in particular, review the meanings of the word "Torah" as these occur in the canonical writings of sages from the Mishnah forward, we shall see nothing to suggest that sages and theologians pursued a single program, defined an issue in one and the same way, appealed to the same set of facts, and employed the same modes of thought. In Christianity the canon reaches closure, but Judaism in the sages' definition yielded no canon, for Torah remained open-ended, a category in which diverse matters, persons, teachings, actions, writings found an ample place. The Christian canon reached closure with the Bible: Old and New Testaments. The Judaic Torah never closed: revelation of Torah continued, as I shall now explain.

The word "Torah" bears a broad range of meanings. Before we can appreciate what is fresh in the treatment, in the Talmud of the Land of Israel, of the Mishnah as part of the Torah, we have to review these possible meanings and discover the one that would encompass even so recent a document as the Mishnah. The meaning of the several categories requires only brief explanation. When the Torah refers to a particular thing, it is to a scroll containing divinely revealed words. The Torah may further refer to revelation, not as an object but as a corpus of doctrine. When one "*does* Torah," the disciple "studies" or "learns," and the master "teaches," Torah. Hence, while "Torah" never appears as a verb, it does refer to an act. The word also bears a quite separate sense, *torah* as category or classification or corpus of rules, e.g., "the torah of driving a car" is a usage entirely acceptable to some documents. This generic usage of the word does occur.

The word "Torah" very commonly refers to a status, distinct from and above another status, as "teachings of Torah" as against "teachings of scribes." Obviously, no account of the meaning of the word can ignore the distinction between the two Torahs, written and oral. Finally, the word refers to a source of salvation, often fully worked out in stories about how the individual and the nation will be saved through Torah. In general, the sense of the word "salvation" is not complicated. It is simply salvation in the way in which Deuteronomy and the Deuteronomic historians understand it: kings who do what God wants win battles; those who do not, lose. So too here, people who study and do Torah are saved from sickness and death, and the way Israel can save itself from its condition of degradation also is through Torah.

Within those categories, we ask, where is there a place for the Mishnah? The one thing that is clear, alas, is negative. The framers of the Mishnah nowhere in their document claim, implicitly or explicitly, that what they have written forms part of the Torah, enjoys the status of God's revelation to Moses at Sinai, or even systematically carries forward secondary exposition and application of what Moses wrote down in the wilderness. Later on, two hundred years beyond the closure of the Mishnah, the need to explain its standing and origin led some to posit two things. First, God's revelation of the Torah at Sinai encompassed the Mishnah as much as Scripture. Second, the Mishnah was handed on through oral formulation and oral transmission from Sinai to the framers of the document as we have it. These two convictions in fact emerge from the references of both Talmuds to the dual Torah. One part is in writing; the other was oral and now is in the Mishnah. As for the Mishnah itself, however, we find not a hint that anyone has heard any such tale. The earliest apologists for the Mishnah, represented in Abot and the Tosefta alike, know nothing of the fully realized myth of the dual Torah of Sinai. It may be that the authors of those documents stood too close to the Mishnah to see its standing as a problem or to recognize the task of accounting for its origins. Certainly they never refer to the Mishnah as something "out there," nor do they speak of the document as autonomous and complete. Only the two Talmuds, which serve the Mishnah as systematic commentaries to passages, taken one by one and episodically, reveal that conception. This treatment of the Mishnah as a whole and as a separate document, demanding explanation, proves congruent with the perspective of the authors of the Talmuds. They see it as a document to be cut into bits and pieces and explained, just as, in the same period, others would see Scripture in the same way and compose for it the same sort of commentary. The two Talmuds, beginning of course with the Talmud of the Land of Israel, find it necessary to provide a mythic explanation of where the document came from and why it should be obeyed. In any event, the absence of explicit expression of such a claim of status in behalf of the Mishnah as Torah requires little specification. It is just not there.

But the absence of an implicit claim demands explanation. When ancient Jews wanted to gain for their writings the status of revelation, of torah, or at least to link what they thought to what the Torah had said, they could do one of four things. They could sign the name of a holy man of old, for instance, Adam, Enoch, Ezra. They could imitate the Hebrew style of Scripture. They could claim that God had spoken to them. They could, at the very least, cite a verse of Scripture and impute to the cited passage their own opinion. These four methods—pseudepigraphy, stylistic imitation (hence, forgery), claim of direct revelation from God, and eisegesis—found no favor with the Mishnah's framers. To the contrary, they signed no name to their book. Their Hebrew was new in its syntax and morphology, completely unlike that of the Mosaic writings of the Pentateuch. They never claimed that God had anything to do with their opinions. They rarely cited a verse of Scripture as authority. It follows that, whatever the authors of the Mishnah said about their document, the implicit character of the book tells us that they did not claim God had dictated or even approved what they had to say. The framers simply ignored all the validating conventions of the world in which they lived. And, as I said, they failed to make explicit use of any others. It follows that we do not know whether the Mishnah was supposed to be part of the Torah or to enjoy a clearly defined relationship to the existing Torah. We also do not know what else, if not the Torah, was meant to endow the Mishnah's laws with heavenly sanction. To state matters simply, we do not know what the framers of the Mishnah said they had made, nor do we know what the people who received and were supposed to obey the Mishnah thought they possessed.

That the compositors of materials in the Talmud of the Land of Israel treated the Mishnah as if it was part of the Torah is evident not solely from what they say about the Mishnah or about the concept of an oral Torah. It is also evident from how they treat the Mishnah. Specifically, in the Talmud of the Land of Israel, sages treat the Mishnah precisely as they do the written Torah. They subject both to exactly the same methods of exegesis, for one thing. They cite both and explain, in much the same modes of thought, the meanings they find. This equivalence of Mishnah and Scripture, moreover, emerges not only in implicit but also in explicit ways. We find sayings that weigh the merit of studying the Torah against the merit of studying the Mishnah—something without parallel in the documents surveyed above. In these same sayings, discourse takes up such other categories as laws (*halakhot*). Whether or not people reached the conclusion that, since the Mishnah enjoyed the status of the (written) Torah, therefore the Mishnah constituted part of the (one whole) Torah revealed to Moses, our rabbi, makes no difference. The most subtle, yet most consequential, step is the first one. Once something is perceived as like the Torah, or at the level of the Torah, things will move in the direction in which we know they ultimately did. What is like the Torah enters the status of, and ultimately becomes, Torah. If, then, we survey the treatment of the Mishnah in the Talmud of the Land of Israel, what do we find? The Mishnah is held equivalent to Scripture (Y. Hor. 3:5). But the Mishnah is not called Torah. Still, as I have pointed out, once the Mishnah entered the status of Scripture, it needed but a short step to reach a theory of the Mishnah as part of the revelation at Sinai—hence, oral Torah.

In the Talmud at hand, we find the first glimmerings of an effort to theorize in general, not merely in detail, about how specific teachings of Mishnah relate to specific teachings of Scripture.[11] The citing of scriptural proof-texts for mishnaic propositions would not have caused much surprise to the framers of the Mishnah; they themselves included such passages, though not often. But what conception of the Torah underlies such initiatives, and how do sages in the Talmud of the Land of Israel propose to explain the phenomenon of the Mishnah as a whole? The following passage gives us one statement. It refers to the assertion at M. Hag. 1 : 8D that the laws on cultic cleanness presented in the Mishnah rest on deep and solid foundations in Scripture.

Y. Hag. 1:7.V

[A] **The laws of the Sabbath** [M. Hagigah 1:8B]: R. Jonah said R. Hama bar Uqba raised the question [in reference to M. Hag. 1:8D's view that there are many verses of Scripture on cleanness], "And lo, it is written only, 'Nevertheless a spring or a cistern holding water shall be clean; but whatever touches their carcass shall be unclean' (Lev. 11:36). And from this verse you derive many laws. [So how can M. 1:8D say what it does about many verses for laws of cultic cleanness?]"

[B] R. Zeira in the name of R. Yohanan: "If a law comes to hand and you do not know its nature, do not discard it for another one, for lo, many laws were stated to Moses at Sinai, and all of them have been embedded in the Mishnah."

The truly striking assertion appears at B. The Mishnah now is claimed to contain statements made by God to Moses. Just how these statements found their way into the Mishnah, and which passages of the Mishnah contain them, we do not know. That is hardly important, given the fundamental assertion.

The next passage proceeds to a further, and far more consequential, proposition. It asserts that part of the Torah was written down and part was preserved in memory and transmitted orally. In context, moreover, that distinction must encompass the Mishnah, thus explaining its origin as part of the Torah. Here I believe we have clear and unmistakable expression of the distinction between two forms in which a single Torah was revealed and handed on at Mount Sinai, part in writing, part orally. While the passage below does not make use of the language, Torah-in-writing and Torah-by-memory, it does refer to "the written" and "the oral." I believe myself fully justified in supplying the word "Torah" in square brackets. The reader will note, however, that the word "Torah" likewise does not occur at K, L. Only when the passage reaches its climax, at M, does it break down into a number of categories— Scripture, Mishnah, Talmud, laws, lore. It there makes the additional point that everything comes from Moses at Sinai. So the fully articulated theory of

---

11. We have noted the same issue preoccupied the framers of Sifra, on Leviticus, and Sifré to Numbers.

two Torahs (not merely one Torah in two forms) does not reach final expression in this passage. But short of explicit allusion to Torah-in-writing and Torah-by-memory, which (so far as I am able to discern) we find mainly in the Talmud of Babylonia, the ultimate theory of Torah of formative Judaism is at hand in what follows.

Y. Hag. 1:8.V

[D]   R. Zeirah in the name of R. Eleazar: " 'Were I to write for him my laws by ten thousands, they would be regarded as a strange thing' (Hos. 8:12). Now is the greater part of the Torah written down? [Surely not. The oral part is much greater.] But more abundant are the matters which are derived by exegesis from the written [Torah] than those derived by exegesis from the oral [Torah]."

[E]   And is that so?

[F]   But more cherished are those matters which rest upon the written [Torah] than those which rest upon the oral [Torah]

[J]   R. Haggai in the name of R. Samuel bar Nahman, "Some teachings were handed on orally, and some things were handed on in writing, and we do not know which of them is the more precious. But on the basis of that which is written, 'And the Lord said to Moses, Write these words; in accordance with these words I have made a covenant with you and with Israel' (Ex. 34:27), [we conclude] that the ones which are handed on orally are the more precious."

[K]   R. Yohanan and R. Yudan b. R. Simeon—One said, "If you have kept what is preserved orally and also kept what is in writing, I shall make a covenant with you, and if not, I shall not make a covenant with you."

[L]   The other said, "If you have kept what is preserved orally and you have kept what is preserved in writing, you shall receive a reward, and if not, you shall not receive a reward."

[M]   [With reference to Deut. 9:10: "And on them was written according to all the words which the Lord spoke with you in the mount,"] said R. Joshua b. Levi, "He could have written, 'On them,' but wrote, 'And on them.' He could have written, 'All,' but wrote, 'According to all.' He could have written, 'Words,' but wrote, 'The words.' [These then serve as three encompassing clauses, serving to include] Scripture, Mishnah, Talmud, laws, and lore. Even what an experienced student in the future is going to teach before his master already has been stated to Moses at Sinai."

[N]   What is the Scriptural basis for this view?

[O]   "There is no remembrance of former things, nor will there be any remembrance of later things yet to happen among those who come after" (Qoh. 1:10).

[P]   If someone says, "See, this is a new thing," his fellow will answer him, saying to him, "This has been around before us for a long time."

Here we have absolutely explicit evidence that people believed part of the Torah had been preserved not in writing but orally. Linking that part to the Mishnah remains a matter of implication. But it surely comes fairly close to the surface, when we are told that the Mishnah contains Torah traditions revealed at Sinai. From that view it requires only a small step to the allegation that the Mishnah is part of the Torah, the oral part.

At the risk of repetitiousness, let us consider yet another example in which the same notion occurs. The following passage moves from the matter of translating from the written Torah into Aramaic, so that the congregation may understand the passage, to a distinction between two forms of the Torah. The same discourse then goes over the ground we have just reviewed. The importance of the issue to the larger argument justifies our reviewing the whole. The first point is that when the Torah (the written Scripture) is read in the synagogue, the original revelation is reenacted. God used Moses as intermediary. So the one who proclaims the Torah (in the place of God) must not be the one who then repeats Torah to the congregation (in the place of Moses). This further leads, at J, to the explicit statement that parts of the Torah were stated orally and parts in writing. Here, however, the part that is oral clearly means the Aramaic translation (Targum). In context, we need not invoke the conception of two kinds of one Torah, let alone of two Torahs constituting the one whole Torah of Moses, our rabbi. That does not appear. Then, with Kff., comes the familiar discussion about two modes of one Torah. This passage precipitates a statement of what constitutes that whole Torah, written and oral. Here, as before, "Mishnah, Talmud, and lore" join Scripture. The main point again is the assertion that whatever a sage teaches falls into the category of the Torahs of Sinai. That point, of course, is familiar and conventional. First, what the sage says is Torah. Second, the sage cites Mishnah. Third, Mishnah is Torah.

Y. Megillah 4:1.II

[G]   R. Samuel bar R. Isaac went to a synagogue. He saw someone standing and serving as translator, leaning on a post. He said to him, "It is forbidden to you [to lean while standing]. For just as the Torah was given, originally, in fear and trembling, so we have to treat it with fear and trembling."

[H]   R. Haggai said R. Samuel bar R. Isaac went to a synagogue. He saw Hunah standing and serving as translator, and he had not set up anyone else in his stead [so he was both reading and translating himself]. He said to him, "It is forbidden to you, for just as it was given through an intermediary [namely, Moses] so we have to follow the custom of having an intermediary [so that the same person may not both read from the Torah and translate]."

[I]   R. Judah bar Pazzi went in and treated the matter as a question: " 'The Lord spoke with you face to face at the mountain . . . while I stood between the Lord and you at that time, to declare to you the word of the Lord'" (Deut. 5:4–5).

[J]   R. Haggai said R. Samuel bar R. Isaac went into a synagogue. He saw a teacher [reading from] a translation spread out, presenting the materials from the book. He said to him, "It is forbidden to do it that way. Things which were stated orally must be presented orally. Things which were stated in writing must be prepared in writing."

[K]   R. Haggai in the name of R. Samuel bar Nahman: "Some teachings were stated orally, and some teachings were stated in writing, and we do not know which of the two is more precious.

[L]   "But on the basis of that which is written, 'And the Lord said to Moses, Write these words; in accordance with these words I have made a covenant with you and with Israel' (Ex. 34:27), that is to say that the ones which are handed on orally are more precious."

[M]   R. Yohanan and R. Judah b. R. Simeon—one said, "[The meaning of the verse is this:] 'If you have kept what is handed on orally and if you have kept what is handed on in writing, then I shall make a covenant with you, and if not, I shall not make a covenant with you.'"

[N]   The other one said, "'If you have kept what is handed on orally, and if you have kept what is handed on in writing, then you will receive a reward, and if not, you will not receive a reward.'"

[O]   [With reference to the following verse: "And the Lord gave me the two tablets of stone written with the finger of God; and on them were all the words which the Lord had spoken with you on the mountain of the midst of the fire on the day of the assembly (Deut. 9:10),] said R. Joshua b. Levi, "[It is written,] 'on them,' 'and on them,' 'words,' 'the words,' 'all,' 'with all.' [These additional usages serve what purpose?]

[P]   "The reference is to Scripture, Mishnah, Talmud, and lore—and even what an experienced disciple is destined to teach in the future before his master has already been stated to Moses at Sinai."

[Q]   That is in line with the following verse of Scripture: "Is there a thing of which it is said, 'See, this is new'? He and his fellow will reply to him, 'It has been already in the ages before us'" (Qoh.1:10).

Here again, the penultimate statement of the theory of the Torah of formative Judaism lies at hand. The final step is not taken here, but it is a short step indeed.

Let me briefly review the stages in the unfolding of the meanings of the word "Torah" as these pertain to the case at hand. For I wish to show that the identification of the Mishnah as part of the Torah would have taken place even if Constantine had not converted to Christianity. The reason is that the processes of thought, with special reference to symbolization, that ultimately led to that identification had long been underway. And the precipitating force derived wholly from the place and function of the Mishnah within the circles of sages and within their administration of the Jewish nation's affairs, both in the Land of Israel and in Babylonia.

The word "Torah" reached the apologists for the Mishnah in its long-established meanings: Torah-scroll, contents of the Torah-scroll. But even in the Mishnah itself, these meanings provoked a secondary development, the status of Torah as distinct from other (lower) status, hence, Torah-teaching in contradistinction to scribal-teaching. With that small and simple step, the Torah ceased to denote only a concrete and material thing—a scroll and its contents. It now connotated an abstract matter of status. And once made abstract, the symbol entered a secondary history beyond all limits imposed by the concrete object, including its specific teachings, the Torah-scroll. I believe that Pirqé Abot stands at the beginning of this process. In the history of the word "Torah" as abstract symbol, a metaphor serving to sort out one abstract status from another regained concrete and material reality of a new order entirely.

For the message of Abot was that the Torah served the sage. How so? The Torah indicated who was a sage and who was not. Accordingly, the apology of Abot for the Mishnah was that the Mishnah contained things sages had said— and these are explicitily identified as "Torah" that "Moses received from God at Sinai and handed on" to named authorities, down to sages of the generation of the closure of the Mishnah itself. And what each sage "said" in the chain of tradition from Sinai is something other than a citation of a verse from Scripture. So this is Torah, but it is not in Scripture, hence it is not written Torah but Torah that is received and handed on not in writing, hence by memory, thus: Oral Torah. The situation could not have been stated with greater force. What sages said formed a chain of tradition extending back to Sinai. Hence it was equivalent to the Torah. The upshot is that words of sages enjoyed the status of the Torah. The small step beyond, I think, was to claim that what sages said was Torah, as much as what Scripture said was Torah. And, a further, equally small step (and the steps need not have been taken separately or in the order here suggested) moved matters to the position that there were two forms in which the Torah reached Israel: one (Torah) in writing, the other (Torah) handed on orally, that is, in memory. Now to return to the exercise of falsification and verification that has led us into the byways of the history of Judaism.

The Absence of Confrontation

Let me cite the language used above: when they read the shared Scriptures— the Old Testament/Written Torah—did the two sides work on the same agendum or on different agenda? They worked on different agenda. Sages asked questions provoked by issues within their circles, on the relative value of reason as against exegesis in the formation of the law. Jerome pursued questions of a different order altogether. Whatever he wished to find out in Scripture or

tell people about Scripture, it had nothing to do with the philosophical program paramount in the generative literary structures of Sifré to Numbers.
Does that fact matter, or is it just how things were? The answer becomes clear
when we recall that sages and theologians did deal with the same issue, in the
same terms. They could, after all, compose intersecting arguments, so achieving a clear confrontation, on the meaning of history from creation forward, on
the claim of Jesus to be the Messiah (with all that that entailed), and on the
identity of Israel and the issue of the salvation of the Jewish people, Israel
after the flesh. Did they ask the same questions, adduce the same facts in evidence, work out the same logic, or did they ask different questions, deal with
different evidence, and think in different logical patterns? In these three
matters, the questions seem to me essentially uniform. The evidence derives
from the same set of historical facts. The mode of argument—appeal to what
has happened, as Scripture records it—of each side coheres with that of the
other.

We come finally to the issue of the canon. The effort to compare the Old
Testament and the New Testament as the Bible to the Written Torah and the
Oral Torah as the one whole Torah of Moses, our rabbi, yields results I can
regard only as derisive. Once the comparison gets under way, we discover that
the categories in no way cohere. The Torah is not the Bible, and the Bible is
not the Torah. The Bible emerges from the larger process of establishing
Church order and doctrine. I cannot pretend to know whether or not von
Campenhausen's arguments about the emergence of the New Testament in response to Montanism prove valid. I can flatly state that the issue—providing a
basis to sort out the claims of living prophets, with direct access to divine
teachings—bears no point of intersection, let alone comparison and contrast,
with anything known to me in the entire corpus of rabbinic writing of late
antiquity. The Torah (Oral and Written) for its part derives from the larger
process of working out, within the political life of the Jewish nation, the authority and standing of two critical components of that life: the sage and the
Mishnah. We deal with matters of public policy and political status. Neither
the Bible nor the Torah emerged in the time of Constantine or in response to
the political revolution that took place at that time. With respect to neither
scriptural exegesis nor the determination of the canon of Scripture do Christian theologians and Judaic sages ever confront the same issue.

Since the answer to our original question is one-sidedly negative, we must
further ask why the confrontation with Scripture did not provoke for Judaic
sages and Christian theologians, a confrontation *over* Scripture, in the way in
which the confrontation with the categories of history, Messiah, and Israel
clearly produced a confrontation over those categories. When, in 325, Constantine called a worldwide assembly of Church authorities to take up urgent
questions of doctrine and Church order, conspicuous by its absence from the
agendum was the program of issues on which we have constructed our imaginary debate between Judaic sages and Christian theologians. A sage who by

some odd chance wandered into the meeting would probably have understood not a word of the discussion, even though he may have known Greek. For at issue were matters of Christology in no way pertinent to outsiders, including Jews. These issues demanded attention as the Church grew and changed, since the task at hand was to produce a cogent and acceptable protocol of faith to hold matters together. It was, in part, a political problem, but not one to attract Judaic sages' attention.

And, to continue the story, if we were to compose an imaginary debate within a sages' assembly, basing our dialogue on arguments in the Talmud of the Land of Israel of the same time, we should in vain try to explain to a Basil of Caesarea or a Eusebius or a Jerome what the Judaic sages found worthy of so much heated debate. For the things on which religious thinkers focus concern the religious community at hand. The outsider takes a place on the edges of thought, not at the center, and debate with the outsider ordinarily proceeds along lines that radiate from the center. So, for instance, Luther thought the depraved condition of the Church, as it appeared to him, kept the Jews from converting; when reformed, the Church would present an irresistible attraction to them. But that, to his exasperation, did not happen.

The real question is not why religious intellectuals of one circle do *not* intersect with those of another. To that question the answer is clear: issues well up from within the springs of the faith. The more difficult question is why religious intellectuals of one side *ever* discuss issues that engage religious intellectuals of the other side, as I believe I have shown, in the age of Constantine, on some few matters, they did. When the issues are defined by both groups in a single way, the facts are not at issue, and the modes of argument are common to the two parties, then we have a situation requiring explanation in a way in which the absence of confrontation does not demand attention. When different people talk about different things to different people, we have no reason to wonder why. When different people talk about the same things to different people, we do.

When political change affects everyone, then a single program of thought superimposes its issues on the inner-facing concerns of diverse groups. At that point both sides will end up talking about one thing—but only that one thing that politics has forced upon the attention of each, in the same way, in the same terms. The one thing no one in 300 expected is what the world of 400 produced: a Christian Rome, firmly in command of the state. That constituted a change in the politics, not of the Church alone, but of all the peoples of the Empire. Mediated into the language of self-understanding supplied by Scripture to both Judaic sages and Christian theologians, the political change provoked thought on what were, fundamentally, political issues. That same change did not require public, therefore shared, discourse on issues that were not matters of public policy. The explanation of the epochs of history, from the beginning to the present, bore immediate consequences for public policy. Every biographer of Eusebius has noted how his high evaluation of Constantine constituted a political, not merely a theological, judgment. The resort to proof from politics that Jesus really was, and is, the Christ, the demonstration of convictions of faith through facts of political change—that is what made the Messiah issue urgent as well. The creation of the Christian state, claiming to carry forward the ancient Israelite state and to appeal to its precedents, brought to a critical stage the long-term Christian claim that Christians formed the New Israel.[12]

But what of the twin issues of exegesis and canon? The ambiguities strike us with force. First, I cannot show the temporal coincidence of the processes of the canonization of the Bible, the Old Testament and the New Testament, with the processes of the "canonization" of the Torah of the two media. The one process—the Christian process of canon—seems to have reached its final stages before the other process got under way. The issues hardly coincided. The precipitating causes within the Church bore no resemblance to those that raised counterpart issues among Judaic sages. Second, while recognizing episodic points of intersecting comments, I cannot demonstrate that the overall exegetical program of an important commentary of sages pursued the issues important to the overall exegetical program of an important Christian exegete. I do not even know that, at the time of Jerome, equivalent exercises among sages to produce systematic, word-for-word commentaries of the same sort went forward.[13] So here too I cannot find evidence of the temporal coincidence of the labor, and, furthermore, I also do not know that the labor of the one party intersected, in its definition of the issues at hand, with the labor of the other. The difference from the points of intersection in exercises of definition of Israel, Messiah, and the meaning and end of history hardly requires specification. There, as chapters 2, 3, and 4 showed us, we do find the same program in writings of the same period, namely, the fourth century. The twin issues of exegesis and canon hardly brought the two sides together into an equivalent confluence, a genuine debate. I do not believe that the one side meant by exegesis what the other did, nor do the processes that led to the canonization of "the Bible" for Christianity in any way correspond to those that yielded "the one whole Torah of Moses, our rabbi, oral and written" for Judaism.

The difference between debate and mere confrontation, the reason to expect the one and not the other, is easy to discern: Nicaea once more calls us. For when we listen to the arguments at Nicaea, we understand why shared discourse on a single topic, unpacked in the same way, formulated on the basis of the same logic, and settled by appeal to the same verses of Scripture or other facts, requires external, political motivation—indeed, provocation. For from

12. I have repeatedly pointed to the political dimensions of these theological issues, and the consequences, for public policy for Israel as well as for Rome (the unequal counterparts in sages' political fantasy) hardly require reiteration.
13. My problem here is that Onqelos, the one Targum that all parties concede falls within the sages' sector, cannot be definitively dated to the century at hand.

Nicaea we hear what can only have been nonsense-talk to Jews, which of course was also discourse on profound and holy truth to Christians. To state the question clearly: Why did a Judaic position on the issue of the nature of Christ not come to the fore? Because the debate made no difference to Jews. And why no common program of debate on canon and exegesis (except, again, at odd and anecdotal points)? For the same reason, on both sides. I doubt that Christians cared about Jews' exegetical program and canonical doctrine, except as the relationship to Judaism made a difference. Christians may well have claimed that the Mishnah came from man, not God. But the theory of the dual Torah cannot be shown to derive from, or to respond in a pointed way to, that allegation as Christians made it. It seems to me beyond argument that Christians found as interesting the debates on the role of logic and exegesis in the study of the law as did Jews on the nature of Christ: like God, not like God, how like God, how God. There is mutual indifference because, to begin with, what mattered to Christian theologians ordinarily made no difference to Judaic sages, and vice versa; and, second, what would matter to both was made to matter by issues neither could evade and both had to sort out and settle. And the state, for its reasons, would define those issues and render them acute. When it did, the intellectuals of Christianity and Judaism took note. Otherwise, neither side had much reason to bother.

Epilogue:
The Shape of the Initial Encounter and the Enduring Confrontation

Sages' Success in the Initial Encounter

Judaism endured in the West for two reasons. First, Christianity permitted it to endure, and, second, Israel, the Jewish people, wanted it to. The fate of paganism in the fourth century shows the importance of the first of the two factors (Geffcken 1978, 115–222). We see, in particular, that it was not the intellectual power of sages alone that secured the long-term triumph of Judaism. It also was the character of the Christian emperors' policy toward Judaism that afforded to Jews and their religion such toleration as they would enjoy then and thereafter. The religious worship of Judaism never was prohibited. Pagan sacrifice, by contrast, came under interdict in 341. Festivals went on into the fifth century, but the die was cast. When, after 350, Constantius won the throne over a contender who had enjoyed pagan support, he closed all the pagan temples in the empire, prohibited access under penalty of death, and tolerated the storming and destruction of the temples. Churches took the place of the pagan temples. That is not to suggest that paganism was extirpated overnight, or that all the laws against it were kept. It is an indication of an ongoing policy. The Christian emperors never instituted a parallel policy toward Judaism and the synagogue. The reason for the limited toleration accorded to Judaism need not detain us, even though, as a political fact, it is the single most important reason for the continued survival of the Jews, therefore also of Judaism, in Western civilization.[1]

Pagan intellectuals, counterparts to the Judaic sages, responded with profound and systematic answers to Christian doctrine. No one familiar with

1. It suffices to note, following Dr. Rosemary Ruether (letter, June 25, 1986), the following: "This protection of the Jews and Judaism, even if under hostile and punitive laws, flowed from one aspect of that same Christian theology that saw itself as God's elect vis-à-vis a superseded Judaism. Just as the Jews saw Christian Rome as a 'brother' but a discarded brother, so Christianity saw Judaism as brother, but as unbelieving brother. To reconcile the conflict it constructed an eschatology that mandated eventual Jewish conversion and reconciliation to Christianity (on

their writings can suppose paganism lacked the power of ideas that was afforded to Israel by the Judaic sages. The contrary was the case. Iamblichus, a principal figure in the first half of the century, accomplished what Geffcken calls "the inner strengthening of paganism." This he did not by a negative statement on Christianity but a positive reassertion of pagan doctrine, in a profoundly philosophical idiom bearing deep overtones of religious feeling. Geffcken cites the following statement, "It is the fulfillment of ineffable rites the fitting accomplishment of which surpasses an intellectual understanding and the power of unspeakable signs which are intelligible to the gods alone that effect theurgic union." Iamblichus inspired Julian, and, for a brief moment, it appeared that paganism would enjoy a renaissance. On intellectual grounds, it might have. But afterward a severe repression set in, and the Christian emperors Gratian, Valentinian II, and Theodosius undertook a systematic counterattack.

The laws came one after the other. In 381 pagans were denied the right to bequeath property; sacrifice was again prohibited; Gratian deprived the temples and cults of their property and subsidies. So the institutions of paganism lost their foundations. And that was a fact of state policy and politics, to which doctrine, on the pagan side, hardly pertained. The upshot, as Geffcken says, was the end of pagan cult: "For without the substructure of religious observance within the framework of the state, there could be no pagan cult, on ancestral worship." True enough, Christian people, led by monks, implemented the laws' spirit through their own actions, destroying temples (as well as synagogues). For their part, pagan intellectuals at the end of the century, typified by Libanius, responded with a program of argument and rhetoric. But the issue was not to be resolved through rhetoric nor was the fate of the temples settled by mobs. It was a political attack that paganism confronted, and, with the throne in Christian hands, the policy of the Church settled matters. Antipagan legislation won the day, to be sure not everywhere and all at once, but ultimately and completely. That fact proves what might have happened to Judaism. But it did not happen, as I said, in part because the Church-state did not choose to extirpate Judaism. The other reason is the intellectual achievements of the Judaic sages.

These require only a rapid reprise. With the triumph of Christianity through Constantine and his successors in the West, Christianity's explicit claims, now validated in world-shaking events of the age, demanded a reply. The sages of the Talmud of the Land of Israel, Genesis Rabbah, and Leviticus Rabbah provided it. At those very specific points at which the Christian challenge met

Christian terms, of course). This notion that the Jews had a future destiny in God's design for history required the survival of the Jews as a religious community. In Christian eschatology the Jews as a religious group had finally to accept Jesus as the Christ and be included in redemption. In this backhanded way Christianity acknowledged that the Jews were still God's chosen people and could not be simply discarded by God."

head-on Israel's worldview, sages' doctrines responded. What did Israel's sages have to present as the Torah's answer to the cross? It was the Torah, with its doctrine of history, Messiah, and Israel. History in the beginning, in Genesis, accounted for the events of the day. The Messiah will be a sage of the Torah. Israel today comprises the family, after the flesh, of the founders of Israel. The Torah therefore served as the encompassing symbol of Israel's salvation. The Torah would be embodied in the person of the Messiah who, of course, would be a rabbi. The Torah confronted the cross, with its doctrine of the triumphant Christ, Messiah and king, ruler now of earth as of heaven. In the formulation of the sages who wrote the fourth- and early fifth-century documents, the Talmud of the Land of Israel and Genesis Rabbah and Leviticus Rabbah, the Torah thus confronted the challenge of the cross of Christianity as, later on, the Torah, with its ample doctrines of history, Messiah, and Israel, would meet and in Israel in particular overcome the sword and crescent of Islam. Within Israel, the Jewish people, the Torah everywhere triumphed. That is why, when Christianity came to power and commenced to define the civilization of the West, Judaism met and overcame its greatest crisis before modern times. And it held. As a result, Jews remained within the Judaic system of the dual Torah. That is why they continued for the entire history of the West to see the world through the worldview of the dual Torah and to conduct life in accord with the way of life of the Torah as the rabbis explained it. The Judaism of the dual Torah took shape in response to the crisis of Constantine's conversion and came to its systematic literary expression in the writings of the following century, from the Talmud of the Land of Israel, ca. 400, through Genesis Rabbah, Leviticus Rabbah, Pesiqta deRav Kahana, The Fathers According to Rabbi Nathan, and beyond. The Judaism of that time took up the ineluctable and urgent question of salvation as Christianity framed that question. And, for believing Israel, the answer proved self-evidently true, then, and for long centuries afterward.

The consequence was stunning success for that society for which, to begin with, sages, and, in sages' view, God, cared so deeply: eternal Israel after the flesh. For Judaism in the rabbis' statement did endure in the Christian West, imparting to Israel the secure conviction of constituting that Israel after the flesh to which the Torah continued to speak. How do we know sages' Judaism won? Because when, in turn, Islam gained its victory, Christianity throughout the Middle East and North Africa gave way. Christianity endured, to be sure, but not as the religion of the majorities of the Roman Middle East and North Africa, areas that for many centuries prior to Islam had formed the heartland of Christianity. Chalcedonian and non-Chalcedonian Christian churches continued under Islamic rule and endure even today. But the Islamic character of the Near and Middle East and North Africa tells the story of what really happened, which was a debacle for Christianity. But sages' Judaism in those same vast territories retained the loyalty and conviction of the people of the Torah. The cross would rule only where the crescent and its sword did not. But the

Torah of Sinai everywhere and always sanctified Israel in time and promised secure salvation for eternity. So Israel believed, and so does faithful Israel, those Jews who also are Judaists, believe today. The entire history of Judaism is contained within these simple propositions.

The Enduring Confrontation

The political circumstances of the fourth century—ascendant Christianity, a still political Judaism—hardly could remain stable. By the turn of the fifth century the state was firmly Christian and its successors in Europe would remain so for fifteen hundred years. The sages' framing of a Judaic system attained the status of a norm. So far as Christianity in all of its European forms raised challenges to Judaism in its one, now normative, form, answers found in the fourth century retained for Jews the standing of self-evident truth. We therefore should anticipate no rehearsal of that odd moment at which, each in his own idiom, a Judaic sage and a Christian theologian could address the same issue and compose a position based on the same facts and modes of argument. When, under the conditions that prevailed eight hundred to a thousand years later, new encounters took place, they bore no resemblance in intellectual structure to the one we have reviewed. Then, as before the fourth century, different people talked about different things to different people—even when they met face-to-face.

Why the initial confrontation produced no later continuation finds its answer, in my view, in an essentially political circumstance. Conditions for debate later on did not accord equal standing to both sides, such as, in their minds at least, the Judaic sages of the fourth century assuredly enjoyed, and the Christian theologians accorded, as best they could. What this meant, curiously, was that the confrontation later on took place jointly—not by indirection, through sustained writings on a given theological issue treated wholly in its own terms—and through direct interlocution of one side by the other. In that respect, too, the later, and enduring confrontation did not replicate the mode of discourse of the initial phase, which was marked by the composition of large-scale writings clear of all marks of an argument such as I have composed: same issues, same facts, same mode of thought.

We do not have to imagine what one side would have said to the other. We know what each did say to the other. In no way can we characterize this later discourse as an interesting argument about issues important to each side, defined in the same way by each party to the discussion. Quite to the contrary, the issues facing the Judaic participants bore a political, not an intellectual, character. The rights of Jews to live where and how they did were at stake in the disputations; the beliefs of the Jews about the meaning and end of history, the Messiah in the end of days, and the definition of Israel, scarcely came up. And, when they did, Christians framed the issue—Why do you *not* believe?—and Jews responded. Nor, in their response, did the Jewish participants vastly improve on matters. They simply ridiculed the Christians' convictions: "they lacked both *ratio* and *auctoritas*," being devoid of scriptural foundation and without logical justification—so Berger (1979, 13). No debate there, scarcely an intellectual confrontation.[2]

The next major intellectual confrontation, on the side of Judaism, took place eight hundred years later, in the twelfth century. Then the Christian side took the offensive, and, in Berger's judgment, "We find Jews arguing that Christianity is so inherently implausible that only the clearest biblical evidence could suffice to establish its validity" (1979, 7n.2). Issues of the initial confrontation scarcely occur in the medieval debates between Judaic and Christian officials, at least not in their classical formulation. An account of the disputations of the Middle Ages—Paris, 1240; Barcelona, 1263; and Tortosa, 1413–14—therefore carries us into a world far removed from the one in which the issues of history, Messiah, and Israel produced a genuine confrontation on the same set of issues, defined in the same terms.[3]

Of special interest here is the bearing these later debates have on the thesis at hand. Specifically, can we identify a political foundation that made common discourse necessary, even urgent? By that question, I mean to ask whether we can find points of public policy, not merely theological doctrine, that debate was meant to settle. The answer is one-sidedly affirmative, according to Maccoby: "The authority of the Inquisition did extend to some regulation of Judaism." The presence of kings and high lords temporal as well as lords spiritual who bore considerable responsibility in public administration leaves no doubt on that score. Yet in other ways I see no important continuity at all. In the fourth century, when Judaic sages and Christian theologians constructed what I take to have been an argument, they addressed issues of mutual interest. The argument was joined fairly on matters of theological substance, each side working out its position free of the intervention of the other. But in the medieval disputations, Judaism stood in the dock, the accused. The charge for Paris, in 1240, was that Judaism in the Talmud taught blasphemies against the Christian religion, made remarks against Christians, revered holy books that contained unedifying material, e.g., nonsense or obscenity.

The issues at Barcelona, in 1263, prove somewhat more interesting. Maccoby sees it as a debate rather than an inquisition. The Christian approach now was "to attempt to prove the truth of Christianity from the Jewish writings, including the Talmud. . . . Various Aggadic passages, collected from Talmud and Midrash, were thought to support Christian doctrines, especially the divinity of the Messiah, his suffering on the Cross, the date of his advent, and his promulgation of a new Law. Nahmanides immediately challenged the rationale of this contention." In consequence of this approach, a further issue

    2. Cf. Berger: "Christians were genuinely puzzled at the Jewish failure to accept the overwhelming array of scriptural arguments which they had marshalled" (1979, 11).
    3. Berger: "Anti-Christian works by Jews . . . are virtually nonexistent before the twelfth century" (1979, 8).

derived from the authority of the so-called Aggadic portions of the Talmud. The Judaic side treated the passages as unimportant, though the rabbis of the day revered them. Maccoby's judgment that there was a basic "lack of rapprochement and mutual understanding in the disputations" proves definitive: no argument here, only a confrontation lacking all shared discourse (Maccoby 1981, 11, 23, 26–38, 41–42).

As to Tortosa, in 1413–14, chaired by a pope and joined by representatives of the Jewish communities of Aragon and Catalonia, the disputation aimed at the conversion of the Jews. Maccoby's judgment is this: "As far as the larger issues of Jewish-Christian confrontation were concerned, it added little to the Barcelona Disputation." But one thing is clear from Maccoby's fine summary: a matter of public policy greatly engaged the Judaic side, specifically, religious toleration. As one of the Jewish spokesmen stated: "I say that all disputation about a principle of religion is prohibited, so that a man may not depart from the principles of his religion. It seems that only science should be made the subject of dispute and argument, but religion and belief ought to be consigned willingly to faith, not argument, so that he may not retreat from it." Europe would have to endure the devastation, in the name of religion, of Germany and much else before even that much toleration might win support as a political party, then in the form, after all, of *cuius regio eius religio*—not much toleration, but better than nothing. In any event the focus of discourse was this: "to prove the truth of Christian doctrines about the Messiah from certain passages in the Talmud." Judaic sages cannot have found very urgent the needs of such an agenda (Maccoby 1981, 82, 86, 89).

I see no point of contact between the shape of the initial confrontation in the fourth century and the intellectual program—such as it was—of the medieval continuation. In fact, the two programs for debate seem to me, in selection and definition of the issues, in the manner of argument, and in the kinds of proofs people adduced in evidence of their propositions, wholly different from one another. Form and substance, context and content, the initial confrontation generated no succession. The reason for this can be seen in the politics of the later confrontation, for these proved wholly different in character from the politics of the fourth-century encounter. In the fourth century two political entities confronted one another out of rough parity, meeting for a brief moment as the one ascended, the other declined. In the medieval confrontations political parity hardly characterized both parties to the dispute, which yielded confrontation but no debate, and certainly not dialogue.

In the fourth century, Christian theologians could consider in essentially the same terms as Judaic sages the scriptural issues they (correctly) deemed critical for Judaism. Aphrahat of course forms the exemplary figure, arguing carefully on the basis of ancient Israelite writings when addressing contemporary Jews. But I do not see the others as much different from Aphrahat. Eusebius addressed issues of world-historical interpretation, doing so in a rational and civil manner. Jerome wanted to engage in serious, equal argument with Jews, and so he took most seriously the lessons they had to teach—again, an encounter between equals. Chrysostom—alas! But he did not argue as an equal in competition with Jews, rather as a beleaguered and harassed figure, fearful of the future of Christians new to the Church and impressed by the synagogue. Eusebius, Chrysostom, Aphrahat, each in his way, addressed the other side by indirection, each with dignity, each in defense of the new faith. Later on, when the encounter became a confrontation that was direct and provocative, it was not between equals, not conducted with much dignity, and not aimed at clarifying, for the faith within, the issues of the challenge from the counterpart without. And this shift in tone and in substance, in the symbolic expression of the issues, expresses a more profound shift in the political realities which dictated and defined the terms of the tragic confrontation of the Middle Ages. In the fourth century sages of Judaism could pretend to ignore the challenge of Christianity, while at the same time systematically countering that challenge. Christian theologians forthrightly could enter the encounter with Judaism as with an equal. In the twelfth, thirteenth, and fourteenth centuries circumstances in no way afforded such an encounter.

The relevance to our own day demands only passing attention. Today Christianity controls few governments but much moral authority, exercises little power to dictate public policy, though (in my view, quite properly) much power of public persuasion. Not hiding in the catacombs, but also not determining the shape of the West, Christianity enjoys a position in the world of politics more like what it had in the time of Constantine—influential, but not (yet) in charge—than in the age of the medieval disputations. And, for its part, Judaism, in the persons of Israel after the flesh, in the West (not to mention in the State of Israel!) enjoys the protection of law that in medieval times proved not entirely reliable. So argument between people equal at both a political and an intellectual level may now go forward once more. Consequently, because of the character of politics in the contemporary West, civil equality exists for both sides. Civil discourse, with subtlety, by indirection, through learning, once more regains the platform. People can now, again, agree on issues, negotiate modes of common argument, concur on the facts that will be probative—that is to say, write books for one another to read.

Genesis Rabbah on Israel's History

LXI:VII

1. A. "But to the sons of his concubines, Abraham gave gifts, and while he was still living, he sent them away from his son Isaac, eastward to the east country" (Gen. 25:6):

   B. In the time of Alexander of Macedonia the sons of Ishmael came to dispute with Israel about the birthright, and with them came two wicked families, the Canaanites and the Egyptians.

   C. They said, "Who will go and engage in a disputation with them?"

   D. Gebiah b. Qosem [the enchanter] said, "I shall go and engage in a disputation with them."

   E. They said to him, "Be careful not to let the Land of Israel fall into their possession."

   F. He said to them, "I shall go and engage in a disputation with them. If I win over them, well and good. And if not, you may say, 'Who is this hunchback to represent us?'"

   G. He went and engaged in a disputation with them. Said to them Alexander of Macedonia, "Who lays claim against whom?"

   H. The Ishmaelites said, "We lay claim, and we bring our evidence from their own Torah: 'But he shall acknowledge the firstborn, the son of the hated' (Deut. 21:17). Now Ishmael was the firstborn. [We therefore claim the land as heirs of the first-born of Abraham.]"

   I. Said to him Gebiah b. Qosem, "My royal lord, does a man not do whatever he likes with his sons?"

   J. He said to him, "Indeed so."

   K. "And lo, it is written, 'Abraham gave all that he had to Isaac' (Gen. 25:2)."

   L. [Alexander asked,] "Then where is the deed of gift to the other sons?"

   M. He said to him, " 'But to the sons of his concubines, Abraham gave gifts, [and while he was still living, he sent them away from his son Isaac, eastward to the east country]' (Gen. 25:6)."

N. [The Ishmaelites had no claim on the land.] They abandoned the field in shame.

O. The Canaanites said, "We lay claim, and we bring our evidence from their own Torah. Throughout their Torah it is written, 'the land of Canaan.' So let them give us back our land."

P. Said to him Gebiah b. Qosem, "My royal lord, does a man not do whatever he likes with his slave?"

Q. He said to him, "Indeed so."

R. He said to him, "And lo, it is written, 'A slave of slaves shall Canaan be to his brothers' (Gen. 9:25). So they are really our slaves."

S. [The Canaanites had no claim to the land and in fact should be serving Israel.] They abandoned the field in shame.

T. The Egyptians said, "We lay claim, and we bring our evidence from their own Torah. Six hundred thousand of them left us, taking away our silver and gold utensils: 'They despoiled the Egyptians' (Ex. 12:36). Let them give them back to us."

U. Gebiah b. Qosem said, "My royal lord, six hundred thousand men worked for them for two hundred and ten years, some as silversmiths and some as goldsmiths. Let them pay us our salary at the rate of a *denar* a day."

V. The mathematicians went and added up what was owing, and they had not reached the sum covering a century before the Egyptians had to forfeit what they had claimed. They abandoned the field in shame.

W. [Alexander] wanted to go up to Jerusalem. The Samaritans said to him, "Be careful. They will not permit you to enter their most holy sanctuary."

X. When Gebiah b. Qosem found out about this, he went and made for himself two felt shoes, with two precious stones worth twenty thousand pieces of silver set in them. When he got to the mountain of the house [of the Temple], he said to him, "My royal lord, take off your shoes and put on these two felt slippers, for the floor is slippery, and you should not slip and fall."

Y. When they came to the most holy sanctuary, he said to him, "Up to this point, we have the right to enter. From this point onward, we do not have the right to enter."

Z. He said to him, "When we get out of here, I'm going to even out your hump."

AA. He said to him, "You will be called a great surgeon and get a big fee."

2. A. "[But to the sons of his concubines, Abraham gave gifts, and while he was still living,] he sent them away from his son Isaac, eastward to the east country]'" (Gen. 25:6):

B.   He said to them, "Go as far to the east as you can, so as not to be burned by the flaming coal of Isaac."

C.   But because Esau came to make war with Jacob, he took his appropriate share on his account: "Is this your joyous city, whose feet in antiquity, in ancient days, carried her afar off to sojourn? Who has devised this against Tyre, the crowning city?" (Is. 23:7).

D.   Said R. Eleazar, "Whenever the name of Tyre is written in Scripture, if it is written out [with all of the letters], then it refers to the province of Tyre. Where it is written without all of its letters [and so appears identical to the word for enemy], the reference of Scripture is to Rome. [So the sense of the verse is that Rome will receive its appropriate reward.]"

E.   [As to the sense of the word for] "the crowning city,"

F.   R. Abba bar Kahana said, "It means that they surrounded the city like a crown."

G.   R. Yannai, son of R. Simeon b. R. Yannai, said, "They surrounded it with a fence of thorns."

LV:VIII

1.   A.   "And Abraham rose early in the morning, [saddled his ass, and took two of his young men with him, and his son Isaac, and he cut the wood for the burnt offering and arose and went to the place which God had told him]" (Gen. 22:3):

B.   Said R. Simeon b. Yohai, "Love disrupts the natural order of things, and hatred disrupts the natural order of things.

C.   "Love disrupts the natural order of things we learn from the case of Abraham: '. . . he saddled his ass.' But did he not have any number of servants? But that proves love disrupts the natural order of things.

D.   "Hatred disrupts the natural order of things we learn from the case of Balaam: 'And Balaam rose up early in the morning and saddled his ass' (Num. 22:21). But did he not have any number of servants? But that proves hatred disrupts the natural order of things.

E.   "Love disrupts the natural order of things we learn from the case of Joseph: 'And Joseph made his chariot ready' (Gen. 46:29). But did he not have any number of servants? But that proves love disrupts the natural order of things.

F.   "Hatred disrupts the natural order of things we learn from the case of Pharoah: 'And he made his chariot ready' (Ex. 14:6). But did he not have any number of servants? But that proves hatred disrupts the natural order of things."

2.   A.   Said R. Simeon b. Yohai, "Let one act of saddling an ass come and counteract another act of saddling the ass. May the act of saddling the ass done by our father Abraham, so as to go and carry out the

will of him who spoke and brought the world into being counteract the act of saddling that was carried only by Balaam when he went to curse Israel.

B. "Let one act of preparing counteract another act of preparing. Let Joseph's act of preparing his chariot so as to meet his father serve to counteract Pharoah's act of preparing to go and pursue Israel."

C. R. Ishmael taught on Tannaite authority, "Let the sword held in the hand serve to counteract the sword held in the hand.

D. "Let the sword held in the hand of Abraham, as it is said, 'Then Abraham put forth his hand and took the knife to slay his son' (Gen. 22:10) serve to counteract the sword taken by Pharoah in hand: 'I will draw my sword, my hand shall destroy them' (Ex. 15:9)."

LVIII:II

1. A. "The sun rises and the sun goes down" (Qoh. 1:5):

B. Said R. Abba, "Now do we not know that the sun rises and the sun sets? But the sense is this: before the Holy One, blessed be he, makes the sun of one righteous man set, he brings up into the sky the sun of another righteous man.

C. "On the day that R. Aqiba died, Our Rabbi [Judah the Patriarch] was born. In his regard, they recited the following verse: 'The sun rises and the sun goes down' (Qoh. 1:5).

D. "On the day on which Our Rabbi died, R. Adda bar Ahbah was born. In his regard, they recited the following verse: 'The sun rises and the sun goes down' (Qoh. 1:5).

E. "On the day on which R. Ada died, R. Abin was born. In his regard, they recited the following verse: 'The sun rises and the sun goes down' (Qoh. 1:5).

F. "On the day on which R. Abin died, R. Abin his son was born. In his regard, they recited the following verse: 'The sun rises and the sun goes down' (Qoh. 1:5).

G. "On the day on which R. Abin died, Abba Hoshaiah of Taraya was born. In his regard, they recited the following verse: 'The sun rises and the sun goes down' (Qoh. 1:5).

H. "On the day on which Abba Hoshaiah of Taraya died, R. Hoshaiah was born. In his regard, they recited the following verse: 'The sun rises and the sun goes down' (Qoh. 1:5).

I. "Before the Holy One, blessed be he, made the sun of Moses set, he brought up into the sky the sun of Joshua: 'And the Lord said to Moses, Take you Joshua, the son of Nun' (Num. 27:18).

J. "Before the Holy One, blessed be he, made the sun of Joshua set, he brought up into the sky the sun of Othniel, son of Kenaz: 'And Othniel the son of Kenaz took it' (Joshua 15:17).

K. "Before the Holy One, blessed be he, made the sun of Eli set, he brought up into the sky the sun of Samuel: 'And the lamp of God was not yet gone out, and Samuel was laid down to sleep in the Temple of the Lord' (1 Sam. 3:3)."

L. Said R. Yohanan, "He was like an unblemished calf."

M. [Reverting to K:] "Before the Holy One, blessed be he, made the sun of Sarah set, he brought up into the sky the sun of Rebecca: 'Behold Milcah also has borne children' (Gen. 22:20). 'Sarah lived a hundred and twenty-seven years. These were the years of the life of Sarah' (Gen. 23:1)."

XLII:III

1. A. R. Tanhuma and R. Hiyya the Elder state the following matter, as does R. Berekhiah in the name of R. Eleazar [the Modite], "The following exegetical principle came up in our possession from the exile.

   B. "Any passage in which the words, 'And it came to pass' appear is a passage that relates misfortune."

   C. Said R. Samuel bar Nahman, "There are five such passages marked by the words, 'and it came to pass,' that bear the present meaning.

   D. " 'And it came to pass in the days of Amraphel, king of Shinar . . . these kings made war with Bera, king of Sodom' (Gen. 14:1).

   E. "The matter [of Abram's defending the local rulers] may be compared to the ally of a king who came to live in a province. On his account the king felt obligated to protect that entire province. Barbarians came and attacked him. Now when the barbarians came and attacked him, the people said, 'Woe, the king is not going to want to protect the province the way he used to [since it has caused him trouble].' That is in line with the following verse of Scripture, 'And they turned back and came to En Mishpat [source of justice], that is Kadesh [holy] [and subdued all the country of the Amalekites]' (Gen. 14:7)." [This concludes the first of the five illustrations.] [Lev. R. XI:VII.2.E adds: So too, Abraham was the ally of the King, the Holy One, blessed be he, and in his regard it is written, 'And in you shall all the families of the earth be blessed' (Gen. 12:4). So it was on his account that the Holy One, blessed be he, felt obligated to protect the entire world.]

   F. Said R. Aha, "They sought only to attack the orb of the Eye of world. The eye that had sought to exercise the attribute of justice in the world did they seek to blind: 'That is Kadesh' (Gen. 14:7)."

   G. Said R. Aha, "It is written, 'that is . . . ,' meaning, that is the particular one who has sanctified the name of the Holy One, blessed be he, by going down into the fiery furnace."

H.   [Reverting to the discourse suspended at the end of E:] When the barbarians came and attacked, they began to cry, "Woe, woe!"

I.   "And it came to pass in the days of Amraphel" (Gen. 14:1).

2. A.   "And it came to pass in the days of Ahaz" (Is. 7:1):

B.   "The Aramaeans on the east and the Philistines on the west devour Israel with open mouth" (Is. 9:12):

C.   The matter [of Israel's position] may be compared to the case of a king who handed over his son to a tutor, who hated the son. The tutor thought, "If I kill him now, I shall turn out to be liable to the death penalty before the king. So what I'll do is take away his wet-nurse, and he will die on his own."

D.   So thought Ahaz, "If there are no kids, there will be no he-goats. If there are no he-goats, there will be no flock. If there is no flock, there will be no Shepherd, if there is no Shepherd, there will be no world."

E.   So did Ahaz plan, "If there are no children, there will be no adults. If there are no adults, there will be no disciples. If there are no disciples, there will be no sages. If there are no sages, there will be no prophets. If there are no prophets, the Holy One, blessed be he, will not allow his presence to come to rest in the world." [Lev. R.: . . . Torah. If there is no Torah, there will be no synagogues and schools. If there are no synagogues and schools, then the Holy One, blessed be he, will not allow his presence to come to rest in the world.]

F.   That is in line with the following verse of Scripture: "Bind up the testimony, seal the Torah among my disciples" (Is. 8:16).

G.   R. Huna in the name of R. Eleazar: "Why was he called Ahaz? Because he seized [*ahaz*] synagogues and schools."

H.   R. Jacob in the name of R. Aha: "Isaiah said, 'I will wait for the Lord, who is hiding his face from the house of Jacob, and I will hope in him' (Is. 8:17). You have no more trying hour than that moment concerning which it is written, 'And I shall surely hide my face on that day' (Deut. 31:18).

I.   "From that hour: 'I will hope in him' (Is. 8:17). For he has said, 'For it will not be forgotten from the mouth of his seed' (Deut. 31:21).

J.   "What good did hoping do for Isaiah?

K.   " 'Behold I and the children whom the Lord has given me are signs and portents in Israel from the Lord of hosts who dwells on Mount Zion' (Is. 8:18). Now were they his children? Were they not his disciples? But this teaches that they were precious to him so that he regarded them as his children."

L.   [Reverting to G:] Now since everyone saw that Ahaz had seized the synagogues and schools, they began to cry out, "Woe, woe!' " Thus: "And it came to pass [marking the woe] in the days of Ahaz" (Is. 7:1).

3. A. "And it came to pass in the days of Jehoiakim, son of Josiah" (Jer. 1:3).
   B. "I look on the earth and lo, it was waste and void" (Jer. 4:23).
   C. The matter may be compared to the case of royal edicts which came into a province. What did the people do? They took the document, tore it up and burned the bits in fire. That is in line with the following verse of Scripture: "And it came to pass, as Jehudi read three or four columns, that is, three or four verses, the king would cut them off with a penknife and throw them into the fire in the brazier until the entire scroll was consumed in the fire that was in the brazier" (Jer. 36:23).
   D. When the people saw all this, they began to cry out, "Woe, woe."
   E. "And it came to pass in the days of Jehoiakim" (Jer. 1:3).
4. A. "And it came to pass in the days in which the judges ruled" (Ruth 1:1). "There was a famine in the land" (Ruth 1:1).
   B. The matter may be compared to a province which owed taxes in arrears to the king, so the king sent a revenuer to collect. What did the inhabitants of the province do? They went and hung him, hit him, and robbed him. They said, "Woe is us, when the king gets word of these things. What the king's representative wanted to do to us, we have done to him."
   C. So too, woe to the generation that has judged its judges.
   D. "And it came to pass in the days in which the judges themselves were judged" (Ruth 1:1).
5. A. "And it came to pass in the days of Ahasuerus" (Est. 1:1). "Haman undertook to destroy, to slay, and to annihilate all the Jews, young and old, women and children, in one day" (Est. 3:13).
   B. The matter may be compared to the case of a king who had a vineyard, and three of his enemies attacked it. One of them began to clip off the small branches, the next began to take the pendants off the grape clusters, and the last of them began to uproot the vines altogether.
   C. Pharoah [began by clipping off the small branches]: "Every son that is born will you throw into the river" (Ex. 1:22).
   D. Nebuchadnezzar [began to clip off the pendants of the grape clusters,] deporting the people: "And he carried away captive the craftsmen and smiths, a thousand" (2 Kgs. 24:16).
   E. R. Berekhiah in the name of R. Judah and rabbis:
   F. R. Berekhiah in the name of R. Judah: "There were a thousand craftsmen and a thousand smiths."
   G. Rabbis say, "This group and that group all together added up to a thousand."
   H. The wicked Haman began to uproot the vines altogether. He uprooted Israel from its roots: "To destroy, to slay, and to annihilate all the Jews" (Est. 3:13).

I.   When everybody saw that [Ahasuerus had sold and Haman had bought the Jews], they began to cry, "Woe, woe,"

J.   "And it came to pass in the days of Ahasuerus" (Est. 1:1).

6. A.   R. Simeon b. Abba in the name of R. Yohanan: "Any context in which the words, 'And it came to pass . . . ,' appear serves to signify either misfortune or good fortune. If it is a case of misfortune, it is misfortune without parallel. If it is a case of good fortune, it is good fortune without parallel."

B.   R. Samuel b. Nahman came and introduced this distinction: "Any context in which the words, 'And it came to pass . . .' occur signifies misfortune, and any context in which the words, 'And it shall come to pass . . .' are used signifies good fortune."

C.   They objected [to this claim], "And God said, 'Let there be light,' and it came to pass that there was light" (Gen. 1:3).

D.   He said to them, "This too does not represent good fortune, for in the end the world did not enjoy the merit of actually making use of that light."

E.   R. Judah [b. R. Simeon] said, "With the light that the Holy One, blessed be he, created on the first day of creation, a person could look and see from one side of the world to the other. When the Holy One, blessed be he, foresaw that there would be wicked people, he did it away for the [exclusive use of the] righteous. 'But the path of the righteous is as the light of the dawn that shines more and more to the perfect day' (Prov. 4:18)."

F.   They further objected, "And it came to pass that there was evening and morning, one day" (Gen. 1:5).

G.   He said to them, "This too does not signify good fortune. For whatever God created on the first day of creation is destined to be wiped out. That is in line with the following verse of Scripture: 'For the heaven shall vanish away like smoke, and the earth shall wax old like a garment' (Is. 51:6)."

H.   They further objected, "And it came to pass that there was evening and it came to pass that there was morning, a second day . . . , a third day . . . , a fifth day . . . , a sixth day . . ." (Gen. 1:8, 13, 19, 23, 31).

I.   He said to them, "This too does not signify good fortune. For everything which God created on the six days of creation was incomplete and would require further processing. Wheat has to be milled, mustard to be sweetened, [lupine to impart sweetness]."

J.   They further objected, "And it came to pass that the Lord was with Joseph, and Joseph was a prosperous man" (Gen. 39:2).

K.   He said to them, "This too does not signify good fortune, for on this account that she-bear [Potiphar's wife] came his way."

L.   They further objected, "And it came to pass on the eighth day that

Moses called Aaron and his sons for consecration in the priesthood" (Lev. 9:1).

M. He said to them, "This too does not signify good fortune, for on that same day Nadab and Abihu died."

N. They further objected, "And it came to pass on the day on which Moses made an end of setting up the tabernacle" (Num. 7:1).

O. He said to them, "This too does not signify good fortune. For on the day on which the Temple was built, the tabernacle was hidden away."

P. They further objected, "And it came to pass that the Lord was with Joshua and his fame was in all the land" (Joshua 6:27).

Q. He said to them, "This too does not signify good fortune, for he still had to tear his garments [on account of the defeat at Ai (Joshua 7:6)]."

R. They further objected, "And it came to pass that the king dwelt in his palace, and the Lord gave him rest round about" (2 Sam. 7:1).

S. He said to them, "This too does not signify good fortune. On that very day Nathan the prophet came to him and said, 'You will not build the house' (1 Kgs. 8:19)."

T. They said to him, "We have given our objections, now you give your proofs about good fortune."

U. He said to them, " 'And it shall come to pass in that day that living waters shall go out of Jerusalem' (Zech. 14:8). 'And it shall come to pass in that day that a great horn shall be blown' (Is. 27:13). 'And it shall come to pass in that day that a man shall rear a youngling' (Is. 7:21). 'And it shall come to pass in that day that the Lord will set his hand again a second time to recover the remnant of his people' (Is. 11:11). 'And it shall come to pass in that day that the mountains shall drop down sweet wine' (Joel 4:18). [All of these represent good fortune without parallel.]"

V. They said to him, "And it shall come to pass on the day on which Jerusalem is taken . . .' (Jer. 38:28)."

W. He said to them, "This too does not signify misfortune but good fortune [without parallel], for on that day the Israelites received a full pardon for all their sins.

X. "That is in line with what R. Samuel b. Nahman said, 'The Israelites received a full pardon for all their sins on the day on which the Temple was destroyed. That is in line with the following verse of Scripture, "The punishment of your inquiry is completed, daughter of Zion, and he will no more take you away into exile" (Lam. 4:22).' "

XLIII:VIII

1. A. "And blessed be God Most High, who has delivered your enemies into your hand" (Gen. 14:20):
   B. [Since the word for "deliver" yields the letters that serve for the word for plans or schemes,] R. Huna said, "It is that he turned your plans against your enemies."
   C. R. Yudan said, "How many schemes did I work out to place them under your hand. They were friendly with one another, sending one another dry dates and other gifts. But I made them rebel against one another so that they would fall into your hand."
2. A. "And Abram gave him a tenth of everything" (Gen. 14:20):
   B. R. Judah in the name of R. Nehorai: "On the strength of that blessing the three great pegs on which the world depends, Abraham, Isaac, and Jacob, derived sustenance.
   C. "Abraham: 'And the Lord blessed Abraham in *all* things' (Gen. 24:1) on account of the merit that 'he gave him a tenth of *all* things' (Gen. 14:20).
   D. "Isaac: 'And I have eaten of *all*' (Gen. 27:33), on account of the merit that 'he gave him a tenth of *all* things' (Gen. 14:20).
   E. "Jacob: 'Because God has dealt graciously with me and because I have all' (Gen. 33:11) on account of the merit that 'he gave him a tenth of *all* things' (Gen. 14:20)."
3. A. Whence did Israel gain the merit of receiving the blessing of the priests?
   B. R. Judah said, "It was from Abraham: '*So* shall your seed be' (Gen. 15:5), while it is written in connection with the priestly blessing: '*So* shall you bless the children of Israel' (Num. 6:23)."
   C. R. Nehemiah said, "It was from Isaac: 'And I and the lad will go *so* far' (Gen. 22:5), therefore said the Holy One, blessed be he, '*So* shall you bless the children of Israel' (Num. 6:23)."
   D. And rabbis say, "It was from Jacob: 'So shall you say to the house of Jacob' (Ex. 19:3) (in line with the statement, '*So* shall you bless the children of Israel' (Num. 6:23)."
4. A. When shall "I magnify your children like the stars"?
   B. R. Eleazar and R. Yose bar Hanina:
   C. One of them said, "When I shall be revealed to them with the word '*so:*' 'So shall you say to the house of Jacob' (Ex., 19:3)."
   D. The other said, "When I shall be revealed to them through their leaders and give a message invoking the word '*so:*' 'So says the Lord, Israel is my son, my firstborn' (Ex. 4:22)."

XLIV:XVII

4. A. "[And it came to pass, as the sun was going down,] lo, a deep sleep fell on Abram, and lo, a dread and great darkness fell upon him" (Gen. 15:12):

   B. ". . . lo, a dread" refers to Babylonia, as it is written, "Then was Nebuchadnezzar filled with fury" (Gen. 3:19).

   C. "and darkness" refers to Media, which darkened the eyes of Israel by making it necessary for the Israelites to fast and conduct public mourning.

   D. ". . . great . . ." refers to Greece.

   E. R. Simon said, "The kingdom of Greece set up one hundred and twenty commanders, one hundred and twenty hyparchs, and one hundred and twenty generals."

   F. Rabbis said, "It was sixty of each, as it is written, 'Serpents, fiery serpents, and scorpions' (Gen. 8:15). Just as the scorpion produces sixty eggs at a time, so the kingdom of Greece set up sixty at a time."

   G. ". . . fell upon him" refers to Edom, as it is written, "The earth quakes at the noise of their fall" (Jer. 49:21).

   H. Some reverse matters:

   I. ". . . fell upon him" refers to Babylonia, since it is written, "Fallen, fallen is Babylonia" (Is. 21:9).

   J. ". . . great . . ." refers to Media, in line with this verse: "King Ahasuerus did make great" (Est. 3:1).

   K. "and darkness" refers to Greece, which darkened the eyes of Israel by its harsh decrees.

   L. ". . . lo, a dread" refers to Edom, as it is written, "After this I saw . . . a fourth beast, dreadful and terrible" (Dan. 7:7).

XLIV:XVIII

1. A. "Then the Lord said to Abram, 'Know of a surety [that your descendants will be sojourners in a land that is not theirs, and they will be slaves there, and they will be oppressed for four hundred years; but I will bring judgment on the nation which they serve, and afterward they shall come out with great possessions']" (Gen. 15:13–14):

   B. "Know" that I shall scatter them.

   C. "Of a certainty" that I shall bring them back together again.

   D. "Know" that I shall put them out as a pledge [in expiation of their sins].

   E. "Of a certainty" that I shall redeem them.

   F. "Know" that I shall make them slaves.

G. "Of a certainty" that I shall free them.

2. A. ". . . that your descendants will be sojourners in a land that is not theirs and they will be slaves there, and they will be oppressed for four hundred years:"

B. It is four hundred years from the point at which you will produce a descendant. [The Israelites will not serve as slaves for four hundred years, but that figure refers to the passage of time from Isaac's birth.]

C. Said R. Yudan, "The condition of being outsiders, the servitude, the oppression in a land that was not theirs all together would last for four hundred years, that was the requisite term."

XLIV:XIX

1. A. "But I will also bring judgment on the nation which they serve" (Gen. 15:14):

B. Said R. Helbo, "Rather than, 'and that nation,' the passage states, 'But I will *also* bring judgment on the nation which they serve' (Gen. 15:14). Also they, also Egypt and the four kingdoms who will enslave you [will God judge]."

2. A. "I will bring judgment" (Gen. 15:14):

B. R. Eleazar in the name of R. Yose: "With these two letters, namely, the letters that form the word for 'judge,' the Holy One, blessed be he, promised our ancestor that he would redeem his children. But should they carry out an act of repentance, he will redeem them with seventy-two letters [and not only with two]."

C. Said R. Yudan, "The verse that follows presents seventy-two letters [in illustration of the foregoing statement]: 'Or has God tried to go and take him a nation from the midst of another nation, by trials, by signs, and by wonders, and by war, and by a mighty hand, and by an outstretched arm, and by great terrors' (Deut. 4:34). Here there are seventy-two letters. But if you propose that there are seventy-five, not seventy-two, take off the three letters that make up the second reference to the word 'nation,' which do not count."

D. R. Abin said, "It is by his name that he will redeem them, and the name of the Holy One, blessed be he, contains seventy-two letters."

XLV:IX

1. A. "He shall be a wild ass of a man, [his hand against every man and every man's hand against him, and he shall dwell over against all his kinsmen]" (Gen. 16:12):

B. R. Yohanan and R. Simeon b. Laqish:

C. R. Yohanan said, "[The term is used figuratively.] For most people grow up in a settled community, while he grew up in the wilderness."

D. R. Simeon b. Laqish said, " 'A wild ass of a man' is meant literally, for most people plunder property, but he plundered lives."

2. A. ". . . his hand against every man and every man's hand against him" (Gen. 16:12):

B. [Reading the consonants for "every . . . against him" with different vowels, we produce the meaning:] His hand and the hand of his dog were alike. Just as his dog ate carrion, so he ate carrion.

3. A. Said R. Eleazar, "When is it the case that 'his hand is against every man and every man's hand against him'?

B. "When he comes concerning whom it is written: 'And whatsoever the children of men, the beasts of the field and the fowl of the heaven dwell, has he given them into your hand' (Dan. 2:38). [Freedman, p. 386, n. 2: In the days of Nebuchadnezzar, whose ruthless policy of conquest aroused the whole world against him.]

C. "That is in line with the following verse of Scripture: 'Of Kedar and of the kingdoms of Hazor, which Nebuchadrezzar smote' (Jer. 49: 28). His name is spelled, 'Nebuchadrezzar' because he shut them up in the wilderness and killed them. [Freedman, p. 386, n. 4: A play on the name, which, with the present spelling, ends in *asar,* spelled with an *alef,* as though it were *asar,* spelled with an *ayin* and yielding the meaning, shut up.]"

4. A. [". . . and he shall dwell over against all his kinsmen]" (Gen. 16:12):

B. Here the word-choice is "dwell" while later on it is "he fell" (Gen. 25:18).

C. So long as Abraham was alive, "he [Ishmael] shall dwell." Once he died, "he fell." [His father's merit no longer protected him.]

D. Before he laid hands on the Temple, "he shall dwell." After he laid hands on the Temple, "he fell."

E. In this world "he shall dwell." In the world to come, "he fell."

XLVIII:X

2. A. "Let a little water be brought" (Gen. 18:4):

B. Said to him the Holy One, blessed be he, "You have said, 'Let a little water be brought' (Gen. 18:4). By your life, I shall pay your descendants back for this: 'Then sang Israel this song, "spring up O well, sing you to it" ' (Num. 21:7)."

C. The recompense took place in the wilderness. Where do we find that it took place in the Land of Israel as well?

D. "A land of brooks of water" (Deut. 8:7).

E. And where do we find that it will take place in the age to come?

F. "And it shall come to pass in that day that living waters shall go out of Jerusalem" (Zech. 14:8).

G. ["And wash your feet" (Gen. 18:4)]: [Said to him the Holy One, blessed be he,] "You have said, 'And wash your feet.' By your life, I shall pay your descendants back for this: 'Then I washed you in water' (Ez. 16:9)."

H. That recompense took place in the wilderness. Where do we find that it took place in the Land of Israel as well?

I. "Wash you, make you clean" (Is. 1:16).

J. And where do we find that it will take place in the age to come?

K. "When the Lord will have washed away the filth of the daughters of Zion" (Is. 4:4).

L. [Said to him the Holy One, blessed be he,] "You have said, 'And rest yourselves under the tree' (Gen. 18:4). By your life, I shall pay your descendants back for this: 'He spread a cloud for a screen' (Ps. 105:39)."

M. That recompense took place in the wilderness. Where do we find that it took place in the Land of Israel as well?

N. "You shall dwell in booths for seven days" (Lev. 23:42).

O. And where do we find that it will take place in the age to come?

P. "And there shall be a pavilion for a shadow in the day-time from the heat" (Is. 4:6).

Q. [Said to him the Holy One, blessed be he,] "You have said, 'While I fetch a morsel of bread that you may refresh yourself' (Gen. 18:5). By your life, I shall pay your descendants back for this: 'Behold I will cause to rain bread from heaven for you' (Ex. 16:45)"

R. That recompense took place in the wilderness. Where do we find that it took place in the Land of Israel as well?

S. "A land of wheat and barley" (Deut. 8:8).

T. And where do we find that it will take place in the age to come?

U. "He will be as a rich cornfield in the land" (Ps. 82:16).

V. [Said to him the Holy One, blessed be he,] "You ran after the herd ['And Abraham ran to the herd' (Gen. 18:7)]. By your life, I shall pay your descendants back for this: 'And there went forth a wind from the Lord and brought across quails from the sea' (Num. 11:27)."

W. That recompense took place in the wilderness. Where do we find that it took place in the Land of Israel as well?

X. "Now the children of Reuben and the children of Gad had a very great multitude of cattle" (Num. 32:1).

Y. And where do we find that it will take place in the age to come?

Z. " 'And it will come to pass in that day that a man shall rear a young cow and two sheep" (Is. 7:21).

AA. [Said to him the Holy One, blessed be he,] "You stood by them: 'And he stood by them under the tree while they ate' (Gen. 18:8). By your life, I shall pay your descendants back for this: 'And the Lord went before them' (Ex. 13:21)."

BB. That recompense took place in the wilderness. Where do we find that it took place in the Land of Israel as well?

CC. "God stands in the congregation of God" (Ps. 82:1).

DD. And where do we find that it will take place in the age to come?

EE. "The breaker is gone up before them . . . and the Lord at the head of them" (Mic. 2:13).

XLVIII:XII

3. A. R. Jonah and R. Levi in the name of R. Hama b. R. Hanina: "The wilderness of Sin [Ex. 16:1ff.] and the wilderness of Alush [Num. 33:13] are the same place.

    B. "On account of what merit did the Israelites merit having mana given to them? It was because of the statement, 'knead it and make cakes.' [The word for knead is *lushi,* hence because of the kneading of the dough by Sarah, the later Israelites had the merit of receiving mana in the wilderness of Alush which is the same as the wilderness of Sin, where, in the biblical account, the mana came down, so Ex. 16:1ff.]"

LIII:IV

1. A. "For ever, O Lord, your word stands fast in heaven" (Ps. 119:89):

    B. But does God's word not stand fast on earth?

    C. But what you said to Abraham in heaven, "At this season I shall return to you" (Gen. 18:14) [was carried out:]

    D. "The Lord remembered Sarah as he had said and the Lord did to Sarah as he had promised" (Gen. 21:1).

2. A. R. Menahamah and R. Nahman of Jaffa in the name of R. Jacob of Caesarea opened discourse by citing the following verse: " 'O God of hosts, return, we beseech you' (Ps. 80:15).

    B. " 'Return and carry out what you promised to Abraham: "Look from heaven and behold" (Ps. 80:15). "Look now toward heaven and count the stars" ' (Gen. 15:5).

    C. " 'And be mindful of this vine' (Ps. 80:15). 'The Lord remembered Sarah as he had said and the Lord did to Sarah as he had promised' (Gen. 21:1)."

3. A. R. Samuel bar Nahman opened discourse with this verse: "God is not a man, that he should lie" (Num. 23:19).

    B. Said R. Samuel bar Nahman, "The beginning of this verse does not correspond to its end, and the end does not correspond to its beginning.

    C. " 'God is not a man that he should lie' (Num. 23:18), but the verse ends, 'When he has said, he will not do it, and when he has spoken, he will not make it good' (Num. 23:18).

D.   "[That obviously is impossible. Hence:] When the Holy One, blessed be he, makes a decree to bring good to the world: 'God is not a man that he should lie' (Num. 23:18).

E.   "But when he makes a decree to bring evil on the world: 'When he has said, he [nonetheless] will not do it, and when he has spoken, he will not make it good' (Num. 23:18).

F.   "When he said to Abraham, 'For through Isaac shall your descendants be named,' 'God is not a man that he should lie' (Num. 23:18).

G.   "When he said to him, 'Take your son, your only son' (Gen. 22:2), 'When he has said, he will not do it, and when he has spoken, he will not make it good' (Num. 23:18).

H.   "When the Holy One, blessed be he, said to Moses, 'I have surely remembered you' (Ex. 3:16), 'God is not a man that he should lie' (Num. 23:18).

I.   "When he said to him, 'Let me alone, that I may destroy them' (Deut. 9:14), 'When he has said, he will not do it, and when he has spoken, he will not make it good' (Num. 23:18).

J.   "When he said to Abraham, 'And also that nation whom they shall serve will I judge' (Gen. 15:14), 'God is not a man that he should lie' (Num. 23:18).

K.   "When he said to him, 'And they shall serve them and they shall afflict them for four hundred years' (Gen. 15:13), 'When he has said, he will not do it, and when he has spoken, he will not make it good' (Num. 23:18).

L.   "When God said to him, 'I will certainly return to you' (Gen. 18:10, 'God is not a man that he should lie' (Num. 23:18).

M.   " 'The Lord remembered Sarah as he had said and the Lord did to Sarah as he had promised' (Gen. 21:1)."

LIII.X

1.   A.   "And the child grew and was weaned, [and Abraham made a great feast on the day that Isaac was weaned]" (Gen. 21:8):

     B.   R. Hoshaia the Elder said, "He was weaned from the evil impulse."

     B.   Rabbis say, "He was weaned from relying upon milk."

2.   A.   ". . . and Abraham made a *great* feast on the day that Isaac was weaned" (Gen. 21:8):

     B.   R. Judah said, "The *Great* One of the ages was there."

     C.   R. Yudan in the name of R. Yose bar Haninah: " 'The king made a great feast' (Est. 2:18). The *Great* One of the ages was there. That is in line with this verse: 'For the Lord will again rejoice over you for good' (Deut. 30:9), in the days of Mordecai and Esther, 'As he rejoiced over your fathers' (Deut. 30:9), in the days of Abraham, Isaac, and Jacob."

3. A. Said R. Judah, " 'A great feast' refers to a feast for the great ones of the age. Og and all the great ones were there. They said to Og, 'Did you not say that Abraham was a barren mule, who cannot product a child?'

   B. "He said to them, 'Now what is this gift of his? Is he not puny? If I put my finger out on him, I can crush him.'

   C. "Said to him the Holy One, blessed be he, 'Now are you treating my gift with contempt? By your life, you will see a thousand myriads of his children, and you will fall in the end to his children.'

   D. "So it is said: 'And the Lord said to Moses, "Fear him not, for I have delivered him into your hand"' (Num. 21:34)."

   E. [Freedman:] (R. Levi said, "The cradle was rocked for the first time in the house of our father Abraham.")

   F. [Continuing A–D,] for R. Joshua bar Nehemiah said, "Those thirty-one kings whom Joshua killed were all present at the feast made by Abraham."

   G. But there were not thirty-one. The matter accords with what R. Berekhiah and R. Helbo, R. Parnakh in the name of R. Yohanan [said], " 'The king of Jericho, one' (Joshua 12:9). Scripture states, 'One,' meaning, 'he and his regent.' "

LIV:IV

1. A. "Abraham set seven ewe lambs of the flock apart" (Gen. 21:28):

   B. Said the Holy One, blessed be he, to him, "You have given him seven ewe lambs. By your life I shall postpone the joy of your descendants for seven generations.

   C. "You have given him seven ewe lambs. By your life matching them his descendants [the Philistines] will kill seven righteous men among your descendants, and these are they: Hofni, Phineas, Samson, Saul and his three sons.

   D. "You have given him seven ewe lambs. By your life, matching them the seven sanctuaries of your descendants will be destroyed, namely, the tent of meeting, the altars at Gilgal, Nob, Gibeon, Shiloh, and the two eternal houses of the sanctuary.

   E. "You have given him seven ewe lambs. [By your life, matching them] my ark will spend seven months in the fields of the Philistines."

2. A. R. Jeremiah in the name of R. Samuel bar R. Isaac: "If the mere chicken of one of them had been lost, would he not have gone looking for it by knocking on doors, so as to get it back, but my ark spent seven months in the field and you pay not mind to it. I on my own will take care of it: His right hand and his holy arm have wrought salvation for him' (Ps. 98:1).

   B. "That is in line with this verse: 'And the kine took the straight way'

(1 Sam. 6:12). They went straight forward, turning their faces to the ark and [since the word for 'straight forward' contains the consonants for the word for 'song'] singing."

C. And what song did they sing?

D. R. Meir said, " 'The song of the sea. Here it is said, 'They went along . . . lowing as they went' (1 Sam. 6:12), and in that connection: 'For he is highly exalted' (Ex. 15:1). [The word for 'lowing' and the word for 'exalted' share the same consonants.]"

E. R. Yohanan said, " 'O sing to the Lord a new song' (Ps. 98:1)."

F. R. Eleazar said, " 'O Give thanks to the Lord, call upon his name' (Ps. 105:1)."

G. Rabbis said, " 'The Lord reigns, let the earth rejoice' (Ps. 97:1)."

H. R. Jeremiah said, "The three: 'O sing to the Lord a new song, sing to the Lord, all the earth' (Ps. 96:1). 'The Lord reigns, let the peoples tremble' (Ps. 99:1)."

I. Elijah taught, "[Freedman:] 'Rise, rise, you acacia, soar, soar, in your abundant glory, beautiful in your gold embroidery, extolled in the innermost shrine of the sanctuary, encased between the two cherubim.' "

J. Said R. Samuel bar. R. Isaac, "How much did [Moses,] son of Amram labor so as to teach the art of song to the Levites. But you beasts are able to sing such a song on your own, without instruction. All power to you!"

LVI:I

1. A. "On the third day Abraham lifted up his eyes and saw the place afar off" (Gen. 22:4):

    B. "After two days he will revive us, on the third day he will raise us up, that we may live in his presence" (Hos. 16:2).

    C. On the third day of the tribes: "And Joseph said to them on the third day, 'This do and live' " (Gen. 42:18).

    D. On the third day of the giving of the Torah: "And it came to pass on the third day when it was morning" (Ex. 19:16).

    E. On the third day of the spies: "And hide yourselves there for three days" (Josh. 2:16).

    F. On the third day of Jonah: "And Jonah was in the belly of the fish three days and three nights" (Jonah 2:1).

    G. On the third day of the return from the Exile: "And we abode there three days" (Ezra 8:32).

    H. On the third day of the resurrection of the dead: "After two days he will revive us, on the third day he will raise us up, that we may live in his presence" (Hos. 16:2).

    I. On the third day of Esther: "Now it came to pass on the third day that Esther put on her royal apparel" (Est. 5:1).

J. She put on the monarchy of the house of her fathers.

K. On account of what sort of merit?

L. Rabbis say, "On account of the third day of the giving of the Torah."

M. R. Levi said, "It is on account of the merit of the third day of Abraham: 'On the third day Abraham lifted up his eyes and saw the place afar off' (Gen. 22:4)."

LVI:II

1. A. He said, "Isaac, my son, do you see what I see?"

    B. He said to him, "Yes."

    C. He said to the two lads, "Do you see what I see?"

    D. They said to him, "No."

    E. He said, "Since you do not see, 'Stay here with the ass' (Gen. 22:5), for you are like an ass."

    F. On the basis of this passage we learn that slaves are in the category of asses.

    G. Rabbis derive proof from the matter of the giving of the Torah: "Six days you shall labor and do all your work, you . . . your daughter, your man-servant, your maid-servant, your cattle" (Ex. 20:10).

2. A. Said R. Isaac: "Will this place [the Temple mount] ever be distant from its owner [God]? Never, for Scripture says, 'This is my resting place for ever; here I will dwell, for I have desired it' (Ps. 132:14).

    B. "It will be when the one comes concerning whom it is written, 'Lowly and riding upon an ass' (Zech. 1:9)."

3. A. "I and the lad will go thus far [and worship and come again to you]" (Gen. 22:5):

    B. Said R. Joshua b. Levi, "[He said], 'We shall go and see what will be the end of "thus."'" [Freedman, p. 492, n. 5: God had said, "Thus shall your seed be" (Gen. 15:5). So the sense is, "We will see how that can be fulfilled, now that I am to lose my son."]

4. A. ". . . and we will worship [through an act of prostration] and come again to you" (Gen. 22:5):

    B. He thereby told him that he would come back from Mount Moriah whole and in peace [for he said that *we* shall come back].

5. A. Said R. Isaac, "And all was on account of the merit attained by the act of prostration.

    B. "Abraham returned in peace from Mount Moriah only on account of the merit owing to the act of prostration: '. . . and we will worship [through an act of prostration] and come [then, on that account] again to you' (Gen. 22:5).

    C. "The Israelites were redeemed only on account of the merit owing to the act of prostration: 'And the people believed . . . then they bowed their heads and prostrated themselves' (Ex. 4:31).

D.   "The Torah was given only on account of the merit owing to the act of prostration: 'And worship [prostrate themselves] you afar off' (Ex. 24:1).

E.   "Hannah was remembered only on account of the merit owing to the act of prostration: 'And they worshipped before the Lord' (1 Sam. 1:19).

F.   "The exiles will be brought back only on account of the merit owing to the act of prostration: 'And it shall come to pass in that day that a great horn shall be blown and they shall come that were lost . . . and that were dispersed . . . and they shall worship the Lord in the holy mountain at Jerusalem' (Is. 27:13).

G.   "The Temple was built only on account of the merit owing to the act of prostration: 'Exalt you the Lord our God and worshp at his holy hill' (Ps. 99:9).

H.   "The dead will live only on account of the merit owing to the act of prostration: 'Come let us worship and bend the knee, let us kneel before the Lord our maker' (Ps. 95:6)."

LVI:IX

1.   A.   "And Abraham lifted up his eyes and looked, and behold, behind him was a ram, [caught in a thicket by his horns. And Abraham went and took the ram and offered it up as a burnt offering instead of his son]" (Gen. 22:13):

B.   What is the meaning of the word for "behind"?

C.   Said R. Yudan, " 'Behind' in the sense of 'after,' that is, after all that happens, Israel nonetheless will be embroiled in transgressions and perplexed by sorrows. But in the end, they will be redeemed by the horns of a ram: 'And the Lord will blow the horn' (Zech. 9:14)."

D.   Said R. Judah bar Simon, " 'After' all generations Israel nonetheless will be embroiled in transgressions and perplexed by sorrows. But in the end, they will be redeemed by the horns of a ram: 'And the Lord God will blow the horn' (Zech. 9:14)."

E.   Said R. Hinena bar Isaac, "All through the days of the year Israelites are embroiled in transgressions and perplexed by sorrows. But on the New Year they take the ram's horn and sound it, so in the end, they will be redeemed by the horns of a ram: 'And the Lord God will blow the horn' (Zech. 9:14)."

F.   R. Abba bar R. Pappi, R. Joshua of Siknin in the name of R. Levi: "Since our father, Abraham, saw the ram get himself out of one thicket only to be trapped in another, the Holy One, blessed be he, said to him, 'So your descendants will be entangled in one kingdom after another, struggling from Babylonia to Media, from Media to Greece, from Greece to Edom. But in the end, they will be redeemed by the horns of a ram: 'And the Lord God will blow the horn . . . the Lord of Hosts will defend them' (Zech. 9:14–5)."

2. A. ". . . And Abraham went and took the ram and offered it up as a burnt offering instead of his son:" (Gen. 22:13):

B. R. Yudan in the name of R. Benaiah: "He said before him, 'Lord of all ages, regard the blood of this ram as though it were the blood of Isaac, my son, its innards as though they were the innards of Isaac my son.'"

C. That [explanation of the word "instead"] accords with what we have learned in the Mishnah: **"Lo, this is instead of that, this is in exchange for that, this is in place of that"—lo, such is an act of exchanging [one beast for another in the sacrificial rite, and both beasts then are held to be sanctified] [M. Tem. 5:5].**

D. R. Phineas in the name of R. Benaiah: "He said before him, 'Lord of all ages, regard it as though I had offered up my son, Isaac, first, and afterward had offered up the ram in his place.'"

E. That [sense of the word "instead"] is in line with this verse: "And Jotham his son reigned in his stead" (2 Kgs. 15:7).

F. That accords with what we have learned in the Mishnah: **[If one says, "I vow a sacrifice] like the lamb," or "like the animals of the Temple stalls" [it is a valid vow] [M. Ned. 1:3].**

G. R. Yohanan said, "That is in the sense of 'like the lamb of the daily whole offering.'" [One who made such a statement has vowed to bring a lamb.]

H. R. Simeon b. Laqish said, ". . . 'like the ram of Abraham, our father.'" [One who has made such a statement has vowed to bring a ram.]

I. There they say, ". . . 'like the offspring of a sin-offering.'"

J. Bar Qappara taught on Tannaite authority, ". . . 'like a lamb which has never given suck' [thus, a ram]."

LXIII:III

1. A. "These are the descendants of Isaac, Abraham's son: Abraham was the father of Isaac" (Gen. 25:19):

B. Abram was called Abraham: "Abram, the same is Abraham" (1 Chr. 1:27).

C. Isaac was called Abraham: "These are the descendants of Isaac, Abraham's son, Abraham."

D. Jacob was called Israel, as it is written, "Your name shall be called no more Jacob but Israel" (Gen. 32:29).

E. Isaac also was called Israel: "And these are the names of the children of Israel, who came into Egypt, Jacob and his" (Gen. 46:8).

F. Abraham was called Israel as well.

G.   R. Nathan said, "This matter is deep: 'Now the time that the children of Israel dwelt in Egypt' (Ex. 12:40), and in the land of Canaan and in the land of Goshen 'was four hundred and thirty years' (Ex. 12:40)." [Freedman, p. 557, n. 6: They were in Egypt for only 210 years. Hence their sojourn in Canaan and Goshen must be added, which means, from the birth of Isaac, hence the children of Israel commence with Isaac. And since he was Abraham's son, it follows that Abraham was called Israel.]

LXV:XIII

1. A.   "[He said, 'Behold I am old; I do not know the day of my death.] Now then take your weapons, [your quiver and your bow, and go out to the field and hunt game for me, and prepare for me savory food, such as I love, and bring it to me that I may eat; that I may bless you before I die']" (Gen. 27:2–4):

    B.   "Sharpen your hunting gear, so that you will not feed me carrion or an animal that was improperly slaughtered.

    C.   "Take your *own* hunting gear, so that you will not feed me meat that has been stolen or grabbed."

2. A.   "Your quiver."

    B.   [Since the word for "quiver" and the word for "held in suspense" share the same consonants, we interpret the statement as follows:] he said to him, "Lo, the blessings [that I am about to give] are held in suspense. For the one who is worthy of a blessing, there will be a blessing."

3. A.   Another matter: "Now then take your weapons, your quiver and your bow and go out to the field:"

    B.   "Weapons" refers to Babylonia, as it is said, "And the weapons he brought to the treasure house of his god" (Gen. 2:2).

    C.   "Your quiver" speaks of Media, as it says, "So they suspended Haman on the gallows" (Est. 7:10). [The play on words is the same as at No. 2.]

    D.   "And your bow" addresses Greece: "For I bend Judah for me, I fill the bow with Ephraim and I will store up your sons, O Zion, against your sons, O Javan [Greece]" (Zech. 9:13).

    E.   "and go out to the field" means Edom: "Unto the land of Seir, the field of Edom" (Gen. 32:4).

4. A.   "And prepare for me savory food:"

    B.   R. Eleazar in the name of R. Yose b. Zimra: "Three statements were made concerning the tree, that it was good to eat, a delight to the eyes, and that it added wisdom,

    C.   "and all of them were stated in a single verse:

    D.   "'So when the woman saw that the tree was good for food,' on which basis we know that it was good to eat;

E.   " 'and that it was a delight to the eyes,' on which basis we know that it was a delight for the eyes,

F.   " 'and that the tree was to be desired to make one wise,' on which basis we know that it added to one's wisdom.

G.   "That is in line with the following verse of Scripture: 'A song of wisdom of Ethan the Ezrahite' (Ps. 89:1)" [and the root for "song of wisdom" and that for "to make one wise" are the same].

H.   "So did Isaac say, ' "And prepare for me savory food." I used to enjoy the appearance [of food], but now I get pleasure only from the taste.'

I.   "And so did Solomon say, 'When goods increase, those who eat them are increased, and what advantage is there to the owner thereof, saving the beholding of them with his eyes' (Qoh. 5:10).

J.   "The one who sees an empty basket of bread and is hungry is not equivalent to the one who sees a full basket of bread and is satisfied."

5.   A.   "And Rebecca was listening when Isaac spoke to his son Esau. So when Esau went to the field to hunt for game and bring it . . ." (Gen. 27:5):

B.   If he found it, well and good.

C.   And if not, ". . . to bring it" even by theft or violence.

LXV:XXIII

1.   A.   ["See the smell of my son is as the smell of a field which the Lord has blessed" (Gen. 27:27):] Another matter: this teaches that the Holy One, blessed be he, showed him the house of the sanctuary as it was built, wiped out, and built once more.

B.   "See the smell of my son:" This refers to the Temple in all its beauty, in line with this verse: "A sweet smell to me shall you observe" (Num. 28:2).

C.   ". . . is as the smell of a field:" This refers to the Temple as it was wiped out, thus: "Zion shall be ploughed as a field" (Mic. 3:12).

D.   ". . . which the Lord has blessed:" This speaks of the Temple as it was restored once more in the age to come, as it is said, "For there the Lord commanded the blessing, even life for ever" (Ps. 133:3).

LXVI:II

1.   A.   R. Berekhiah opened [discourse by citing the following verse:] " 'Return, return, O Shulamite, return, return that we may look upon you' (Song 7:1):

B.   "The verse at hand refers to 'return' four times, corresponding to the four kingdoms in which Israel enters in peace and from which Israel comes forth in peace.

C.   " 'O Shulamite:' the word refers to the nation who every day is

blessed with a blessing ending with peace [which shares the consonants of the word at hand], as it is said, 'And may he give you peace'
(Num. 7:26).

D.   "It is the nation in the midst of which dwells the Peace of the ages,
as it is said, 'And let them make me a sanctuary that I may dwell
among them' (Ex. 25:8).

E.   "It is the nation to which I am destined to give peace: 'And I will
give peace in the land' (Lev. 26:6).

F.   "It is the nation over which I am destined to spread peace: 'Behold, I
will extend peace to her like a river' (Is. 66:12)."

G.   R. Samuel bar Tanhum, R. Hanan bar Berekiah in the name of R.
Idi: "It is the nation that makes peace between me and my world.
For if it were not for that nation, I would destroy my world."

H.   R. Hana in the name of R. Aha: " 'When the earth and all the inhabitants thereof are dissolved' (Ps. 75:4), as in the statement, 'All the
inhabitants of Canaan are melted away'(Ex. 15:15).

I.   " 'I' (Ps. 75:4), that is, when they accepted upon themselves [the
Ten Commandments, beginning,] 'I am the Lord your God' (Ex.
20:2), I established the pillars of it'(Ps. 75:4), and the world was
set on a solid foundation."

J.   Said R. Eleazar bar Merom, "This nation preserves [makes whole]
the stability of the world, both in this age and in the age to come."

K.   R. Joshua of Sikhnin in the name of R. Levi: "This is the nation on
account of the merit of which whatever good that comes into the
world is bestowed. Rain comes down only for their sake, that is, 'to
you' [as in the base verse], and the dew comes down only 'to you.'

L.   "May God give you of the dew of heaven."

LXVII:IV

1. A.   When Esau heard the words of his father, he cried out with an exceedingly great and bitter cry [and said to his father, 'Bless me, even
me also, O my father!']" (Gen. 27:34):

B.   Said R. Hanina, "Whoever says that the Holy One, blessed be he, is
lax, may his intestines become lax. While his is patient, he does collect what is coming to you.

C.   "Jacob made Esau cry out one cry, and where was he penalized? It
was in the castle of Shushan: 'And he cried with a loud and bitter
cry' (Est. 4:1)."

2. A.   "But he said, 'Your brother came with guile and he has taken away
your blessing'" (Gen. 33:35):

B.   R. Yohanan said, "[He came] with the wisdom of his knowledge of
the Torah."

3. A.   "Esau said, 'Is he not rightly named Jacob? [For he has supplanted

me these two times. He took away my birthright and behold, now he has taken away my blessing.' Then he said, 'Have you not reserved a blessing for me?]" (Gen. 27:36):

B. " 'He took away my birthright, and I kept silence, and now he has taken away my blessing.' "

4. A. "Then he said, 'Have you not reserved a blessing for me?' " (Gen. 27:36):

B. —even an inferior one?

LXVIII:XII

3. A. Bar Qappara taught on Tannaite authority, "There is no dream without a proper interpretation.

B. " 'That there was a ladder:' refers to the ramp to the altar.

C. " '. . . set up on the earth:' that is the altar, 'An altar of dirt you will make for me' (Ex. 20:24).

D. " '. . . and the top of it reached to heaven:' these are the offerings, for their fragrance goes up to heaven.

E. " '. . . and behold, the angels of God:' these are the high priests.

F. " '. . . were ascending and descending on it:' for they go up and go down on the ramp.

G. " 'And behold, the Lord stood above it:' 'I saw the Lord standing by the altar' (Amos 9:1)."

4. A. Rabbis interpreted the matter to prefigure Sinai: " 'And he dreamed:

B. " '. . . that there was a ladder:' this refers to Sinai.

C. " '. . . set up on the earth:' 'And they stood at the lower part of the mountain' (Ex. 19:17).

D. " '. . . and the top of it reached to heaven:' 'And the mountain burned with fire into the heart of heaven' (Deut. 4:11).

E. " '. . . and behold, the angels of God:' these are Moses and Aaron.

F. " '. . . were ascending:' 'And Moses went up to God' (Ex. 19:3).

G. " '. . . and descending on it:' 'And Moses went down from the mount' (Ex. 19:14).

F. " '. . . And behold, the Lord stood above it:' 'And the Lord came down upon Mount Sinai' (Ex. 19:20)."

5. A. Salomaini in the name of R. Simeon b. Laqish: "He showed him a throne with three legs."

B. R. Joshua of Sikhnin in the name of R. Levi: " 'And you are the third of the three legs.' "

C. That accords with the view of R. Joshua in the name of R. Levi: " 'For the portion of the Lord is his people, Jacob the cord of his inheritance' (Deut. 32:9): as a cord cannot be made of less than three strands [so there were three patriarchs, and hence he told Jacob that he would be the third of the three]."

D. R. Berekhiah said, "He showed him a world and a third of the world.

E. " 'Ascending' [in the plural] speaks of at least two angels, and 'descending' speaks of two, and each angel in size is a third of the world [thus a world and a third].

F. "And how do we know that an angel is the size of a third of the world? 'His body also was like the beryl and his face as the appearance of lightning' (Dan. 10:6)."

6. A. R. Hiyya the Elder and R. Yannai:

B. One of them said, " 'They were going up and coming down' on the ladder."

C. The other said, " 'They were going up and coming down' on Jacob."

D. The one who says, " 'They were going up and coming down' on the ladder," has no problems.

E. As to the one who says, " 'They were going up and coming down' on Jacob," the meaning is that they were raising him up and dragging him down, dancing on him, leaping on him, abusing him.

F. For it is said, "Israel, in whom I will be glorified" (Is. 49:3).

G. [So said the angels,] "Are you the one whose visage is incised above?" They would then go up and look at his features and go down and examine him sleeping.

H. The matter may be compared to the case of a king who was in session and judging cases in a judgment chamber. So people go up to the basilica and find him asleep. They go down to the judgment chamber and find him judging cases.

I. Above, whoever speaks in favor of Israel rises up, and whoever condemns Israel goes down. Below, whoever speaks in his favor goes down, and whoever condemns him goes up.

7. A. The angels who accompany a person in the Land do not accompany him outside the Land.

B. "Ascending" are the ones who accompanied him in the land, and "descending" are the ones who will accompany him outside the land.

8. A. R. Levi in the name of R. Samuel: "Because the ministering angels revealed the mystery of the Holy One, blessed be he, [telling Lot what he was about to do], they were sent into exile from their appropriate dwelling for a hundred and thirty-eight years."

B. R. Tanhuma stated it in the word for "stalk," which contains the letters of a numerical value adding up to 138.

C. Said R. Hama bar Hanina, "It was because they puffed themselves up, saying, 'for *we* are about to destroy this place' (Gen. 19:13)."

D. When did they return? Here: "ascending" and only then "descending." [Freedman, p. 627, n. 3: The banished angels were now permitted to reascend to heaven and then bidden to descend to accompany Jacob.]

LXX:VI

1. A.   ". . . so that I come again to my father's house in peace, then the Lord shall be my God" (Gen. 28:20–22):

    B.   R. Joshua of Sikhnin in the name of R. Levi: "The Holy One, blessed be he, took the language used by the patriarchs and turned it into a key to the redemption of their descendants.

    C.   "Said the Holy One, blesesd be he, to Jacob, 'You have said, "Then the Lord shall be my God." By your life, all of the acts of goodness, blessing, and consolation which I am going to carry out for your descendants I shall bestow only by using the same language:

    D.   "'"Then, in that day, living waters shall go out from Jerusalem" (Zech. 14:8). "Then, in that day, a man shall rear a young cow and two sheep" (Is. 7:21). "Then, in that day, the Lord will set his hand again the second time to recover the remnant of his people" (Is. 11:11). "Then, in that day, the mountains shall drop down sweet wine" (Joel 4:18). "Then, in that day, a great horn shall be blown and they shall come who were lost in the land of Assyria" (Is. 27:13).'"

LXX:XV

1. A.   "Now Laban had two daughters, the name of the older was Leah, and the name of the younger was Rachel" (Gen. 29:16):

    B.   They were like two beams running from one end to of the world to the other.

    C.   This one produced captains and that one produced captains, this one produced kings and that one produced kings, this one produced lion-tamers and that one produced lion-tamers, this one produced conquerors of nations and that one produced conquerers of nations, this one produced those who divided countries and that one produced dividers of countries.

    D.   The offering brought by the son of this one overrode the prohibitions of the Sabbath, and the offering brought by the son of that one overrode the prohibitions of the Sabbath.

    E.   The war fought by this one overrode the prohibitions of the Sabbath, and the war fought by that one overrode the prohibitions of the Sabbath.

    F.   To this one were given two nights, and to that one were given two nights.

    G.   The night of Pharaoh and the night of Sennacherib were for Leah, and the night of Gideon was for Rachel, and the night of Mordecai was for Rachel, as it is said, "On that night the king could not sleep" (Est. 6:1).

2. A. "The name of the older [greater] was Leah:"
   B. She was greater in the gifts that came to her, receiving the priesthood forever and the throne forever.
   C. ". . . and the name of the younger [lesser] was Rachel" (Gen. 29:16):
   D. She was lesser in the gifts she received, Joseph for a while, Saul for a while.

LXXIII:VII

1. A. "When Rachel had borne Joseph, [Jacob said to Laban, 'Send me away, that I may go to my own home and country. Give me my wives and my children for whom I have served you and let me go; for you know the service which I have given you']" (Gen. 30:25):
   B. Once the "satan" of Esau was born [namely, Joseph], then: "Jacob said to Laban, 'Send me away, that I may go to my own home and country.'"
   C. For R. Phineas in the name of R. Samuel bar Nahman: "It is a tradition that Esau will fall only by the hand of the descendants of the children of Rachel: 'Surely the youngest of the flock shall drag them away' (Jer. 49:20).
   D. "And why does Scripture call them 'the youngest of the flock'? Because they are the youngest of the tribes."

LXXVIII:XIII

1. A. "[Then Esau said, 'Let us journey on our way, and I will go before you.'] But Jacob said to him, 'My lord knows [that the children are frail, and that the flocks and herds giving suck are a care to me; and if they are overdriven for one day, all the flocks will die. Let my lord pass on before his servant, and I will lead on slowly, according to the pace of the cattle which are before me and according to the pace of the children, until I come to my lord in Seir']" (Gen. 33:12–14):
   B. Said R. Berekhiah, "'My lord knows that the children are frail' refers to Moses and Aaron.
   C. "'. . . and that the flocks and herds giving suck are a care to me' speaks of Israel: 'And you, my flock, the flock of my pasture, are men' (Ez. 34:31)."
   D. R. Huna in the name of R. Aha: "If it were not for the tender mercies of the Holy One, blessed be he, 'and if they are overdriven for one day, all the flocks will die' in the time of Hadrian."
   E. R. Berekhiah in the name of R. Levi: "'My lord knows that the children are frail' speaks of David and Solomon.

F.   " '. . . the flocks and herds' refer to Israel: 'And you, my flock, the flock of my pasture, are men' (Ez. 34:31)."

G.   Said R. Huna in the name of R. Aha, "If it were not for the tender mercies of the Holy One, blessed be he,' 'and if they are overdriven for one day, all the flocks will die' in the time of Haman."

LXXXII:X

1.   A.   "So Rachel died and she was buried on the way to Ephrath, [that is, Bethlehem, and Jacob set up a pillar upon her grave; it is the pillar of Rachel's tomb, which is there to this day. Israel journeyed on and pitched his tent beyond the tower of Eder]" (Gen. 35:16–21):

     B.   Why did Jacob bury Rachel on the way to Ephrath?

     C.   Jacob foresaw that the exiles would pass by there [en route to Babylonia].

     D.   Therefore he buried her there, so that she should seek mercy for them: "A voice is heard in Ramah . . . Rachel weeping for her children. . . . Thus says the Lord, 'Keep your voice from weeping . . . and there is hope for your future' " (Jer. 31:15–16).

XCVI:I

1.   A.   "And Jacob lived in the land of Egypt seventeen years, so the days of Jacob, the years of his life, were a hundred and forty-seven years" (Gen. 47:28):

     B.   [The basis of the question to follow is explained by Freedman, p. 885, n. 1: This passage is the beginning of a new lection, which normally is separated from the previous one by the space of nine letters, while sections in the same lection are separated by not less than three letters' space. This one, however, is separated from the previous one by the space of one letter only, and is therefore called closed.] Why then is this passage, among all of the passages that are in the Torah, closed [and not open, as explained by Freedman]?

     C.   At the point at which our father, Jacob, died, the subjugation of Israel by Egypt began.

2.   A.   Why then is this passage, among all of the passages that are in the Torah, closed?

     B.   Because Jacob wanted to reveal the mysteries of the end, and they were closed off from him.

3.   A.   Why then is this passage, among all of the passages that are in the Torah, closed?

     B.   Because from him all of the troubles of the world were closed off [since he enjoyed life in Egypt].

LXXXIV:V

2. A.   "These are the generations of the family of Jacob. Joseph [being sev-
         enteen years old, was shepherding the flock with his brothers]"
         (Gen. 37:2):
    B.   These generations came along only on account of the merit of
         Joseph.
    C.   Did Jacob go to Laban for any reason other than for Rachel?
    D.   These generations thus waited until Joseph was born, in line with
         this verse: "And when Rachel had borne Joseph, Jacob said to Laban,
         'Send me away'" (Gen. 30:215).
    E.   Who brought them down to Egypt? It was Joseph.
    F.   Who supported them in Egypt? It was Joseph.
    G.   The sea split open only on account of the merit of Joseph: "The
         waters saw you, O God" (Ps. 77:17). "You have with your arm re-
         deemed your people, the sons of Jacob and Joseph" (Ps. 77:16).
    H.   R. Yudan said, "Also the Jordan was divided only on account of the
         merit of Joseph."

LXXXVI:I

1. A.   "Now Joseph was taken down to Egypt, [and Potiphar, an officer of
         Pharaoh, the captain of the guard, an Egyptian, bought him from the
         Ishmaelites who had brought him down there] (Gen. 39:1):
    B.   "I drew them with cords of a man, [with bands of love. Yet I was to
         them as those who lift up a yoke, on account of their jaws. I reached
         out food to them]" (Hos. 11:4):
    C.   "I drew them with cords of a man:" this refers to Israel: "Draw me,
         we will run after you" (Song 1:4).
    D.   "With bands of love" (Hos. 11:4): "I have loved you, says the Lord"
         (Mal 1:2).
    E.   "Yet I was to them as those who lift up a yoke:" "For I raised their
         enemies over them." Why so?
    F.   "On account of their jaws:" On account of something that they
         issued from their jaws, saying to the golden calf, "These are your
         Gods, Israel" (Ex. 32:8).
    G.   And at the end: "I reached out food to them:" [God says,] "I pro-
         vided much food for them. 'May he be as a rich grain field in the
         land' (Ps. 72:16)."
2. A.   Another interpretation: "I drew them with cords of a man:" this re-
         fers to Joseph: "And they drew and lifted up Joseph" (Gen. 37:28).
    B.   ". . . with bands of love:" "Now Israel loved Joseph" (Gen. 37:3).
    C.   ". . . Yet I was to them as those who lift up a yoke:" [God speaks,]

"I raised up his enemies over him, and who is this? It is the wife of Potiphar." All this why?

D. ". . . on account of their jaws:" It was on account of something that they issued from their jaws, saying, "And Joseph brought an evil report of them to their father" (Gen. 37:2).

E. But in the end, ". . . I reached out food to them:" "I gave him much food: "And Joseph was the governor over the land" (Gen. 42:6).

LXXXVII:VI

1. A. "And although she spoke to Joseph [day after day, he would not listen to her, to lie with her or to be with her. But one day, when he went into the house to do his work and none of the men of the house was there in the house, she caught him by his garment, saying, 'Lie with me.' But he left his garment in her hand and fled and got out of the house]" (Gen. 39:10–13):

    B. R. Yudan in the name of R. Benjamin bar Levi: "As to the sons of Levi, the trials affecting them were the same, and the greatness that they achieved was the same.

    C. ". . . the trials affecting them were the same: 'And although she spoke to Joseph day after day.' 'Now it came to pass, when they spoke to him day by day' (Est. 3:4). [Mordecai, descended from Benjamin, was nagged every day.] 'He would not listen to her.' 'And he did not listen to them' (Est. 3:4).

    D. ". . . and the greatness that they achieved was the same: 'And Pharaoh took off his signet ring from his hand and put it upon Joseph's hand' (Gen. 41:42). 'And the king took off his ring, which he had taken from Haman and gave it to Mordecai' (Est. 8:2).

    E. " 'And arrayed him in fine linen clothing and put a gold chain about his neck' (Gen. 41:42). 'And Mordecai went forth from the presence of the king in royal apparel of blue and white, and with a great crown of gold and with a robe of fine linen and purple' (Est. 8:15).

    F. " 'And he made Joseph ride in the second chariot which he had' (Gen. 41:43). 'And cause Mordecai to ride on horseback through the street of the city' (Est. 6:9).

    G. " 'And they cried before him, Abrech' (Gen. 41:43). 'And proclaimed before Mordecai, "Thus shall it be done to the man" ' (Est. 6:11)."

2. A. ". . . he would not listen to her, to lie with her or to be with her."

    B. ". . . to lie with her" in this world, that he would not have children with her.

    C. ". . . or to be with her" in the world to come.

3. A. ". . . he would not listen to her, to lie with her or to be with her:"

B.   ". . . to lie with her:" even lying without sexual relations.
4. A.   A noble lady asked R. Yose, "Is it possible that Joseph, at the age of seventeen, in his full vigor, could have done such a thing?"
    B.   He produced for her a copy of the book of Genesis. He began to read the story of Reuben and Judah. He said to her, "If these, who were adults and in their father's domain, were not protected by the Scripture [but were revealed by Scripture in all their lust], Joseph, who was a minor and on his own, all the more so [would have been revealed as lustful, had he done what the lady thought he had]."

LXXXVIII:III

1. A.   "And Pharoah was angry with his two officers" (Gen. 40:2):
    B.   R. Judah bar Simon, R. Hanan in the name of R. Yohanan: " 'Come and see the works of God' (Ps. 66:5).
    C.   "He made servants angry with their masters so as to bestow greatness on the righteous, he made masters angry with their servants in order to bestow greatness on the righteous.
    D.   "Thus: 'And Pharoah was angry with his two officers' so as to bestow greatness on Joseph.
    E.   " 'Bigthan and Teresh were angry' (Est. 2:21) with Ahasuerus, so that he might bestow greatness on Mordecai."
2. A.   [(Freedman:) As to the plots of Bigthan and Teresh against Ahasuerus:] R. Yudan said, "These are the views:
    B.   "Rab said, 'Short daggers did they hide in their shoes.'
    C.   "R. Hanan said, 'They made an instrument with which to strangle him.'
    D.   "Samuel said, 'They hid a snake in his dish.'
    E.   "In respect to all these views: 'Inquisition was made of the matter and it was found to be so' (Est. 2:23)."

LXXXVIII:V

1. A.   ["So the chief butler told his dream to Joseph and said to him, 'In my dream there was a vine before me, and on the vine there were three branches; as soon as it budded, its blossoms shot forth, and the clusters ripened into grapes. Pharaoh's cup was in my hand, and I took the grapes and pressed them into Pharaoh's cup and placed the cup in Pharaoh's hand' " (Gen. 49:11–13)]. ". . . there was a vine before me:" this refers to Israel: "You plucked up a vine out of Egypt" (Ps. 80:9).
    B.   ". . . and on the vine there were three branches:" this refers to Moses, Aaron, and Miriam.

C. ". . . as soon as it budded, its blossoms shot forth:" specifically, the blossoming of the redemption of Israel.

D. ". . . and the clusters ripened into grapes:" as soon as the vine budded, it blossomed, and as soon as the grapes blossomed, the clusters ripened.

2. A. " 'Pharaoh's cup was in my hand, and I took the grapes and pressed them into Pharaoh's cup and placed the cup in Pharaoh's hand. And I took the grapes and pressed them into Pharaoh's cup and placed the cup in Pharaoh's hand.'. . . 'you shall place Pharaoh's cup in his hand:' "

B. On what basis did sages ordain that there should be four cups of wine for Passover?

C. R. Hunah in the name of R. Benaiah: "They correspond to the four times that redemption is stated with respect to Egypt: 'I will bring you out . . . and I will deliver you . . . and I will redeem you . . . and I will take you' (Ex. 6:6–7)."

D. R. Samuel b. Nahman said, "They correspond to the four times that 'cups' are mentioned here: 'Pharaoh's *cup* was in my hand, and I took the grapes and pressed them into Pharaoh's *cup* and placed the *cup* in Pharaoh's hand. And I took the grapes and pressed them into Pharaoh's *cup*.' "

E. R. Levi said, "They correspond to the four kingdoms."

F. R. Joshua b. Levi said, "They correspond to the four cups of fury that the Holy One, blessed be he, will give the nations of the world to drink: 'For thus says the Lord, the God of Israel, to me, "Take this cup of the wine of fury" '" (Jer. 25:15). 'Babylon has been a golden cup in the Lord's hand' (Jer. 51:7). 'For in the hand of the Lord there is a cup' (Ps. 75:9). 'And burning wind shall be the portion of their cup' (Ps. 11:6).

G. "And in response to these, the Holy One, blessed be he, will give Israel four cups of salvation to drink in the age to come: 'O Lord, the portion of my inheritance and of my cup, you maintain my lot' (Ps. 16:5). 'You prepare a table before me in the presence of my enemies, you have anointed my head with oil, my cup runs over' (Ps. 23:5). 'I will lift up the cup of salvations and call upon the name of the Lord' (Ps. 116:13).

H. "What is said is not 'cup of salvation' but 'cup of salvations,' one in the days of the Messiah, the other in the time of Gog and Magog."

3. A. Joseph said to him, "[Since the dream refers to Israel's coming redemption,] you have brought me a good gospel, so I shall now give you a good gospel: 'within three days Pharaoh will lift up your head and restore you to your office.'

4. A. "But remember me, when it is well with you, and do me the kind-

ness, I pray you, to make mention of me to Pharaoh, and so get me out of this house. For I was indeed stolen out of the land of the Hebrews, and here also I have done nothing that they should put me into the dungeon" (Gen. 40:14–15):

B.   Said R. Aha, "On the basis of the use of the verb 'stolen' twice [in the statement, 'indeed stolen,'] we learn that he was stolen twice."

5.   A.   ". . . that they should put me into the dungeon:"

B.   Said R. Abin, "The meaning is that they put [One] with me in prison. [Freedman, p. 817, n. 4: The divine Presence accompanied me.]"

XCIII:XII

1.   A.   "Then he fell upon his brother Benjamin's necks and wept, and Benjamin wept upon his necks:"

B.   [The Hebrew repeatedly uses the plural for the word "neck," so we ask:] how many necks did Benjamin have?

C.   Said R. Eleazar, "He foresaw through the Holy Spirit that two sanctuaries were destined to be built in the share of Benjamin and were destined to be destroyed."

D.   ". . . and Benjamin wept upon his necks:"

E.   He foresaw that the tabernacle of Shilo was destined to be built in the share of Joseph and destined to be destroyed.

2.   A.   "And he wept out loud" (Gen. 45:2):

B.   Just as Joseph conciliated his brothers only through weeping, so the Holy One, blessed be he, will redeem Israel only through weeping.

C.   So it is said, "They shall come with weeping and with supplications will I lead them, I will cause them to walk by rivers of waters" (Jer. 31:9).

LXXXIV:XX

1.   A.   "Then Jacob tore his garments and put sackcloth upon his loins and mourned for his son many days" (Gen. 37:34):

B.   R. Phineas in the name of R. Hoshaiah: "The tribal fathers caused their father to tear his garments, and where were they paid back? In Egypt: 'And they tore their clothes' (Gen. 44:13).

C.   "Joseph caused the tribal fathers to tear their clothes. He was paid back in the case of the son of his son: 'And Joshua tore his clothes' (Josh. 7:6).

D.   "Benjamin caused the tribal fathers to tear their clothes. He was paid back in Shushan, the capital: 'Mordecai tore his clothes' (Est. 4:1).

E.   "Manasseh caused the tribal fathers to tear their clothes. He was paid back by having his inheritance divided into half, half on the other side of the Jordan, and half in the land of Canaan."

2. A.   ". . . and put sackcloth upon his loins:"

B.   Said R. Aibu, "Because Jacob took hold of sackcloth, therefore sackcloth did not leave him or his children to the end of all generations:

C.   "Ahab: 'And he put sackcloth on his flesh and fasted' (1 Kgs. 21:27).

D.   "Joram: 'And the people looked, and behold, he had sackcloth within upon his flesh' (2 Kgs. 6:30).

E.   "Mordecai: 'And he put sackcloth and ashes' (Est. 4:1).

3. A.   ". . . and mourned for his son many days:"

B.   Twenty-two years. [Freedman, p. 785, n. 5: Joseph was seventeen years old, and he was thirty when he stood before Pharaoh. To this must be added seven years of plenty, and Jacob's reunion with him took place after two years of famine.]

XCVIII:II

7. A.   "Then Jacob called his sons and said, 'Gather yourselves together, that I may tell you what shall befall you in days to come:"

B.   R. Simon said, "He showed them the fall of Gog, in line with this usage: 'It shall be in the end of days . . . when I shall be sanctified through you, O Gog' (Ez. 38:165). 'Behold, it shall come upon Edom' (Is. 34:5)."

C.   R. Judah said, "He showed them the building of the house of the sanctuary: 'And it shall come to pass in the end of days that the mountain of the Lord's house shall be established' (Is. 2:2)."

D.   Rabbis say, "He came to reveal the time of the end to them, but it was hidden from him."

E.   R. Judah in the name of R. Eleazar bar Abina: "To two men the secret of the time of the end was revealed, but then it was hidden from them, and these are they: Jacob and Daniel.

F.   "Daniel: 'But you, O Daniel, shut up the words and seal the book' (Dan. 12:4).

G.   "Jacob: 'Then Jacob called his sons and said, "Gather yourselves together, that I may tell you what shall befall you in days to come. Assemble and hear, O sons of Jacob, and hearken to Israel, your father. Reuben, you are my first-born."' "

H.   "This teaches that he came to reveal the time of the end to them, but it was hidden from him."

I.   The matter may be compared to the case of the king's ally, who was departing this world, and his children surrounded his bed. He said to them, "Come and I shall tell you the secrets of the king." Then he looked up and saw the king. He said to them, "Be most meticulous about the honor owing to the king."

J. So our father Jacob looked up and saw the Presence of God standing over him. He said to them, "Be most meticulous about the honor owing to the Holy One, blessed be he."

XCVIII:IX

1. A. "Binding his foal to the vine [and his ass's colt to the choice vine, he washes his garments in wine, and his vesture in the blood of grapes; his eyes shall be red with wine, and his teeth white with milk]" (Gen. 49:8–12):

F. R. Nehemiah said, " 'Binding his foal to the vine:' God binds to the vine, that is Israel, his city, namely, 'the city which I have chosen.'

G. " '. . . and his ass's colt to the choice vine:' the strong sons which are destined to arise from him."

H. Rabbis said, " 'I am bound to the vine and the choice vine' [that is Israel].

I. " 'Binding his foal to the vine and his ass's colt to the choice vine:' when the one concerning whom it is written, 'Lowly and riding upon an ass, even upon a colt of the foal of an ass' (Zech. 9:9).

J. " '. . . he washes his garments in wine:' for he will link together words of Torah.

K. " '. . . and his vesture in the blood of grapes:' for he will explain their errors to them."

2. A. Said R. Hanin, "Israel does not require the learning of the king-messiah in the age to come, as it is said, 'Unto him shall *the nations* seek' (Is. 11:1)—but not Israel.

B. "If so, why will the king-messiah come? And what will he come to do? It is to gather together the exiles of Israel and to give them thirty religious duties: 'And I said to them, If you think good, give me my hire, and if not, forbear. So they weighed for my hire thirty pieces of silver' (Zech. 11:12)."

C. Rab said, "These refer to thirty heroes."

D. R. Yohanan said, "These refer to thirty religious duties."

E. They said to R. Yohanan, "Have you not accepted the view of Rab that the passage speaks only of the nations of the world?"

F. In the view of Rab, "And I said to them" speaks of Israel, and in the view of Israel, "And I said to them" speaks of the nations of the world.

G. In the view of Rab, when the Israelites have sufficient merit, the greater number of the thirty heroes are in the Land of Israel, and the lesser number in Babylonia, and when the Israelites do not have sufficient merit, the greater number is in Babylonia and the smaller number in the Land of Israel.

XCIX:II

1. A. "For the Lord God will do nothing unless he reveals his secret to his servants the prophets" (Amos 3:7).

   B. Jacob linked two of his sons, corresponding to two of the monarchies, and Moses linked two of the tribes, corresponding to two of the monarchies.

   C. Judah corresponds to the kingdom of Babylonia, for this is compared to a lion and that is compared to a lion. This is compared to a lion: "Judah is a lion's whelp" (Gen. 49:9), and so too Babylonia: "The first was like a lion" (Dan. 7:4).

   D. Then by the hand of which of the tribes will the kingdom of Babylonia fall? It will be by the hand of Daniel, who comes from the tribe of Judah.

   E. Benjamin corresponds to the kingdom of Media, for this is compared to a wolf and that is compared to a wolf. This is compared to a wolf: "Benjamin is a ravenous wolf, [in the morning devouring the prey, and at evening dividing the spoil.]" And that is compared to a wolf: "And behold, another beast, a second, like a wolf" (Dan. 7:5).

   F. R. Hanina said, "The word for 'wolf' in the latter verse is written as 'bear.' It had been called a bear."

   G. That is the view of R. Yohanan, for R. Yohanan said, " 'Wherefore a lion of the forest slays them' (Jer. 5:6) refers to Babylonia, and 'a wolf of the deserts spoils them' refers to Media."

   H. [Reverting to E:] Then by the hand of which of the tribes will the kingdom of Media fall? It will be by the hand of Mordecai, who comes from the tribe of Benjamin.

   I. Levi corresponds to the kingdom of Greece. This is the third tribe in order, and that is the third kingdom in order. This is written with a word that is made up of three letters, and that is written with a word which consists of three letters. This one sounds the horn and that one sounds the horn, this one wears turbans and that one wears helmets, his one wears pants and that one wears knee-cuts.

   J. To be sure, this one is very populous, while that one is few in numbers. But the many came and fell into the hand of the few.

   K. On account of merit deriving from what source did this take place? It is on account of the blessing that Moses bestowed: "Smiter through the loins of them that rise up against him" (Deut. 33:11).

   L. Then by the hand of which of the tribes will the kingdom of Greece fall? It will be by the hand of sons of the Hasmoneans, who come from the tribe of Levi.

M. Joseph corresponds to the kingdom of Edom [Rome], for this one has horns and that one has horns. This one has horns: "His firstling bullock, majesty is his, and his horns are the horns of the wild ox" (Deut. 33:17). And that one has horns: "And concerning the ten horns that were on its head" (Dan. 7:20). This one kept away from fornication while that one cleaved to fornication. This one paid respect for the honor owing to his father, while that one despised the honor owing to his father. Concerning this one it is written, "For I fear God" (Gen. 42:18), while in regard to that one it is written, "And he did not fear God" (Deut. 25:18). [So the correspondence in part is one of opposites.]

N. Then by the hand of which of the tribes will the kingdom of Edom fall? It will be by the hand of the anointed for war, who comes from the tribe of Joseph.

O. R. Phineas in the name of R. Samuel b. Nahman: "There is a tradition that Esau will fall only by the hand of the sons of Rachel: 'Surely the least of the flock shall drag them away' (Jer. 49:20). Why the least? Because they are the youngest of the tribes."

APPENDIX 2

Aphrahat on Israel

Demonstration Sixteen
"On the Peoples which are in the place of the People"

1. Vocation of the Gentiles

[760](320)XVI-1. The peoples which were of all languages were called first, before Israel, to the inheritance of the Most High, as God said to Abraham, "I have made you the father of a multitude of peoples" (Gen. 17:5). Moses proclaimed, saying, "The peoples will call to the mountain, and there will they offer sacrifices of righteousness" (Deut. 33:19). And in the hymn of testimony he said to the people, "I shall provoke you with a people which is no people, and with a foolish nation I shall anger you" (Deut. 32:21). Jacob our father testified concerning the peoples when he blessed Judah, saying to him, "The staff shall not depart from Judah, the lawgiver from between his feet, until there shall come he who possesses dominion, and for him the peoples will hope" (Gen. 49:10).

Isaiah said, "The mountain of the house of the Lord will be established at the head of the mountains and high above the heights. All the peoples will look to it, [761] and (321) many peoples from a distance will come and say, "Come, let us go up to the mountain of the Lord, to the house of the God of Jacob. He will teach us his ways, and we shall walk in his paths. For from Zion law will go forth, and the word of the Lord from Jerusalem. He will judge among peoples and will correct all the distant peoples" (Is. 2:2–4). When he judges and corrects them, then will they accept instruction, be changed, and be humbled from their hardheartedness. "And they shall beat their swords into ploughshares, and their spears into pruning hooks. No longer will a nation take the sword against a nation; no longer will they learn how to make war" (Is. 2:2–4). From of old, those peoples who did not know God would do battle against robbers and against wrongdoers with swords, spears, and lances. When the redeemer, the Messiah, came, "he broke the bow of war and spoke peace with the peoples" (Zech. 9:10). He had them turn "their

swords into ploughshares, and their spears they made into pruning hooks," so
that they would eat from the works of their hands, and not from spoil.

Furthermore, it is written, "I shall turn chosen lips for the peoples, so that
they will all of them call upon the name of the Lord" (Zeph. 3–9). From of
old the nations did not have chosen lips, nor did they call on the name of the
Lord, for with their lips they would praise the idols which they had made with
their hands, and on the name of their gods [764] they would call, but not on
the name of the Lord. Furthermore, also the prophet Zechariah said, "Many
and strong peoples will adhere to the Lord" (Zech. 2:11). Jeremiah the
prophet publicly and clearly proclaimed concerning the peoples, when he
said, "The peoples will abandon their idols, and they will cry and proclaim,
saying, The lying idols, which our fathers left us as an inheritance, are
nothing" (Jer. 16:19).

II. Rejection of Israel

(322)XVI-2. To his people Jeremiah preached, saying to them, "Stand by the
ways and ask the wayfarers, and see which is the good way. Walk in it." But
they in their stubbornness answered, saying to him, "We shall not go." Again
he said to them, "I established over you watchmen, that you might listen for
the sound of the trumpet." But they said to him again, "We shall not hearken."
And this openly, publicly did they do in the days of Jeremiah when he preached
to them the word of the Lord, and they answered him, saying, "To the word
which you have spoken to us in the name of the Lord we shall not hearken.
But we shall do our own will and every word which goes out of our mouths, to
offer up incense-offerings to other gods" (Jer. 44:16–17). When he saw that
they would not listen to him, he turned to the peoples, saying to them, "Hear
O peoples, and know, O church which is among them, and hearken, O land, in
its fullness" (Jer. 6:18–19). And when he saw that they rashly rose against
him and impudently responded to him, then he abandoned them as he had
prophesied, saying [765], "I have abandoned my house. I have abandoned my
inheritance. I have given the beloved of my soul into the hands of his
enemies. And in his place a painted bird has become my inheritance" (Jer.
12:7–9). And this is the church which is of the peoples, which has been
gathered together from among all languages.

XVI-3. So that you will know he has truly abandoned them (323)[listen to
this]: Isaiah further said concerning them, "You have abandoned your people,
the house of Jacob" (Is. 2:6). He called their name Sodomites and the people
of Gomorrah, and in their place he brought in the peoples and he called them
"House of Jacob." For Isaiah called the peoples by the name of the House of
Jacob, saying to them, "O House of Jacob, come and let us go in the light of
the Lord" (Is. 2:5–6), for the people of the house of Jacob has been abandoned and they have become "the rulers of Sodom and the people of Gomorrah" (Is. 1:10). "Their father is an Amorite and their mother is a Hittite"
(Ez. 16:3, 45); "they have been changed into a strange vine" (Jer. 2:21).

"Their grapes are bitter and their clusters are bitter for them" (Deut. 32:32). [They are] rebellious sons (Is. 30:1), and rejected silver (Jer. 6:30). [They are] "the vine of Sodom and the planting of Gomorrah" (Deut. 32:32); "a vineyard which brings forth thorns instead of grapes" (Is. 5:2). [They are] "a vine whose branches the fire has consumed, they are good for nothing, they are not serviceable, and they are not wanted for any use" (Ez. 15:4).

Two did he call Jacob, one to go in the light of the Lord, one [768] to be abandoned. In place of Jacob they are called "rulers of Sodom." By the name of Jacob [now] are called the people which is of the peoples. Again the prophet said concerning the peoples that they shall bring offerings in place of the people, for he said, "Great is my name among the peoples, and in every place they are offering pure sacrifices in my name" (Mal. 1:11). Concerning Israel the prophet said, "I am not pleased by your sacrifices" (Jer. 6:20). Again he said (324), "Your sacrifices do not smell good to me" (Jer. 6:20).

Furthermore Hosea also said concerning Israel, "In lying they seek the Lord" (Hos. 5:7). Isaiah said that his heart is distant from his God, for he said, "This people honors me with its lips, but its heart is distant from me" (Is. 29:13). Hosea said, "Ephraim has encircled me in lying, and the house of Israel and Judah in deceit until the people of God go down" (Hos. 11:12). And which people [of God go down], if not the righteous and faithful people? If then he said concerning Israel, "He has surrounded me with lying and deceit," and concerning Ephraim, "Lo, the sinning kingdom of Ephraim has arisen in Israel,"—since the name of Judah is not mentioned in this saying, [then] they respond, Judah is the holy and faithful one that has gone down and [still] adheres to the Lord. But the prophet openly and articulately declared, "Ephraim and Israel have surrounded me with lying, [769] for Jeroboam the son of Nobat has publicly turned them aside after the calf." "And Judah in deceit" (Hosea 11:12)—for in deceit and in concealment they are worshipping idols, as he furthermore showed Ezekiel their uncleanness (Ez. 8:10ff). Concerning them Hosea preached when he called them a licentious and adulterous woman. He said concerning the congregation of Israel, "Remove her licentiousness from her face," and concerning the congregation of the house of Judah he said, "Remove her adultery from between her breasts" (Hos. 2:2). Now, so that you should know that the prophet spoke concerning both of their congregations and called them [both] licentiousness from before her face and her adultery from between her breasts, (325) then I shall throw her out naked, and I shall abandon her as on the day on which she was born, and as on the day on which she went forth from the land of Egypt" (Hos. 2:2, 3, 15). [These are] both their congregations, one of Israel and one of Judah. The one of Israel has played the whore, and the one of Judah has committed adultery. And the people which is of the peoples is the holy and faithful people which has gone down and adhered to the Lord. Now why does he say that it has gone down? Because they have gone down from their pride. Ezekiel moreover called them by the name of Ohola and Oholibah, and both of their congregations he called two shoots of the vine which the fire has eaten (Ez. 23:4). David further proclaimed and said concerning the peoples, "The Lord will count the peoples in a book" (Ps. 87:6), [772] and concerning the children of Israel he prophesied, saying, "They shall be blotted out of your book of the living. With your righteous they will not be inscribed" (Ps. 69:28).

XVI-4. You should know, my beloved, that the children of Israel were written in the book of the Holy One, as Moses said before his God, "Either forgive the sin of this people, or blot me out from the book which you have written." He [God] said, "Him who sins against me shall I blot out of my book" (Ex. 32:31–33). When they sinned, David said concerning them, "They are wiped out of your book of the living. With your righteous will they not be inscribed" (Ps. 69:28). But concerning the peoples he said, "The Lord will number the peoples in the book" (Ps. 87:6). For the peoples were not recorded in the book and in the Scripture.

See, my beloved, that the vocation of the peoples was recorded before the vocation of the people. When (326) they sinned in the wilderness, he said to Moses, "Let me blot out this people, and I shall make you into a people which is greater and more worthy than they" (Ex. 32:10). But because the time of the peoples had not come, and another was [to be] their redeemer, Moses was not persuaded that a redeemer and a teacher would come for the people which was of the peoples, which was greater and more worthy than the people of Israel. On this account it is appropriate that we should name the son of God [with] great and abundant praise, as [773] Isaiah said, "This thing is too small, that you should be for me a servant and restore the scion of Jacob and raise up the staff of Israel. But I have made you a light for the peoples, that you may show my redemption until the ends of the earth" (Is. 49:6). Isaiah further preached concerning the peoples, "Hear me, O peoples, and pay attention to me, O nations, for the law has gone forth from before me, and my justice is the light of the peoples" (Is. 51:4). David said, "Alien children will hear me with their ears," and these alien children "will be kept back and will be lamed from their ways" (Ps. 18:45), 46), and for the peoples have heard and have been lamed from the ways of the fear of images and of idols.

XVI-5. If they should say, "Us has he called alien children," they have not been called alien children, but sons and heirs, as Isaiah said, "I have raised up and nurtured children, and they have rebelled against me" (Is. 1:2). The prophet (327) said, "From Egypt I have called him my son" (Hos. 11:1). And the Holy One said to Moses, "Say to Pharaoh, let my son go that he may serve me" (Ex. 4:23). Further he said, "My son, my first born [is] Israel" (Ex. 4:22). But the peoples are those who hearken to God and were lamed and kept back from the ways of their sins. Again Isaiah said, "You will call the peoples who have not known you, and peoples who do not know you will come to you [776] and turn" (Is. 55:5). Again Isaiah said, "Hear, O peoples, the thing which I have done, and know, O distant ones, my power" (Is. 33:13). Concerning the church and the congregation of the peoples, David said, "Remember your church which you acquired from of old" (Ps. 74:2). Again David said, "Praise the Lord all peoples, and praise his name, O nations" (Ps. 117:1). Again he said, "Dominion belongs to the Lord, and he rules over the peoples" (Ps. 22:28). Again the prophet said, "At the end of days I shall pour my spirit over all flesh, and they will prophesy. No longer will a man teach his fellow-citizen nor his brother, and say, 'Know our Lord,' for all will know me from the least of them even to the oldest" (Jer. 31:34).

Concerning the children of Israel he said, "I shall send a famine in the land, not that they shall hunger for bread, nor that they shall thirst for water, but (328) for hearing the word of the Lord. They shall go from the west to the east and from the south to the north to seek the word of the Lord, but they shall not find it, for he has withdrawn it from them" (Amos 8:11, 12). Moses earlier wrote about them, "When in the end of days many evil things will happen to you, you will say, Because the Lord is not in my midst, these evil things have happened to me" (Deut. 31:17). So it was that they said in the days of Ezekiel, "The Lord has abandoned the land, and the Lord no longer sees [777] us" (Ez. 8:12). Isaiah said about them, "Your sins have separated between you and your God, and your iniquities have held back good things from you" (Is. 59:2). Again he said, "You will call in my ears with a loud voice, but I shall not hear you" (Ex. 8:18). Concerning the people which is from the peoples, David said, "All you peoples clap hands, and praise God with the sound of praise" (Ps. 47:1). Again he said, "Hear this, all of you peoples, and pay attention, all who dwell on earth" (Ps. 49:1).

III. Israel and the Nations

XVI-6. Even from of old, whoever from among the peoples was pleasing to God was more greatly justified than Israel. Jethro the priest who was of the peoples and his seed were blessed: "Enduring is his dwelling place, and his nest is set on a rock" (Num. 24:21).

And [to] the Gibeonites from among the unclean peoples Joshua gave his right hand, and they entered, took refuge in the inheritance of the Lord, and were hewers of wood and drawers of water for the congregation and the altar of the Lord. When Saul wanted to kill them, (329) the heavens were closed up from [giving] rain until the sons of Saul were slaughtered. Then the Lord turned toward the land and blessed his inheritors.

Rehab, the prostitute who received the spies, and the house of her fathers received an inheritance in Israel.

Obededom of Gath of the Philistines, into whose house the ark of the Lord entered and by whom it was honored more [780] than by all Israel, and his house were blessed by the Lord. Ethai, the Gathite, fed David when he was persecuted, and his name and seed were honored.

Ebedmelech the Ethiopian, the man of faith, raised up Jeremiah from the pit when the children of Israel his people imprisoned him. This is the matter concerning which Moses said concerning them, "The stranger that is among you will be higher, and you will be lower" (Deut. 28:33). They imprisoned and lowered Jeremiah the prophet into the lowest pit, but Ebedmelech the sojourner from Ethiopia raised up Jeremiah from the pit.

Ruth the Moabite, from the people smitten with wrath, came and was assimilated with the people of Israel, and from her seed arose the leader of kings, from whom was born the redeemer of the peoples.

Uriah the Hittite, from an unclean people, was chief among the men of David. Because David killed him with deceit in the war with the children of Ammon, desired his wife, and married her, David received the judgment that the sword would never depart from his house (II Sam. 12:10).

XVI-7. Furthermore Isaiah said concerning our redeemer, "I have set you as a covenant for the people and as a light for the peoples" (Is. 42:6). Now how was this covenant for the people? From the time that the light and the redeemer (330) [781] of the peoples came, from that time Israel was restrained from the worship of idols, and they had a true covenant. Concerning this matter Moses said, "I shall provoke you with a people which is no people, and with a foolish people I shall anger you" (Deut. 32:21). By us they are provoked. On our account they do not worship idols, so that they will not be shamed by us, for we have abandoned idols and call lies the thing which our fathers left us. They are angry, their hearts are broken, for we have entered and have become heirs in their place. For theirs was this covenant which they had, not to worship other gods, but they did not accept it. By means of us he provoked them, and ours was the light and the life, as he preached, saying when he taught, "I am the light of the world" (John 8:12). Again he said, "Believe while the light is with you, before the darkness overtakes you" (John 12:35). And again he said, "Walk in the light, so that you may be called the children of light" (John 12:36). And further he said, "The light gave light in the darkness" (John 1:5). This is the covenant which the people had, and the light which gave light for all the peoples, and lamed and hindered them from crooked ways, as it is written, "In his coming the rough place will be smoothed, and the high place (331) will be plain, and the glory of the Lord will be revealed, and all flesh will see the life of God" (Is. 40:4, 5; Luke 3:5, 6).

XVI-8. This brief memorial I have written to you concerning the [784] peoples, because the Jews take pride and say, "We are the people of God and the children of Abraham." But we shall listen to John [the Baptist] who, when they took pride [saying], "We are the children of Abraham," then said to them, "You should not boast and say, Abraham is father unto us, for from these very rocks can God raise up children for Abraham" (Matthew 3:9). Our redeemer said to them, "You are the children of Cain, and not the children of Abraham" (John 8:39, 44). The apostle said, "The branches which sinned were broken off. We were grafted on in their place and are partners in the fat of the olive tree. Now let us not take pride and sin so that we too may not be broken off. Lo, we have been grafted onto the olive tree" (Rom. 11:17, 18).

This is the apology against the Jews, because they take pride saying, "We are the children of Abraham, and we are the people of God."

The demonstration of the people and the peoples is completed.

Demonstration Nineteen
"Against the Jews, on account of their saying that they are destined to be gathered together"

1. Early Redemptions

[845] (357) XIX-1. The voice of the Holy One was heard by Moses. He sent him to take his people out of Egypt, out of the house of Pharaoh, the bondage of the Egyptians, saying to him, "Say to Pharaoh: My son, my first-born in Israel. I say to you: Send out my son to worship me" (Ex. 4:22–3). When he took them forth from Egypt with signs and wonders, with a mighty hand, with a high arm, and with great visions, he brought them through the wilderness and led them there forty years. He led them to the Promised Land, took them across the Jordan, and caused them to inherit it, having destroyed its inhabitants from before them. They dwelt in it four hundred and forty years before Solomon built the holy house, and then four hundred [848] years before the king of Babylonia conquered them.

On account of their sins, which were many, he uprooted and scattered them among every nation, for they did not listen to his prophets, whom he had sent to them. When they had been in Babylonia seventy years, he again gave thought in their behalf to the covenant of their fathers. He proclaimed concerning them through his prophets that they should go up from Babylonia (358) at the end of seventy years. When the seventy years were fulfilled, as Jeremiah had prophesied, Daniel prayed and offered supplication that he should restore their captivity and have mercy upon them. "And the Lord aroused the spirit of Cyrus, and he issued a proclamation through his entire kingdom. He announced to them saying, Whoever remains of all the people of the Lord, may his God be with him. Let him return and go to Jerusalem which is in Judah" (Ezra 1:1, 3).

But because they were assimilated among the peoples, had built, planted, and acquired [property] in the place of their captivity, not all of them entirely wanted to go up, but some of them went up, and some of them remained. Because God knew their evil impulse, he did not force them to go up from Babylonia, but without compulsion did Cyrus the king of Persia proclaim to them. For even when he brought them out of Egypt by the hand of Moses, if the bondage of Pharaoh were not strong on them, they would not have wanted [849] to go out of Egypt, as they said to Moses when they were rebelling against him in the wilderness, "This is the word which we spoke to you in Egypt: You should let us serve the Egyptians, for it was good for us in Egypt" (Ex. 14:12). So see that even when they were oppressed by bondage, they did not want to go out of Egypt until the Egyptians forced them to go out of their land when they saw that their first-born were dead, saying, "We are all dead" (Ex. 12:33). It is written, "The Egyptians forced the people to go out of their land" (Ex. 12:33). And also from Babylonia, if (359) the persecutors had gathered together against them, they all would have gone forth.

II. The Jews' Hope

XIX-2. I have written this to you because even today they hope an empty hope, saying, "It is still certain for Israel to be gathered together," for the prophet thus spoke, "I shall leave none of them among the nations" (Ex. 39: 28). But if all of our people is to be gathered together, why are we today scattered among every people?

Concerning these things, my beloved, as best as I am able, I shall instruct you: Israel never is going to be gathered together. For they depend on this: All of the prophets gave Israel hope. Hear, O debater of Israel: [852] No law has been imposed upon God, nor is there anyone above him to censure him for anything that he does. He said, "If I declare concerning a people and a kingdom to be built and to be planted, and afterward it will do that which is evil before me, I shall make my word into a lie and shall turn away from it the good which I promised for it. In its iniquity and sins I shall destroy it. If again I shall declare concerning a people and a kingdom to be built and planted, and afterward to be uprooted, overthrown, destroyed, and wiped out, and it will do that which is right before me, then I shall turn away from it the evil which I promised for it" (Jer. 18:7–10). Isaiah also said, "Woe unto him who despoils. You will not despoil. A liar shall not lie among you. When you want to despoil, you will be despoiled, and when you want to lie, there will be lying among you" (Is. 33:1). And with regard to these things there is none who censures the will of God.

III. God Never Reconciled to Israel

XIX-3. I shall write and show you that never did God accept (360) their repentance [through] either Moses or all of the prophets. For Moses said to them, "You were rebellious before the Lord from the day I knew you" (Deut. 9:24). Again he said, "It is a people whose mind is lost, among whom is no understanding" (Deut. 32:28). Further he said, "They have outraged me with their idols, and with their gods they have provoked me. So shall I provoke them with a people [853] which is no people, and with a foolish people I shall anger them" (Deut. 32:21). And Moses further said to them, "I know that after my death you will certainly become corrupt, and you will turn aside from the way which I have commanded you. Many evil things will happen to you at the end of days. And lo, while I am still alive with you, you are rebelling against the Lord" (Deut. 31:29).

Hosea said, "I have cut off my prophets and have killed them with the word of my mouth" (Hosea 6:5). "And you, O children of Israel, have not turned from your evil, from the days of your fathers" (Mal. 3:7). Again he said to them, "Your goodness is like the clouds of the morning and like the dew which first passes" (Hosea 6:4). And again he said, "Woe to them who wander from me. Evil is upon them" (Hosea 7:13). And again he said, "Go to Baalpeor and become a Nazirite unto its disgrace" (Hosea 9:10). And again he said, "Like a bird has their honor flown from them. If they raise sons, I shall then wipe them out from among men, and I shall smite the delight of their bowels" (Hosea 9:11, 12).

Further, Jeremiah said, (861) "They are called rejected silver, for the Lord has rejected them" (Jer. 6:30). Hosea said, "I shall drive them out of my house, and I shall no longer continue to have mercy on them" (Hosea 9:15). Now that he said, "I shall no longer continue to have mercy on them," what do they have to say? [856]

Again he said, "The Lord has rejected them because they did not listen to him" (Hosea 9:17). Again he said, "They shall be wandering among the peoples" (Hosea 9:17). Again he said concerning them, "According to the good of their land, they have multiplied altars and built high places" (Hosea 10:1). Again he said, "Ephraim will receive shame, and Israel will be confounded into its opinion" (Hosea 10:6). Again he said, "Ephraim has surrounded me with lying, and Judah and the house of Israel with deceit" (Hos. 11:12). Again he said, "I have destroyed you, O Israel. Who will help you?" (Hos. 13:9). Again he said, "I have given to you a king in my anger, and I have taken him away in my wrath" (Hosea 13:11). Micah said, "Do not raise up your face, and do not go standing up straight" (Micah 2:3). Again he said, "Rise up, go, for this was not my rest" (Micah 2:10). Again he said, "Those who see visions will be confounded, and those who divine will be shamed, all their lips will be covered, for God does not answer them" (Micah 3:7).

XIX-4. And why did he say concerning the diviners and those who see visions that they will be confounded, and that their lips will be covered? For this is a plague for which there is no healing. It is written in the law, "When there shall be a leper in Israel, his lips (362) shall be covered, and his clothes shall be ripped, and his head will be disheveled. His dwelling will be outside of the camp. He will call himself unclean all the days he is a leper" (Lev. 13:45–46). [857] On this account the prophet who proclaims with lying lips will receive the plague of leprosy, cover his lips all the days, and sit in confusion, like Uzziah, the king of the house of Judah. Because he wanted to rob the priesthood, a leprosy went out from before the presence of the Holy One and smote him between the eyes, and he dwelt in the house in secret, for he was confounded all the days. There was a great movement [earthquake] in the whole people, as Zechariah said, "You will flee as you fled in the earthquake which was in the days of Uzziah, the king of the house of Judah" (Zech. 14:5).

IV. Israel Rejected

XIX-5. See, then, they have never accepted correction in their lives. He said, "I smote you with a hot wind and with hail stones, and the canker-worm has consumed the multitude of your orchards. But you did not return to me, says the Lord" (Amos 4:9). And again he said, "I overthrew you, as God over-threw Sodom and Gomorrah" (Amos 4:11). I announced that they have no further hope, for "the virgin of Israel has fallen and will no longer continue to rise" (Amos 5:2). Again he said, "She is abandoned upon the ground, and there is none to raise her up" (Amos 5:2). Again he said, "In all of their mar-kets are lamentations, and in all of their streets they will say woe, woe" (Amos 5:16). He rejected and cast them from before him, saying, "I hate and I reject [860] your festivals. I will not smell your offerings" (Amos 5:21). (363) Again he said, "I am not pleased by your offerings, and upon the beauty of your fatted beasts I shall not look" (Amos 56:22). Again he said to them, "For the forty years in the wilderness did you offer to me sacrifices and offer-ings, O children of Israel?" (Amos 5:25). And concerning his abandoning them Jeremiah said, "I have abandoned my house, I have abandoned my in-heritance" (Jer. 12:7). Again he said, "I have given to the daughter of my people a writ of divorce" (Jer. 3:8). Because they take pride [saying] that we are the people of God, the prophet called, saying to them, "Lo, you are like the children of Ethiopians unto me, O children of Israel. Thus the children of Israel I brought forth from the land of Egypt, the Philistines from Cappadocia, and Aram from Kyr. The eyes of the Lord of Lords are upon the sinning king-dom, and I will destroy it from off the face of the earth" (Amos 9:7, 8). Know that he reckoned them like the Philistines. Jeremiah said concerning the congregation of Israel, "I planted you a root which was entirely a true seed. But you have turned and rebelled against me like an alien vine" (Jer. 2:21). Moses said, "Their vine is from the vine of Sodom and from the planting of Gomorrah. Their grapes are bitter grapes, and their clusters are bitter for them" (Deut. 32:32).

David said, "You have brought forth a vine from Egypt [861] and looked upon it, and have planted its root" (Ps. 80:8). He said, "You have destroyed peoples and planted it" (Ps. 80:9). When they had sinned, he said, (364) "The pig of the forest has eaten it, and the wild beasts of the field have pas-tured in it" (Ps. 80:13).

Ezekiel said concerning the vine, "The fire has consumed the two branches and laid waste their inside" (Ez. 15:4). He said, "When the vine was without blemish, it was good for nothing. And now that the fire has consumed and destroyed it, how shall it be good for anything?" (Ez. 15:5). Concerning the entire vineyard, Isaiah prophesied saying, "My beloved had a vineyard on a hill which was a fertile place. He worked it, surrounded it with a fence, and planted it in vines. But when the vineyard brought forth thorns, he tore down its fence, threw over its watch towers, left it unworked, and restrained his clouds from bringing down rain upon it" (Is. 5:1–6).

Concerning the false prophets, he said, "Woe unto those who build Zion in deceit, and Jerusalem in iniquity" (Hab. 2:12; Micah 3:10). He further said concerning them, "From the prophets of Jerusalem has gone forth pollution into all the land" (Jer. 23:15).

V. Peoples Called in Place of People

Concerning the vocation of the peoples, Isaiah said, "It shall come to be in the last days that the mountain of the House of the Lord will be established at the head of the mountains and high above the heights. Peoples will come together to it, and many peoples will go and say, Come, let us go up to the mountain of the Lord, to the House of the God of Jacob. He will teach us his ways, and we shall walk in his paths. [864] For from Zion the law will go forth, and the word of the Lord from Jerusalem" (Is. 2:2, 3). Now when the law went forth from Zion, where did it go? He said, "He will judge between peoples and will chastise many nations who are at a distance" (Is. 2:4). Concerning them [the Jews] Isaiah said, "Separate (365) from them, and call them unclean, for the Lord has rejected them" (Is. 52:11, Lam. 4:15; Jer. 6:30). Again the prophet said, "Their goodness is rejected like a piece of tattered cloth which the moth has eaten" (Micah 7:4, 17). Further he said, "They are enraged by their ways, and by the Lord our God they are terrified and frightened" (Micah 7:17). Again he said, "I shall burn with smoke your gathering places, and your young lions the sword will consume" (Nahum 2:13). Again he said, "Who unto the city of blood, which is entirely filled with lying, in which destruction is not attended" (Nathum 3:1). Micah [sic] said, "Judah has lied, and pollution has been done in Israel and in Jerusalem, for Judah has polluted the sanctity of the Lord" (Malachi 2:11). He said, "You have turned away from the way and have caused many to stumble from the law, and you have corrupted the covenant of Levi. I also have made you contemptible and humiliated among every people, because you did not keep my ways" (Malachi 2:8, 9). Concerning the peoples he said, "I shall turn to them a chosen lip" (Zeph. 3:). Concerning them [the Jews] Malachi said, "You have wearied the Lord with your words" (Malachi 2:17). [865] Again he said, "You, children of Jacob, have not passed from your evil, and from the days of your fathers you have not kept my commandments" (Malachi 3:6, 7).

VI. Israel's Redemption in the Past, Not in the Future

XIX-6. Now hear, my beloved: Two times only did God save Israel: Once from Egypt, the second time from Babylonia; from Egypt by Moses, and from Babylonia by Ezra and by the prophecy of Haggai and Zechariah. Haggai (366) said, "Build this house, and I shall have pleasure in it, and in it I shall be glorified, says the Lord" (Hag. 1:8). Again he said, "Act, for I am with you, and my spirit endures among you. Do not fear, for thus says the Lord almighty: One more time shall I shake the heaven and the earth, the sea and the dry land, and I shall shake all the peoples, and they will bring the treasure of all the peoples and will fill this house with glory. The latter glory of this house will be greater than the former" (Hag. 2:5–8, 10). All of these things were said in the days of Zerubbabel, Haggai, and Zechariah. They were exhorting concerning the building of the house.

Zechariah said, "I have turned to Jerusalem in mercy, and my house do I set in its midst" (Zech. 1:17). Again he said, "Cities will be emptied of goods. The Lord will build Zion and choose Jerusalem again" (Zech. 1:17). Again he said, "I am jealous for Zion [868] and for Jerusalem with great jealousy. I am angry with great wrath against the peoples who are in commotion" (Zech. 1:14–15). Again he said, "In great estates will Jerusalem dwell, with the multitude of men and beasts which are in its midst, and I shall be in it like a wall of copper, and for glory will I be in its midst, says the Lord" (Zech. 2:4, 5). Again he said, "O, O, flee from the land of the North, says the Lord, for to the four winds of heaven have I scattered you. O Zion, escape, [you who] dwell with the daughter of Babylonia" (Zech. 2:6, 7). Again he said, "The Lord will inherit Judah as his portion on (367) his holy land, and he will again take pleasure in Jerusalem" (Zech. 2:12). Again he said, "The hands of Zerubbabel laid the foundations of this house, and his hands are going to complete it" (Zech. 4:9). All these things did Zechariah prophesy, and with the gathering of Israel from Babylonia they were fulfilled and completed. It is not as they say, that Israel is still destined to be gathered together.

XIX-7. Hear then, my beloved, I shall show you that Israel was saved two times, once from Egypt, the second time from Babylonia. Isaiah said, "The Lord will stretch his hand a second time to acquire the remnant of his people that remains in the land of Assyria, Egypt, Tyre, Sidon, Hamath, and from the distant islands" (Is. 11:11). Now if they were destined to be [869] gathered together and redeemed, why did Isaiah say that the Lord would stretch out his hand a second time and acquire the remnant of his people that remained? If there were still [to be] salvation for them, Isaiah should have said, "God will stretch out his hand a third time to possess the remnant of his people," and not say a second time.

Leviticus Rabbah on Israel

Leviticus Rabbah Parashah Two

II:I

1. A. "Speak to the children of Israel [and say to them, when any man of you brings an offering to the Lord, you shall bring your offering of cattle from the herd or from the flock]" (Lev. 1:2).

    B. "Is Ephraim a precious son to me? [Is he a child that is dandled? For as often as I speak of him, I still keep mentioning him]" (Jer. 31:20).

    C. Ten were called precious, and these are they: Torah, prophecy, understanding, knowledge, folly, riches, the righteous, the death of the faithful, faithfulness, and Israel.

    D. Torah, whence? "It [wisdom] is more precious than rubies" (Prov. 3:15).

    E. Prophecy, whence? "And the word of the Lord was precious in those days" (1 Sam. 3:1).

    F. Understanding, whence? "That which is precious of the spirit of man is understanding" (Prov. 17:27).

    G. Knowledge, whence? "The lips of knowledge are a precious jewel" (Prov. 20:15).

    H. Folly, whence? "A little folly is more precious than wisdom and honor" (Qoh. 10:1).

    I. Riches, whence? "Precious is the capital of a diligent man" (Prov. 12:27).

    J. The righteous, whence? "How precious are your friends to me, O God" (Ps. 139:17).

    K. The death of the faithful, whence? "Precious in the sight of the Lord is the death of the faithful ones" (Ps. 116:15).

    L. Faithfulness, whence? "How precious is your faithfulness, O God" (Ps. 36:8).

M. Israel, whence? "Is Ephraim [=Israel] not a precious son to me?" (Jer. 31:20).

2. A. Under ordinary circumstances, if a thousand people start [to study] Scripture, a hundred succeed. If a hundred start [to study] the Mishnah, ten succeed. [If] ten go on to Talmud, one succeeds. That is in line with the following verse of Scripture: "One man among a thousand have I found [M'LP, one who teaches, with the same consonants reads, 'out of a thousand'] but a woman among all those have I not found" (Qoh. 7:28).

B. "One man among a thousand have I found" refers to Abraham.

C. "But a woman among all those have I not found"—even Sarah.

D. Another possibility: "One man among a thousand have I found" refers to Amram.

E. "But a woman among all those have I not found"—even Jochebed.

F. Another possibility: "One man among a thousand have I found" refers to Moses.

G. "But a woman among all those have I not found" refers to the women of the generation of the wilderness. . . .

3. A. Said the Holy One, blessed be he, "I place a high price on Israel."

B. R. Abba bar Kahana and R. Isaac:

C. R. Abba bar Kahana said, "Had Pharaoh demanded the equivalent of the weight of each Israelite in precious stones and pearls, would the Holy One, blessed be he, not have paid it to him?"

D. Said R. Isaac, "Now did [God] not take them out for a price? [He sent] swarms and swarms of vermin, swarms and swarms of evil beasts. Are these not a price [to be paid]?"

E. Accordingly: "I place a high price on Israel."

II:II

1. A. "[Is Ephraim a precious son] to me" (Jer. 31:20).

B. Wherever in Scripture the words, "to me," are written, [that to which the words refer] is not to be moved either in this world or in the world to come [see Sifre Deut. 92].

C. In reference to the priests, it is written, "And they shall serve as priests to me" (Ex. 40:15).

D. The Levites: "And they shall take heave offering for me" (Ex. 25:2).

E. Israel: "For to me belong the children of Israel" (Lev. 25:45).

F. Heave offering: "And they shall take up heave offering for me" (Ex. 25:2).

G. Firstlings: "For to me belongs every firstborn" (Num. 3:13).

H. The Sanhedrin: "Gather to me [seventy elders]" (Num. 11:16).

I. The Land of Israel: "For to me belongs the land" (Lev. 25:23).

J. Jerusalem: "The city which I have chosen for me" (1 Kgs. 11:36).

K.   "For I have seen for myself a king among his sons" (1 Sam. 16:1).

L.   The sanctuary: "And they shall make a sanctuary for me" (Ex. 25:8).

M.   The altar: "An altar of dirt you will make for me" (Ex. 20:21).

N.   To the offerings: "You shall watch to offer to me" (Num. 25:2).

O.   The anointing oil: "This will be for me a holy oil of anointing" (Ex. 30:31).

P.   Lo, every reference in Scripture to "to me" means that that to which reference is made will not be moved either in this world or in the world to come.

II:III

1.   A.   "[Is] Ephraim [a precious son to me]" (Jer. 31:20).

     B.   R. Joshua b. Levi said, "[Ephraim means] a courtier."

     C.   R. Joshua b. Nehemiah said, "It means an aristocrat."

2.   A.   Said R. Phineas, "With this crown was Ephraim crowned by our father, Jacob, when he departed to his eternal dwelling.

     B.   "He said to him, 'Ephraim, head of the tribe, head of the session, one who is beautiful and exalted above all of my sons will be called by your name: [Samuel, the son of Elkanah, the son of Jeroham,] the son of Tohu, the son of Zuph, an Ephraimite' [1 Sam. 1:1]; 'Jeroboam son of Nabat, an Ephraimite' [1 Sam. 11:26]. 'And David was an Ephraimite, of Bethlehem in Judah'" (1 Sam. 17:12).

4.   A.   [Is Ephraim a darling son unto me? Is he a child that is dandled?] For as often as (MDY) I speak (DBRY) to him I still remember him (Jer. 31:20).

     B.   R. Judan in the name of R. Abba bar Kahana, "Sufficient (DYY) is [merely] speaking to him (DYBWRW)."

     C.   Said R. Judah b. R. Simon, "Even when I say that I am not going to speak with him, I cannot bear it."

5.   A.   "For as often (MDY) as I speak to him (DBRY)" —

     B.   For surely (BWD'Y) my speech is with him (DBRY), thus: "Speak to the children of Israel" (Lev. 1:1).

II:IV

1.   A.   Returning to the matter (GWPH): "Speak to the children of Israel" (Lev. 1:2).

     B.   R. Yudan in the name of R. Samuel b. R. Nehemiah [B-P = Pesiqta de R. Kahana Sheqalim 15:2–17]: "The matter may be compared to the case of a king who had an undergarment, concerning which he instructed his servant, saying to him, 'Fold it, shake it out, and be careful about it!'

C. "He said to him, 'My lord, O king, among all the undergarments that you have, [why] do you give me such instructions only about this one?'

D. "He said to him, 'It is because this is the one that I keep closest to my body.'

E. "So too did Moses say before the Holy One, blessed be he, 'Lord of the Universe: Among the seventy distinct nations that you have in your world, [why] do you give me instructions only concerning Israel? [For instance,] "Command the children of Israel" [Num. 28:2], "Say to the children of Israel" [Ex. 33:5], "Speak to the children of Israel"' [Lev. 1:2].

F. "He said to him, 'The reason is that they stick close to me, in line with the following verse of Scripture: "For as the undergarment cleaves to the loins of a man, so have I caused to cleave unto me the whole house of Israel"'" (Jer. 13:11).

G. Said R. Abin, "[The matter may be compared] to a king who had a purple cloak, concerning which he instructed his servant, saying, 'Fold it, shake it out, and be careful about it!'

H. "He said to him, 'My Lord, O king, among all the purple cloaks that you have, [why] do you give me such instructions only about this one?'

I. "He said to him, 'That is the one that I wore on my coronation day.'

J. "So too did Moses say before the Holy One, blessed be he, Lord of the Universe: 'Among the seventy distinct nations that you have in your world, [why] do you give instructions to me only concerning Israel? [For instance,] "Say to the children of Israel," "Command the children of Israel," "Speak to the children of Israel."'

K. "He said to him, 'They are the ones who at the [Red] Sea declared me to be king, saying, "The Lord will be king"'" (Ex. 15:18).

L. Said R. Berekhiah, "[The matter may be compared to an elder, who had a hood [signifying his office as Elder], concerning which he instructed his disciple, saying to him, 'Fold it, shake it out, and be careful about it!'

M. "He said to him, 'My lord, Elder, among all the hoods that you have, [why] do you give me such instructions only about this one?'

N. "He said to him, 'It is because that is the one that I wore on the day on which I was officially named an Elder.'

O. "So too did Moses say before the Holy One, blessed be he, Lord of the Universe: 'Among the seventy distinct nations that you have in your world, [why] do you give instructions to me only concerning Israel?'

P. He said to him, "[It is because] they accepted my dominion on them at Mount Sinai, saying, 'Whatever the Lord has spoken we shall do and we shall hear'" (Ex. 24:7).

2. A.   Said R. Yudan, "Now take note of how the Holy One, blessed be he, cherishes Israel.

    B.   "For he makes mention of them five times in a single verse of Scripture, in line with the following verse: 'And I have given the Levites as a gift to Aaron and his sons [from among the people of Israel, to do the service for the people of Israel at the tent of meeting, and to make atonement for the people of Israel, that there may be no plague among the people of Israel in case the people of Israel should come near the sanctuary]' " (Num. 8 : 19).

II:V

1. A.   Said R. Simeon b. Yohai, "[The matter may be compared] to a king who had an only son. Every day he would give instructions to his steward, saying to him, 'Make sure my son eats, make sure my son drinks, make sure my son goes to school, make sure my son comes home from school.'

    B.   "So every day the Holy One, blessed be he, gave instructions to Moses, saying, 'Command the children of Israel,' 'Say to the children of Israel,' 'Speak to the children of Israel.'"

2. A.   Said R. Judah b. R. Simon, "[The matter may be compared] to a person who was sitting and making a crown for the king. Someone passed by and said to him, 'What are you doing?'

    B.   "He replied, 'Making a crown for the king.'

    C.   "He said to him, 'Whatever [precious stones] that you can affix [to the crown] you should affix, put on emeralds, put on jewels, put on pearls. For that crown is going to be put on the head of the king.'

    D.   "So too did the Holy One, blessed be he, say to Moses, 'In whatever way you can praise Israel, give that praise, if you can magnify them, do it, if you can adorn them, do it. Why? Because through [Israel] I am going to be glorified.' [That is] in line with the following verse of Scripture: 'And he said to me, You are my servant, Israel, in whom I will be glorified' " (Is. 49 : 3).

II:VI

1. A.   R. Joshua of Sikhnin in the name of R. Levi: "Even the Scriptures paid honor to Israel.

    B.   "That is in line with the following verse of Scripture: 'When any man of you brings an offering' [Lev. 1 : 2].

    C.   "Now when [Scripture] proceeds to yet another [but less praiseworthy] topic, [how does it phrase matters?] 'When a man of you has on the flesh of his skin' is not written, but rather, 'When man will have on the flesh of his skin is rising'" (Lev. 13 : 2).

D.   R. Samuel b. R. Nehemiah made two points [in this same manner]:

E.   "It is written, 'But there shall be no needy among you' [Deut. 15:4].

F.   "Now when [Scripture] proceeds to yet another [but less praise-worthy] topic, [how does it phrase matters?]

G.   " 'For there shall be no needy in your midst' is not written here, but rather, 'from the midst of the land' " (Deut. 15:11).

H.   R. Samuel b. R. Nehemiah made yet another point [in the same manner]:

I.   "It is written, 'These shall stand to bless the people on Mount Gerizim' [Deut. 27:12].

J.   "Now when [Scripture] proceeds to yet another [but less praise-worthy] topic, [how does it phrase matters?]

K.   " 'These will stand to curse the people' is not written here, but rather, '. . . these will stand concerning (L) the curse' " (Deut. 27:13).

2. A.   R. Berekhiah, R. Helbo, and R. Ami in the name of R. Ilai: "Not only so, but when punishment comes into the world, the righteous overcome it, in line with that which is written, 'These shall stand against (L) the curse' " (Deut. 27:13).

II:VII

1. A.   Said R. Berekhiah, "Said the Holy One, blessed be He, to this man (Adam) [to whom Scripture refers, 'When any may (Adam) of you brings an offering . . .' (Lev. 1:2)], 'Man, let your offering be like the offering of the first man.'

B.   "Just as the first man had everything under his dominion and so did not bring an offering that had been acquired by robbery or violence, so you, in whose dominion all things [do not fall], should offer nothing acquired by robbery or violence, and, if you conform, 'It will please the Lord more than an ox, [or a bull with horns and hoofs]' " (Ps. 69:32). [In context: "I will praise the name of God with a song, I will magnify him with thanksgiving. This will please the Lord more than an ox. . . . Let the oppressed see it and be glad. . . . For the Lord hears the needy and does not despise his own that are in bonds" (Ps. 69:30–33).]

Leviticus Rabbah Parashah Five

V:VII

1. A.   "[If the whole congregation of Israel commits a sin unwittingly and the thing is hidden from the eyes of the assembly, and they do any

one of the things which the Lord has commanded not to be done and are guilty, when the sin which they have committed becomes known the assembly shall offer a young bull for a sin offering and bring it before the tent of meeting;] and the elders of the congregation shall lay their hands [upon the head of the bull before the Lord]" (Lev. 4: 13–15).

B. [Since, in laying their hands (SMK) on the head of the bull, the elders sustain (SMK) the community by adding to it the merit they enjoy,] said R. Isaac, "The nations of the world have none to sustain them, for it is written, 'And those who sustain Egypt will fall' (Ez. 30:6).

C. "But Israel has those who sustain it, as it is written: 'And the elders of the congregation shall lay their hands [and so sustain Israel]'" (Lev. 4:15).

2. A. Said R. Eleazar, "The nations of the world are called a congregation, and Israel is called a congregation.

B. "The nations of the world are called a congregation: 'For the congregation of the godless shall be desolate' [Job 15:34].

C. "And Israel is called a congregation: 'And the elders of the congregation shall lay their hands' [Lev. 4:15].

D. "The nations of the world are called sturdy bulls and Israel is called sturdy bulls.

E. "The nations of the world are called sturdy bulls: 'The congregation of [sturdy] bulls with the calves of the peoples' [Ps. 68:31].

F. "Israel is called sturdy bulls, as it is said, 'Listen to me, you sturdy [bullish] of heart' [Is. 46:13].

G. "The nations of the world are called excellent, and Israel is called excellent.

H. "The nations of the world are called excellent: 'You and the daughters of excellent nations' [Ex. 32:18].

I. "Israel is called excellent: 'They are the excellent, in whom is all my delight' [Ps. 16:4].

J. "The nations of the world are called sages, and Israel is called sages.

K. "The nations of the world are called sages: 'And I shall wipe out sages from Edom' [Ob. 1:8].

L. "And Israel is called sages: 'Sages store up knowledge' [Prov. 10:14].

M. "The nations of the world are called unblemished, and Israel is called unblemished.

N. "The nations of the world are called unblemished: 'Unblemished as are those that go down to the pit' [Prov. 1:12].

O. "And Israel is called unblemished: 'The unblemished will inherit goodness' [Prov. 28:10].

P. "The nations of the world are called men, and Israel is called men.

Q. "The nations of the world are called men: 'And you men who work iniquity' [Ps. 141:4].

R. "And Israel is called men: 'To you who are men I call' [Prov. 8:4].

S. "The nations of the world are called righteous, and Israel is called righteous.

T. "The nations of the world are called righteous: 'And righteous men shall judge them' [Ez. 23:45].

U. "And Israel is called righteous: 'And your people—all of them are righteous' [Is. 60:21].

V. "The nations of the world are called mighty, and Israel is called mighty.

W. "The nations of the world are called mighty: 'Why do you boast of evil, O mighty man' [Ps. 52:3].

X. "And Israel is called mighty: 'Mighty in power, those who do his word' " [Ps. 103:20].

V:VIII

1. A. R. Simeon b. Yohai taught, "How masterful are the Israelites, for they know how to find favor with their creator."

B. Said R. Yudan, [in Aramaic:], "It is like the case of Samaritan [beggars]. The Samaritan [beggars] are clever at begging. One of them goes to a housewife, saying to her, 'Do you have an onion? Give it to me.' After she gives it to him, he says to her, 'Is there such a thing as an onion without bread?' After she gives him [bread], he says to her, 'Is there such a thing as food without drink?' So, all in all, he gets to eat and drink."

C. Said R. Aha [in Aramaic:], "There is a woman who knows how to borrow things, and there is a woman who does not. The one who knows how to borrow goes over to her neighbor. The door is open, but she knocks [anyhow]. Then she says to her neighbor, 'Greetings, good neighbor. How're you doing? How's your husband doing? How're your kids doing? Can I come in? [By the way], would you have such-and-such a utensil? Would you lend it to me?' [The neighboring housewife] says to her, 'Yes, of course.'

D. "But the one who does not know how to borrow goes over to neighbor. The door is closed, so she just opens it. She says [to the neighboring housewife], 'Do you have such-and such a utensil? Would you lend it to me?' [The neighboring housewife] says to her, 'No.' "

E. Said R. Hunia [in Aramaic:], "There is a tenant farmer who knows how to borrow things, and there is a tenant farmer who does not know how to borrow. The one who knows how to borrow combs his hair, brushes off his clothes, puts on a good face, and then goes over to the overseer of his work to borrow from him. [The overseer] says to him, 'How's the land doing?' He says to him, 'May you have the merit of being fully satisfied with its [wonderful] produce.' 'How are the oxen doing?' He says to him, 'May you have the merit of being fully satisfied with their fat.' 'How are the goats doing?' 'May you have the merit of being fully satisfied with their young.' 'And what would you like?' Then he says, 'Now if you might have an extra ten denars, would you give them to me?' The overseer replies, 'If you want, take twenty.'

F. "But the one who does not know how to borrow leaves his hair a mess, his clothes filthy, his face gloomy. He too goes over to the overseer to borrow from him. The overseer says to him, 'How's the land doing?' He replies, 'I hope it will produce at least what [in seed] we put into it.' 'How are the oxen doing?' 'They're scrawny.' 'How are the goats doing?' 'They're scrawny too.' 'And what do you want?' 'Now if you might have an extra ten denars, would you give them to me?' The overseer replies, 'Go, pay me back what you already owe me!'"

G. Said R. Hunia, "David was one of the good tenant farmers. To begin with, he starts a psalm with praise [of God], saying, 'The heavens declare the glory of God, and the firmament shows his handiwork' [Ps. 19:2]. The Heaven says to him, 'Perhaps you need something?' 'The firmament shows his handiwork.' The firmament says to him, 'Perhaps you need something?'

H. "And so he would continue to sing: 'Day unto day utters speech, and night to night reveals knowledge' [Ps. 19:3].

I. "Said to him the Holy One, blessed be he, 'What do you want?'

J. "He said before him, 'Who can discern errors?' [Ps. 19:13].

K. "'What sort of unwitting sin have I done before you!'

L. "[God] said to him, 'Lo, this one is remitted, and that one is forgiven you.'

M. "'And cleanse me of hidden sins' [Ps. 19:13]—from the secret sins that I have done before you.'

N. "He said to him, 'Lo, this one is remitted, and that one is forgiven to you.'

O. "'Keep back your servant also from deliberate ones.' This refers to transgressions done in full knowledge.

P. "'That they may not have dominion over me. Then I shall be faultless' [Ps. 19:14]. This refers to the most powerful of transgressions.

Q. "'And I shall be clear of great transgression'" (Ps. 19:14).

R. Said R. Levi, "David said before the Holy One, blessed be he, 'Lord of the age[s], you are a great God, and, as for me, my sins are great too. It will take a great God to remit and forgive great sins: "For your name's sake, O Lord, pardon my sin, for [your name] is great"'" (Ps. 25:11).

Leviticus Rabbah Parashah 36

XXXVI:IV

1. A. "But now thus says the Lord, he who created you is Jacob, and he who formed you is Israel" (Is. 43:1).

    B. R. Phineas in the name of R. Reuben said, "[Said] the Holy One, blessed be he, to his world, 'O my world, my world! Shall I tell you who created you? Shall I tell you who formed you? Jacob is the one who created you, Israel is the one who formed you,' as it is written, 'He who created you is Jacob, and he who formed you is Israel'" (Is. 43:1).

    C. R. Joshua of Sikhnin in the name of R. Levi said, "Behemoth was created only on account of the merit of Jacob, as it is written, 'Behold now behemoth, which I made with you'" (Job 40:15).

    D. R. Joshua b. Nehemiah in the name of R. Haninah bar Isaac: "The heaven and the earth were created only on account of the merit of Jacob.

    E. "What is the proof text? 'For he established a testimony on account of Jacob' [Ps. 78:5], and 'testimony' can mean only heaven and earth, as it is written, 'I call heaven and earth to testify against you this day'" (Deut. 4:26).

    F. R. Berekhiah said, "The heaven and earth were created only on account of the merit of Jacob, whose name is Israel.

    G. "What is the proof text? 'On account of the beginning did God create heaven and earth' [Gen. 1:1]. And 'beginning' refers only to Israel, as it is written, 'Israel is holy to the Lord, the beginning of his harvest'" (Jer. 2:3).

    H. Said R. Benaiah, "The heaven and earth were created only on account of the merit of Moses.

    I. "For it is written, 'And he chose a beginning part [namely Moses] for himself'" (Deut. 33:21).

    J. Said R. Abbahu, "Everything was created only on account of the merit of Jacob.

    K. "That is in line with the following verse of Scripture: 'Not like these is the portion of Jacob, for he [that is, Jacob] is the one who formed everything'" (Jer. 10:16).

2. A. R. Berekhiah and R. Levi in the name of Samuel bar Nahman: "Abraham was saved from the furnace of fire only because of the merit of Jacob.

    B. "The matter may be compared. To what is it like? It is like the case of someone who was judged before the ruler, and the judgment came forth from the ruler that he was to be put to death through burning.

    C. "The ruler perceived through his astrological science that [the con-

demned man] was going to beget a daughter, who was going to be
married to a king. He said, 'This one is worthy to be saved through
the merit of the daughter that he is going to beget, who is going to be
married to a king.'

D. "So in the case of Abraham, judgment against him came forth from
Nimrod that he was to be put to death through burning. But the Holy
One, blessed be he, foresaw that Jacob was going to come forth from
him. So he said, 'That one is worthy of being saved on account of
the merit of Jacob.'

E. "That is in line with the following verse of Scripture: 'Thus said the
Lord to the House of Jacob, who redeemed Abraham'" (Is. 29:22).

F. And rabbis say, "Abraham himself was created only on account of
the merit of Jacob.

G. "That is in line with the following verse of Scripture: 'For I have
known him, that he may change his children and his household after
him to keep the way of the Lord by doing righteousness and justice'
(Gen. 18:19).

H. "Now righteousness and justice are only with Jacob, for it is written,
'You have made justice and righteousness in Jacob'" (Ps. 99:4).

XXXVI:V

1. A. Why (at Lev. 26:42) are the patriarchs listed in reverse order [Jacob,
Isaac, Abraham]?

   B. It is as if to say, if the deeds of Jacob are insufficient, there are the
deeds of Isaac, and if the deeds of Isaac are insufficient, there are the
deeds of Abraham.

   C. Each one of them is sufficient for [his merit] to sustain [the world].

2. A. And why is the matter of remembrance stated with respect to Abraham and Jacob but not with respect to Isaac?

   B. R. Berekhiah and rabbis:

   C. R. Berekhiah said, "It was because he was a child born of sorrow."

   D. And rabbis say, "They regard the ashes of Isaac as if they were piled
up on the altar."

3. A. And why is the word "even" used with respect to Abraham and Isaac
but not with respect to Jacob?

   B. It was because the fruit of the bed of Jacob, our father, was whole
[and unblemished], while from the bed of Abraham came forth
dross, Ishmael and the sons of Keturah, and from the bed of Isaac
came forth dross, Esau and all of his nobles.

   C. But in the case of Jacob, his bed was unblemished, for all the sons
that were born of him were righteous men.

4. A. I know that that is the case of the patriarchs. How do I know that
[God remembers the merit of the matriarchs]?

B.   Scripture uses the accusative particle ('T) three times, and these refer only to the matriarchs,

C.   For it is said, "There they buried Abraham and [accusative particle]
Sarah his wife" (Gen. 49:31).

5.   A.   And then why, when the Scripture (at Lev. 26:42) makes mention of
the patriarchs, does it make mention of the merit of the land with
them?

B.   Said R. Simeon b. Laqish, "[The matter may be compared] to a king
who had three sons, and one handmaiden raised them all. When,
therefore, the king would ask about how his sons were, he would
also say, 'Tell me about the welfare of the one who raises them.'

C.   "So the Holy One, blessed be he, makes mention of the merit of the
fathers and alongside he makes mention of the merit of the land:
'Then I will remember my covenant with Jacob, [and I will remember my covenant with Isaac and my covenant with Abraham,] and I
will remember the land'" (Lev. 26:42).

XXXVI:VI

1.   A.   [Returning to] the body [of the matter:] How long does the merit of
the patriarchs endure?

B.   R. Tanhuma made this statement, Rab in the name of R. Hiyya the
Elder, R. Menehama said it, R. Berekhiah and R. Helbo in the name
of R. Abba bar Zabeda: "Down to Jehoahaz. 'But the lord was gracious to them and had compassion on them [and he turned toward
them, because of his covenant with Abraham, Isaac, and Jacob, and
would not destroy them; nor has he cast them from his presence until
now]' [2 Kgs. 13:23].

C.   "Until now [the time of Jehoahaz, 2 Kgs. 13:22] the merit of the
patriarchs has endured."

D.   R. Joshua b. Levi said, "Until the time of Elijah: 'And it came to
pass at the time of the evening offering, that Elijah the prophet came
near and said, "O Lord, [the God of Abraham, Isaac, and Israel, this
day let it be known that you are God"' [1 Kgs. 18:36]. Thus, to this
day the merit endured, but not afterward.]"

E.   Samuel said, "Down to the time of Hosea: 'Now will I uncover her
shame in the sight of her lovers, and no man will [ever again] deliver
her out of my hand' [Hos. 2:12].

F.   "'Man' refers then to Abraham, as it is said in Scripture: 'And now,
return the wife of the man' [Gen. 20:7].

G.   "'Man' refers only to Isaac, as it is said, 'Who is this man?' [Gen.
24:65].

H.   "'Man' refers only to Jacob, as it is said, 'Jacob, a quiet man, dwelling in tents'" (Gen. 28:27).

I. R. Yudan said, "Down to the time of Hezekiah: 'That the government may be increased [and of peace there be no end . . . the zeal of the Lord of hosts [thus: not the merit of the patriarchs] does this'" (Is. 9:6).

J. R. Yudan bar Hanan in the name of R. Berekhiah said, "If you see that the merit of the patriarchs is slipping away, and the merit of the matriarchs is trembling, then go and cleave to the performance of deeds of loving kindness.

K. "That is in line with the following verse of Scripture: 'For the mountains will melt (YMWSW), and the hills will tremble, [but my love will not depart from you]' [Is. 54:10].

L. "'Mountains' refers to the patriarchs, and 'hills' to the matriarchs.

M. "Henceforward: 'But my love will not (YMWS) depart from you'" (Is. 54:10).

N. Said R. Aha, "The merit of the patriarchs endures forever. Forever do people call it to mind, saying, 'For the Lord your God is a merciful God. He will not fail you nor destroy you nor forget the covenant he made with your fathers'" (Deut. 4:31).

Leviticus Rabbah Parashah Thirteen

XIII:V

1. A. Said R. Ishmael b. R. Nehemiah, "All the prophets foresaw what the pagan kingdoms would do [to Israel].

    B. "The first man foresaw what the pagan kingdoms would do [to Israel].

    C. "That is in line with the following verse of Scripture: 'A river flowed out of Eden [to water the garden, and there it divided and became four rivers]' (Gen. 2:10). [The four rivers stand for the four kingdoms, Babylonia, Media, Greece, and Rome]."

2. A. R. Tanhuma said it, [and] R. Menahema [in the name of] R. Joshua b. Levi: "The Holy One, blessed be he, will give the cup of reeling to the nations of the world to drink in the world to come.

    B. "That is in line with the following verse of Scripture: 'A river flowed out of Eden' (Gen. 2:10), the place from which justice [DYN] goes forth."

3. A. "[There it divided] and became four rivers" (Gen. 2:10)—this refers to the four kingdoms.

    B. "The name of the first is Pishon (PSWN); [it is the one which flows around the whole land of Havilah, where there is gold; and the gold of that land is good; bdellium and onyx stone are there]" (Gen. 2:11–12).

    C. This refers to Babylonia, on account [of the reference to Babylonia in the following verse:] "And their [the Babylonians'] horsemen spread themselves (PSW)" (Hab. 1:8).

D. [It is further] on account of [Nebuchadnezzar's being] a dwarf, shorter than ordinary men by a handbreadth.

E. "[It is the one which flows around the whole land of Havilah" (Gen. 2:11).

F. "This [reference to the river's flowing around the whole land] speaks of Nebuchadnezzar, the wicked man, who came up and surrounded the entire Land of Israel, which places its hope in the Holy One, blessed be he.

G. That is in line with the following verse of Scripture: "Hope in God, for I shall again praise him" (Ps. 42:5).

H. "Where the is gold" (Gen. 2:11)—this refers to the words of Torah, "which are more to be desired than gold, more than much fine gold" (Ps. 19:11).

I. "And the gold of that land is good" (Gen. 2:12).

J. This teaches that there is no Torah like the Torah that is taught in the Land of Israel, and there is no wisdom like the wisdom that is taught in the Land of Israel.

K. Bdellium and onyx stone are there" (Gen. 2:12)—Scripture, Mishnah, Talmud, and lore.

4. A. "The name of the second river is Gihon; [it is the one which flows around the whole land of Cush]" (Gen. 2:13).

B. This refers to Media, which produced Haman, that wicked man, who spit out venom like a serpent.

C. It is on account of the verse: "On your belly will you go" (Gen. 3:14).

D. "It is the one which flows around the whole land of Cush" (Gen. 2:13).

E. [We know that this refers to Media, because it is said:] "Who rules from India to Cush" (Est. 1:1).

5. A. "And the name of the third river is Tigris (HDQL), [which flows east of Assyria]" (Gen. 2:14).

B. This refers to Greece [Syria], which was sharp (HD) and speedy (QL) in making its decrees, saying to Israel, "Write on the horn of an ox that you have no portion in the God of Israel."

C. "Which flows east (QDMT) of Assyria" (Gen. 2:14).

D. Said R. Huna, "In three aspects the kingdom of Greece was in advance (QDMH) of the present evil kingdom [Rome]: in respect to ship-building, the arrangement of camp vigils, and language."

E. Said R. Huna, "Any and every kingdom may be called 'Assyria' (ashur), on account of all of their making themselves powerful at Israel's expense."

F. Said R. Yose b. R. Hanina, "Any and every kingdom may be called

Nineveh (NNWH), on account of their adorning (NWY) themselves at Israel's expense."

G. Said R. Yose b. R. Hanina, "Any and every kingdom may be called Egypt (MSRYM), on account of their oppressing (MSYRYM) Israel."

6. A. "And the fourth river is the Euphrates (PRT)" (Gen. 2:14).

B. This refers to Edom [Rome], since it was fruitful (PRT), and multiplied through the prayer of the elder [Isaac at Gen. 27:39].

C. Another interpretation: It was because it was fruitful and multiplied, and so cramped his world.

D. Another explanation: Because it was fruitful and multiplied and cramped his son.

E. Another explanation: Because it was fruitful and multiplied and cramped his house.

F. Another explanation: "Parat"—because in the end, "I am going to exact a penalty from it."

G. That is in line with the following verse of Scripture: "I have trodden (PWRH) the winepress alone" (Is. 63:3).

7. A. [Gen. R. 42:2:] Abraham foresaw what the evil kingdom would do [to Israel].

B. "[As the sun was going down,] a deep sleep fell on Abraham; and lo, a dread and great darkness fell upon him" (Gen. 15:12).

C. "Dread" ('YMH) refers to Babylonia, on account of the statement, "Then Nebuchadnezzer was full of fury (HMH)" (Dan. 3:19).

D. "Darkness" refers to Media, which brought darkness to Israel through its decrees: "to destroy, to slay, and to wipe out all the Jews" (Est. 7:4).

E. "Great" refers to Greece.

F. Said R. Judah b. R. Simon, "The verse teaches that the kingdom of Greece set up one hundred twenty-seven governors, one hundred and twenty-seven hyparchs and one hundred twenty-seven commanders."

G. And rabbis say, "They were sixty in each category."

H. R. Berekhiah and R. Hanan in support of this position taken by rabbis: " 'Who led you through the great terrible wilderness, with its fiery serpents and scorpions and thirsty ground where there was no water]' (Deut. 8:15).

I. "Just as the scorpion produces eggs by sixties, so the kingdom of Greece would set up its administration in groups of sixty."

J. "Fell on him" (Gen. 15:12).

K. This refers to Edom, on account of the following verse: "The earth quakes at the noise of their [Edom's] fall" (Jer. 49:21).

L. There are those who reverse matters.

M. "Fear" refers to Edom, on account of the following verse: "And this I saw, a fourth beast, fearful, and terrible" (Dan. 7:7).

N. "Darkness" refers to Greece, which brought gloom through its decrees. For they said to Israel, "Write on the horn of an ox that you have no portion in the God of Israel."

O.   "Great" refers to Media, on account of the verse: "King Ahasuerus made Haman [the Median] great" (Est. 3:1).

P.   "Fell on him" refers to Babylonia, on account of the following verse: "Fallen, fallen is Babylonia" (Is. 21:9).

8. A.   Daniel foresaw what the evil kingdoms would do [to Israel].

B.   "Daniel said, I saw in my vision by night, and behold, the four winds of heaven were stirring up the great sea. And four great beasts came up out of the sea, [different from one another. The first was like a lion and had eagles' wings. Then as I looked, its wings were plucked off. . . . And behold, another beast, a second one, like a bear. . . . After this I looked, and lo, another, like a leopard. . . . After this I saw in the night visions, and behold, a fourth beast, terrible and dreadful and exceedingly strong; and it had great iron teeth]" (Dan. 7:3–7).

C.   If you enjoy sufficient merit, it will emerge from the sea, but if not, it will come out of the forest.

D.   The animal that comes up from the sea is not violent, but the one that comes up out of the forest is violent.

E.   Along these same lines: "The boar out of the wood ravages it" (Ps. 80:14).

F.   If you enjoy sufficient merit, it will come from the river, and if not, from the forest.

G.   The animal that comes from the river is not violent, but the one that comes up out of the forest is violent.

H.   "Different from one another" (Dan. 7:3).

I.   Differing from [hating] one another.

J.   This teaches that every nation that rules in the world hates Israel and reduces them to slavery.

K.   "The first was like a lion [and had eagles' wings]" (Dan. 7:4).

L.   This refers to Babylonia.

M.   Jeremiah saw [Babylonia] as a lion. Then he went and saw it as an eagle.

N.   He saw it as a lion: "A lion has come up from his thicket" (Jer. 4:7).

O.   And [as an eagle:] "Behold, he shall come up and swoop down as the eagle" (Jer. 49:22).

P.   People said to Daniel, "What do you see?"

Q.   He said to them, "I see the face like that of a lion and wings like those of an eagle: 'The first was like a lion and had eagles' wings. Then, as I looked, its wings were plucked off, and it was lifted up from the ground [and made to stand upon two feet like a man and the heart of a man was given to it]'" (Dan. 7:4).

R.	R. Eleazar and R. Ishmael b. R. Nehemiah:
S.	R. Eleazar said, "While the entire lion was smitten, its heart was not smitten.
T.	"That is in line with the following statement: 'And the heart of a man was given to it' (Dan. 7:4)."
U.	And R. Ishmael b. R. Nehemiah said, "Even its heart was smitten, for it is written, 'Let his heart be changed from a man's' (Dan. 4:17).
X.	"And behold, another beast, a second one, like a bear. [It was raised up on one side; it had three ribs in its mouth between its teeth, and it was told, Arise, devour much flesh]" (Dan. 7:5).
Y.	This refers to Media.
Z.	Said R. Yohanan, "It is like a bear."
AA.	It is written, "similar to a wolf" (DB); thus, "And a wolf was there."
BB.	That is in accord with the view of R. Yohanan, for R. Yohanan said, " 'Therefore a lion out of the forest [slays them]' (Jer. 5:6)—this refers to Babylonia.
CC.	" 'A wolf of the deserts spoils them' (Jer. 5:6) refers to Media.
DD.	" 'A leopard watches over their cities' (Jer. 5:6) refers to Greece.
EE.	" 'Whoever goes out from them will be savaged' (Jer. 5:6) refers to Edom.
FF.	"Why so? 'Because their transgressions are many, and their backslidings still more' (Jer. 5:6)."
GG.	"After this, I looked, and lo, another, like a leopard [with four wings of a bird on its back; and the beast had four heads; and dominion was given to it]" (Dan. 7:6).
HH.	This [leopard] refers to Greece, which persisted impudently in making harsh decrees, saying to Israel, "Write on the horn of an ox that you have no share in the God of Israel."
II.	"After this I saw in the night visions, and behold, a fourth beast, terrible and dreadful and exceedingly strong; [and it had great iron teeth; it devoured and broke in pieces and stamped the residue with its feet. It was different from all the beasts that were before it; and it had ten horns]" (Dan. 7:7).
JJ.	This refers to Edom [Rome].
KK.	Daniel saw the first three visions on one night, and this one he saw on another night. Now why was that the case?
LL.	R. Yohanan and R. Simeon b. Laqish:
MM.	R. Yohanan said, "It is because the fourth beast weighed as much as the first three."
NN.	And R. Simeon b. Laqish said, "It outweighed them."
OO.	R. Yohanan objected to R. Simeon b. Laqish, " 'Prophesy, therefore, son of man, clap your hands [and let the sword come down

twice; yea, thrice. The sword for those to be slain; it is the sword for the great slaughter, which encompasses them]' (Ez. 21:14–15). [So the single word of Rome weighs against the three others]."

PP. And R. Simeon b. Laqish, how does he interpret the same passage? He notes that [the threefold sword] is doubled (Ez. 21:14), [thus outweighs the three swords, equally twice their strength].

9. A. Moses foresaw what the evil kingdoms would do [to Israel].

B. "The camel, rock badger, and hare" (Deut. 14:7). [Compare: "Nevertheless, among those that chew the cud or part the hoof, you shall not eat these: the camel, because it chews the cud but does not part the hoof, is unclean to you. The rock badger, because it chews the cud but does not part the hoof, is unclean to you. And the hare, because it chews the cud but does not part the hoof, is unclean to you, and the pig, because it parts the hoof and is cloven-footed, but does not chew the cud, is unclean to you" (Lev. 11:4–8).]

C. The camel (GML) refers to Babylonia, [in line with the following verse of Scripture: "O daughter of Babylonia, you who are to be devastated!] Happy will be he who requites (GML) you, with what you have done to us" (Ps. 147:8).

D. "The rock badger" (Deut. 14:7)—this refers to Media.

E. Rabbis and R. Judah b. R. Simon.

F. Rabbis say, "Just as the rock badger exhibits traits of uncleanness and traits of cleanness, so the kingdom of Media produced both a righteous man and a wicked one."

G. Said R. Judah b. R. Simon, "The last Darius was Esther's son. He was clean on his mother's side and unclean on his father's side."

H. "The hare" (Deut 14:7)—this refers to Greece. The mother of King Ptolemy was named "Hare" [in Greek: lagos].

I. "The pig" (Deut. 14:7)—this refers to Edom [Rome].

J. Moses made mention of the first three in a single verse and the final one in a verse by itself [(Deut. 14:7, 8)]. Why so?

K. R. Yohanan and R. Simeon b. Laqish.

L. R. Yohanan said, "It is because [the pig] is equivalent to the other three."

M. And R. Simeon b. Laqish said, "It is because it outweighs them."

N. R. Yohanan objected to R. Simeon b. Laqish, "Prophesy, therefore, son of man, clap your hands [and let the sword come down twice, yea thrice] (Ez. 21:14)."

O. And how does R. Simeon b. Laqish interpret the same passage? He notes that [the threefold sword] is doubled (Ez. 21:14).

10. A. [Gen. R. 65:1:] R. Phineas and R. Hilqiah in the name of R. Simon: "Among all the prophets, only two of them revealed [the true evil of Rome], Assaf and Moses.

B. "Assaf said, 'The pig out of the wood ravages it' (Ps. 80:14).

C. "Moses said, 'And the pig, [because it parts the hoof and is cloven-footed but does not chew the cud]' (Lev. 11:7).

D. "Why is [Rome] compared to a pig?

E. "It is to teach you the following: Just as, when a pig crouches and produces its hooves, it is as if to say, 'See how I am clean [since I have a cloven hoof],' so this evil kingdom takes pride, seizes by violence, and steals, and then gives the appearance of establishing a tribunal for justice."

F. There was the case of a ruler in Caesarea, who put thieves, adulterers, and sorcerers to death, while at the same time telling his counsellor, "That same man [I] did all these three things on a single night."

11. A. Another interpretation: "The camel" (Lev. 11:4).

B. This refers to Babylonia.

C. "Because it chews the cud [but does not part the hoof]" (Lev. 11:4).

D. For it brings forth praises [with its throat] of the Holy One, blessed be he. [The Hebrew words for "chew the cud"—bring up cud—are now understood to mean "give praise." GRH is connected with GRWN, throat, hence, "bring forth [sounds of praise through] the throat."

E. R. Berekhiah and R. Helbo in the name of R. Ishmael b. R. Nahman: "Whatever [praise of God] David [in writing a psalm] treated singly [item by item], that wicked man [Nebuchadnezzar] lumped together in a single verse.

F. " 'Now I, Nebuchadnezzar, praise and extol and honor the King of heaven, for all his works are right and his ways are just, and those who walk in pride he is able to abase' (Dan. 4:37).

G. " 'Praise'—'O Jerusalem, praise the Lord' (Ps. 147:12).

H. " 'Extol'—'I shall extol you, O Lord, for you have brought me low' (Ps. 30:2).

I. " 'Honor the king of heaven'—'The Lord reigns, let the peoples tremble! He sits enthroned upon the cherubim, let the earth quake' (Ps. 99:1).

J. " 'For all his works are right'—'For the sake of thy steadfast love and they faithfulness' (Ps. 115:1).

K. " 'And his ways are just'—'He will judge the peoples with equity' (Ps. 96:10).

L. " 'And those who walk in pride'—'The Lord reigns, he is robed in majesty, the Lord is robed, he is girded with strength' (Ps. 92:1).

M. " 'He is able to abase'—'All the horns of the wicked he will cut off' (Ps. 75:11)."

N. "The rock badger" (Lev. 11:5)—this refers to Media.

O. "For it chews the cud"—for it gives praise to the Holy One, blessed be he: "Thus says Cyrus, king of Persia, 'All the kingdoms of the earth has the Lord, the God of the heaven, given me'" (Ezra 1:2).

P. "The hare"—this refers to Greece.

Q. "For it chews the cud"—for it gives praise to the Holy One, blessed be he.

R. Alexander the Macedonian, when he saw Simeon the Righteous, said, "Blessed be the God of Simeon the Righteous."

S. "The pig" (Lev. 11:7)—this refers to Edom.

T. "For it does not chew the cud"—for it does not give praise to the Holy One, blessed be he.

U. And it is not enough that it does not give praise, but it blasphemes and swears violently, saying, "Whom do I have in heaven, and with you I want nothing on earth" (Ps. 73:25).

12. A. Another interpretation [of GRH, cud, now with reference to GR, stranger:]

B. "The camel" (Lev. 11:4)—this refers to Babylonia.

C. "For it chews the cud" [now: brings up the stranger]—for it exalts righteous men: "And Daniel was in the gate of the king" (Dan. 2:49).

D. "The rock badger" (Lev. 11:5)—this refers to Media.

E. "For it brings up the stranger"—for it exalts the righteous men: "Mordecai sat at the gate of the king" (Est. 2:19).

F. "The hare" (Lev. 11:6)—this refers to Greece.

G. "For it brings up the stranger"—for it exalts the righteous.

H. When Alexander of Macedonia saw Simeon the Righteous, he would rise up on his feet. They said to him, "Can't you see the Jew, that you stand up before this Jew?"

I. He said to them, "When I go forth to battle, I see something like this man's visage, and I conquer."

J. "The pig" (Lev. 11:7)—this refers to Rome.

K. "But it does not bring up the stranger"—for it does not exalt the righteous.

L. And it is not enough that it does not exalt them, but it kills them.

M. That is in line with the following verse of Scripture: "I was angry with my people, I profaned my heritage; I gave them into your hand, you showed them no mercy; on the aged you made your yoke exceedingly heavy" (Is. 47:6).

N. This refers to R. Aqiba and his colleagues.

13. A. Another interpretation [now treating "bring up the cud" (GR) as "bring along in its train" (GRR)]:

B. "The camel" (Lev. 11:4)—this refers to Babylonia.

C. "Which brings along in its train"—for it brought along another kingdom after it.

D. "The rock badger" (Lev. 11:5)—this refers to Media.

E. "Which brings along in its train"—for it brought along another kingdom after it.

F. "The hare" (Lev. 11:6)—this refers to Greece.

G. "Which brings along in its train"—for it brought along another kingdom after it.

H. "The pig" (Lev. 11:7)—this refers to Rome.

I. "Which does not bring along in its train"—for it did not bring along another kingdom after it.

J. And why is it then called "pig" (HZYR)? For it restores (MHZRT) the crown to the one who truly should have it [namely, Israel, whose dominion will begin when the rule of Rome ends].

K. That is in line with the following verse of Scripture: "And saviors will come up on Mount Zion to judge the Mountain of Esau [Rome], and the kingdom will then belong to the Lord" (Ob. 1:21).

Genesis Rabbah on Israel

LIII:XII

2. A. "But God said to Abraham, 'Be not displeased because of the lad and because of your slave woman; whatever Sarah says to you, do as she tells you, for through Isaac shall your descendants be named'" (Gen. 21:12):

B. Said R. Yudan bar Shillum, "What is written is not 'Isaac' but 'through Isaac.' [The matter is limited, not through all of Isaac's descendants but only through some of them, thus excluding Esau.]"

3. A. R. Azariah in the name of Bar Hutah, "The use of the B, which stands for two, indicates that he who affirms that there are two worlds will inherit both worlds [this age and the age to come]."

B. Said R. Yudan bar Shillum, "It is written, 'Remember his marvelous works that he has done, his signs and the judgments of his mouth' (Ps. 105:5). I have given a sign, namely, it is one who gives the appropriate evidence through what he says. Specifically, he who affirms that there are two worlds will be called 'your seed.'

C. "And he who does not affirm that there are two worlds will not be called 'your seed.'"

LXIII:VI

11. A. "And the children struggled together [within her, and she said, 'If it is thus, why do I live?' So she went to inquire of the Lord. And the Lord said to her, 'Two nations are in your womb, and two peoples, born of you, shall be divided; the one shall be stronger than the other, and the elder shall serve the younger']" (Gen. 25:22–23):

2. A. R. Berekhiah in the name of R. Levi said, "It is so that you should not say that it was only after he left his mother's womb that [Esau] contended against [Jacob].

    B. "But even while he was yet in his mother's womb, his fist was stretched forth against him: 'The wicked stretch out their fists [so Freedman] from the womb' (Ps. 58:4)."

3. A. "And the children struggled together within her:"

    B. [Once more referring to the letters of the word "struggled," with special attention to the ones that mean "run,"] they wanted to run within her.

    C. When she went by houses of idolatry, Esau would kick, trying to get out: "The wicked are estranged from the womb" (Ps. 58:4).

    D. When she went by synagogues and study-houses, Jacob would kick, trying to get out: "Before I formed you in the womb, I knew you" (Jer. 1:5).

LXIII:VII

2. A. "Two nations are in your womb, [and two peoples, born of you, shall be divided; the one shall be stronger than the other, and the elder shall serve the younger]" (Gen. 25:23):

    B. There are two proud nations in your womb, this one takes pride in his world, and that one takes pride in his world.

    C. This one takes pride in his monarchy, and that one takes pride in his monarchy.

    D. There are two proud nations in your womb.

    E. Hadrian represents the nations; Solomon, Israel.

    F. There are two who are hated by the nations in your womb. All the nations hate Esau, and all the nations hate Israel.

    G. [Following Freedman's reading:] The one whom your creator hates is in your womb: "And Esau I hated" (Mal. 1:3).

3. A. "and two peoples, born of you, shall be divided:"

    B. Said R. Berekhiah, "On the basis of this statement we have evidence that [Jacob] was born circumcised.

4. A. ". . . the one shall be stronger than the other, [and the elder shall serve the younger]" (Gen. 25:23):

    B. R. Helbo in the name of the house of R. Shila: "Up to this point there were Sabteca and Raamah, but from you will come Jews and Romans." [Freedman, p. 561, n. 8: "Hitherto even the small nations such as Sabteca and Raamah counted; but henceforth all these will pale into insignificance before the two who will rise from you.]

5. A. ". . . and the elder shall serve the younger" (Gen. 25:23):

    B. Said R. Huna, "If he has merit, he will be served, and if not, he will serve."

LXIII:VIII

3. A. "The first came forth red:"
   B. R. Haggai in the name of R. Isaac: "On account of the merit attained by obeying the commandment, 'You will take for yourself on the first day . . . ,' (Lev. 23:40),
   C. "I shall reveal myself to you as the First, avenge you on the first, rebuild the first, and bring you the first.
   D. "I shall reveal myself to you the First: 'I am the first and I am the last' (Is. 44:6).
   E. ". . . avenge you on the first: Esau, 'The first came forth red.'
   F. ". . . rebuild the first: that is the Temple, of which it is written, 'You throne of glory, on high from the first, you place of our sanctuary' (Jer. 17:12).
   G. ". . . and bring you the first: that is, the messiah-king: 'A first unto Zion will I give, behold, behold them, and to Jerusalem' (Is. 41:27)."

LXIII:X

1. A. "[When the boys grew up,] Esau was a skillful hunter, [a man of the field, while Jacob was a quiet man, dwelling in tents]" (Gen. 25:27):
   B. He hunted people through snaring them in words [as the Roman prosecutors do:] "Well enough, you did not steal. But who stole with you? You did not kill, but who killed with you?"
2. A. R. Abbahu said, "He was a trapper and a fieldsman, trapping at home and in the field.
   B. "He trapped in the field: 'How do you tithe salt?' [which does not, in fact, have to be tithed at all!]
   C. "He trapped at home: 'How do people give tithe for straw?' [which does not, in fact, have to be tithed at all!]"
3. A. R. Hiyya bar Abba said, "He treated himself as totally without responsibility for himself, like a field [on which anyone tramples].
   B. "Said the Israelites before the Holy One, blessed be he, 'Lord of all ages, is it not enough for us that you have subjugated us to the seventy nations, but even to this one, who is subjected to sexual intercourse just like a woman?'
   C. "Said to them the Holy One, blessed be he, 'I too will exact punishment from him with those same words: 'And the heart of the mighty men of Edom at that day shall be as the heart of a woman in her pangs' (Jer. 49:22)."
4. A. ". . . while Jacob was a quiet man, dwelling in tents" (Gen. 25:27):
   B. There is a reference to two tents, that is, the school house of Shem and the school house of Eber.

5. A. "Now Isaac loved Esau, because he ate of his game:"
   B. It was first-rate meat and wine for Isaac's eating.
6. A. ". . . but Rebecca loved Jacob" (Gen. 25:28):
   B. The more she heard his voice, the more she loved him.

LXV:I

1. A. "When Esau was forty years old, he took to wife Judith, the daughter of Beeri, the Hittite, and Basemath the daughter of Elon the Hittite; and they made life bitter for Isaac and Rebecca" (Gen. 26:34–35):
   B. "The swine out of the wood ravages it, that which moves in the field feeds on it" (Ps. 80:14).
   C. R. Phineas and R. Hilqiah in the name of R. Simon: "Among all of the prophets, only two of them spelled out in public [the true character of Rome, represented by the swine], Asaf and Moses.
   D. "Asaf: 'The swine out of the wood ravages it.'
   E. "Moses: 'And the swine, because he parts the hoof' (Deut. 14:8).
   F. "Why does Moses compare Rome to the swine? Just as the swine, when it crouches, puts forth its hoofs as if to say, 'I am clean,' so the wicked kingdom steals and grabs, while pretending to be setting up courts of justice.
   G. "So Esau, for all forty years, hunted married women, ravished them, and when he reached the age of forty, he presented himself to his father, saying, 'Just as father got married at the age of forty, so I shall marry a wife at the age of forty.'
   H. " 'When Esau was forty years old, he took to wife Judith, the daughter of Beeri, the Hittite, and Basemath the daughter of Elon the Hittite.' "

LXXV:IV

2. A. "And Jacob sent messengers before him:"
   B. To this one [Esau] whose time to take hold of sovereignty would come before him [namely, before Jacob, since Esau would rule, then Jacob would govern].
   C. R. Joshua b. Levi said, "Jacob took off the purple robe and threw it before Esau, as if to say to him, 'Two flocks of starlings are not going to sleep on a single branch' [so we cannot rule at the same time]."
3. A. ". . . to Esau his brother:"
   B. Even though he was Esau, he was still his brother.

LXXV:IX

1. A. Someone else commenced discourse by citing this verse: "Do not
      grant, O Lord, the desires of the wicked, do not advance his evil
      plan" (Ps. 140:9).
   B. "Lord of all ages, do not give to the wicked Esau what his heart has
      devised against Jacob."
   C. What is the meaning of, "Do not advance his evil plan"?
   D. He said before him, "Lord of the ages, Make a bit for the mouth of
      the wicked Esau, so that he will not get full pleasure [from anything
      he does]." [The word for "evil plan" and for "bit" use the same
      consonants.]
   E. What sort of bit did the Holy One, blessed be he, make for Esau?
   F. Said R. Hama bar Haninah, "These are the barbarian nations, the
      Germans whom the Edomites fear."

LXXXIII:I

1. A. "These are the kings who reigned in the land of Edom before any
      king reigned over the Israelites: Bela the son of Beor reigned in
      Edom, the name of his city being Dinhabah" (Gen. 36:31–32):
   B. R. Isaac commenced discourse by citing this verse: "Of the oaks of
      Bashan they have made your oars" (Ez. 27:6).
   C. Said R. Isaac, "The nations of the world are to be compared to a
      ship. Just as a ship has its mast made in one place and its anchor
      somewhere else, so their kings: 'Samlah of Masrekah' (Gen. 36:
      36), 'Shaul of Rehobot by the river' (Gen. 36:27), and: 'These are
      the kings who reigned in the land of Edom before any king reigned
      over the Israelites.'"
2. A. ["An estate may be gotten hastily at the beginning, but the end
      thereof shall not be blessed" (Prov. 20:21)]: "An estate may be got-
      ten hastily at the beginning:" "These are the kings who reigned in
      the land of Edom before any king reigned over the Israelites."
   B. ". . . but the end thereof shall not be blessed:" "And saviors shall
      come up on mount Zion to judge the mount of Esau" (Ob. 1:21).

LXXXIII:II

1. A. "These are the kings who reigned in the land of Edom before any
      king reigned over the Israelites: Bela the son of Beor reigned in
      Edom, the name of his city being Dinhabah" (Gen. 36:31–32):
   B. Said R. Aibu, "Before a king arose in Israel, kings existed in Edom:
      'These are the kings who reigned in the land of Edom before any
      king reigned over the Israelites.'" [Freedman, p. 766, n. 4: "1 Kgs.

22:48 states, 'There was no king in Edom, a deputy was king.' This refers to the reign of Jehoshaphat. Subsequently in Jehoram's reign, Edom revolted and 'made a king over themselves' (2 Kgs. 8:20). Thus from Saul to Jehoshaphat, in which Israel had eight kings, Edom had no king but was ruled by a governor of Judah. Aibu observes that this was to balance the present period, during which Edom had eight kings while Israel had none. For that reason, Aibu employs the word for deputy when he wishes to say 'existed' thus indicating a reference to the verse in the book of Kings quoted above."]

C. R. Yose bar Haninah said, "[Alluding to a mnemonic, with the first Hebrew letter for the word for kings, judges, chiefs, and princes:] When the one party [Edom] was ruled by kings, the other party [Israel] was ruled by judges, when one side was ruled by chiefs, the other side was ruled by princes."

D. Said R. Joshua b. Levi, "This one sets up eight kings and that one set up eight kings. This one set up Bela, Jobab, Husham, Samlah, Shaul, Hadad, Baalhanan, and Hadar. The other side set up Saul, Ishbosheth, David, Solomon, Rehoboam, Abijah, Asa, and Jehoshaphat.

E. "Then Nebuchadnezzar came and overturned both: 'That made the world as a wilderness and destroyed the cities thereof' (Is. 14:17).

F. "Evil-merodach came and exalted Jehoiakin, Ahasuerus came and exalted Haman."

LXXXIII:IV

3. A. "Magdiel and Iram: these are the chiefs of Edom, that is Esau, the father of Edom, according to their dwelling places in the land of their possession" (Gen. 36:42):

B. On the day on which Litrinus came to the throne, there appeared to R. Ammi in a dream this message: "Today Magdiel had come to the throne."

C. He said, "One more king is required for Edom [and then Israel's turn will come]."

4. A. Said R. Hanina of Sepphoris, "Why was he called Iram? For he is destined to amass [a word using the same letters] riches for the king-messiah."

B. Said R. Levi, "There was the case of a ruler in Rome who wasted the treasuries of his father. Elijah of blessed memory appeared to him in a dream. He said to him, 'Your fathers collected treasures and you waste them.'

C. "He did not budge until he filled the treasuries again."

Bibliography

Aland, Kurt. 1985. *A History of Christianity*. Vol. 1, *From the Beginnings to the Threshold of Reformation*. Translated by James L. Schaaf. Philadelphia: Fortress.

Avi-Yonah, Michael. 1976. *The Jews under Roman and Byzantine Rule*. New York: Schocken; Jerusalem: Magnes, on Julian, pp. 185–207.

Bainton, Roland. 1964. *The Penguin History of Christianity*. Vol. 1. Harmondsworth: Penguin Books.

Baron, Salo Wittmayer. 1952. *A Social and Religious History of the Jews*. 2d ed., rev. and enlarged. Vol. 2 of *Ancient Times*, part 2. Philadelphia: Jewish Publication Society of America.

Baynes, N. H. 1972. *Constantine the Great and the Christian Church*. 2d ed. Preface by Henry Chadwick. New York: Oxford University Press.

Berger, David. 1979. *The Jewish-Christian Debate in the High Middle Ages*. A Critical Edition of the *Nizzahon Vetus*. With an Introduction, Translation, and Commentary. Philadelphia: Jewish Publication Society of America.

Blumenkranz, B. 1963. *Les auteurs Chrétiens Latins du Moyen Age sur les Juifs et le Judaisme*. Paris: Le Haye.

Bowersock, G. W. 1978. *Julian the Apostate*. Cambridge: Harvard University Press.

Brown, Peter. 1981. *The Cult of the Saints: Its Rise and Function in Latin Christianity*. Chicago: University of Chicago Press.

———. 1972. *Religion and Society in the Age of Saint Augustine*. New York: Harper and Row.

———. 1971. *The World of Late Antiquity: A.D. 150–750*. New York: Harcourt Brace Jovanovich; on Julian, pp. 92–93.

Burckhardt, Jacob. 1958. *The Age of Constantine the Great*. Translated by Moses Hadas. New York: Doubleday Anchor Books.

Chesnut, Glenn F. 1977. *The First Christian Histories: Eusebius, Socrates, Sozomen, Theodoret, and Evagrius*. Paris: Editions Beauchesne.

Childs, Brevard S. 1985. *The New Testament as Canon: An Introduction.* Philadelphia: Fortress.

Cross, F. L. 1960. *The Early Christian Fathers.* London: Gerald Duckworth.

Duchesne, Louis. 1922. *Early History of the Christian Church. From Its Foundation to the End of the Fifth Century.* New York: Longmans Green. On Christianity in Palestine, pp. 486–91.

Duff, James. 1942. *The Letters of Saint Jerome: A Selection to Illustrate Roman Christian Life in the Fourth Century.* Dublin: Browne and Nolan.

Eusebius. 1961. *Church History,* trans. Arthur Cushman McGiffert. A Select Library of the Nicene and Post-Nicene Fathers of the Christian Church, ed. Philip Schaaf and Henry Wace. 2d ser. Repr., Grand Rapids: Eerdmans.

Filson, Floyd V. 1957. *Which Books Belong in the Bible? A Study of the Canon.* Philadelphia: Westminster Press.

Fremantle, W. H.; Lewis G.; Martley, W. G., translators. 1961. *The Principal Works of St. Jerome.* A Select Library of the Nicene and Post-Nicene Fathers of the Christian Church, ed. Philip Schaff and Henry Wace. 2d ser. Repr., Grand Rapids: Eerdmans.

Frend, W. H. C. 1984. *The Rise of Christianity.* Philadelphia: Fortress.

Gager, John G. 1983. *The Origins of Anti-Semitism: Attitudes toward Judaism in Pagan and Christian Antiquity.* New York: Oxford University Press.

Geffcken, Johannes. 1978. *The Last Days of Greco-Roman Paganism.* Translated by Sabine MacCormack. New York: Elsevier-North Holland Publishing Co. On Julian and paganism, pp. 136–59. I owe this reference to Robert Berchman.

Goodenough, Erwin R. 1970. *The Church in the Roman Empire.* New York: Henry Holt, 1931; repr., New York: Cooper Square Publishers.

Grant, Robert M. 1980. *Eusebius as Church Historian.* Oxford: Clarendon Press.

Grissom, Fred Allen. 1978. *Chrysostom and the Jews: Studies in Jewish-Christian Relations in Fourth-Century Antioch.* Ann Arbor: University Microfilms International.

Harnack, Adolf. 1972. *The Mission and Expansion of Christianity in the First Three Centuries.* Translated and edited by James Moffatt. London, 1908; repr., Gloucester: Peter Smith.

Hruby, Kurt. 1971. *Juden and Judentum bei den Kirchenvaetern.* Zurich: Theologischer Verlag.

Hussey, J. M. 1961. *The Byzantine World.* New York: Harper & Brothers.

Isaac of Troki. 1970. *Faith Strengthened.* Translated by Moses Mocatta. Introduction by Trude Weiss-Rosmarin. New York: Ktav Publishing House.

Jackson, Frederick John Foakes. 1933. *Eusebius Pamphili: Bishop of Caesarea in Palestine and First Christian Historian.* Cambridge: W. Heffer & Sons.

————. 1939. *A History of Church History: Studies of Some Historians of the Christian Church.* Cambridge: W. Heffer & Sons.

Jones, A. H. M. 1966. *The Decline of the Ancient World.* London: Longmans.

————. 1964. *The Later Roman Empire, 284–602: A Social, Economic, and Administrative Survey.* Oxford: Basil Blackwell.

Kasowki, Chaim Josua. 1956. *Thesaurus Mishnae.* Vols. 1, 2, 4. Jerusalem.

————. 1932–61. *Thesaurus Thosephthae.* Vols. 1, 3, 6. Jerusalem.

Kelly, J. N. D. 1975. *Jerome: His Life, Writings, and Controversies.* New York: Harper & Row.

Labriolle, Pierre de. 1953. "Christianity and Paganism in the Middle of the Fourth Century." In Palanque et al. (1953).

Laeuchli, Samuel. 1966. *The Serpent and the Dove. Five Essays on Early Christianity.* Nashville: Abingdon.

Lasker, Daniel J. 1977. *Jewish Philosophical Polemics against Christianity in the Middle Ages.* New York: Ktav Publishing House and Anti-Defamation League of B'nai B'rith.

Lawlor, H. J., and Oulton, J. E. L. 1954. *Eusebius: Bishop of Caesarea.* Vol. 1 of *The Ecclesiastical History and the Martyrs of Palestine.* London: SPCK.

Lietzmann, Hans. 1950. *From Constantine to Julian.* Vol. 3 of *A History of the Early Church.* Translated by Bertram Lee Woolf. New York: Charles Scribner's Sons.

Luibheid, Colm. 1966. *The Essential Eusebius.* New York: Mentor Omega.

Maccoby, Hyam. 1981. *Judaism on Trial: Jewish-Christian Disputations in the Middle Ages.* Rutherford, N. J.: Fairleigh Dickinson University Press.

MacMullen, Ramsay. 1984. *Christianizing the Roman Empire: A.D. 100–400.* New Haven: Yale University Press.

————. 1969. *Constantine.* New York: Dial.

Maxwell, C. Mervyn. 1966. *"Chrysostom's Homilies against the Jews.* An English Translation." Ph.D. diss., University of Chicago. I did not see this item, which is listed in Grissom.

Meeks, Wayne A., and Wilken, Robert L. 1978. *Jews and Christians in Antioch.* Society of Biblical Literature Sources for Biblical Study, vol. 13. Missoula: Scholars Press.

Momigliano, Arnaldo. 1963a. "Christianity and the Decline of the Roman Empire." In Arnaldo Momigliano, ed., *The Conflict between Paganism and Christianity in the Fourth Century.* Oxford: Clarendon Press.

————. 1963b. "Pagan and Christian Historiography in the Fourth Century A.D." In Momigliano, *The Conflict between Paganism and Christianity in the Fourth Century.*

Murray, Robert. 1975. *Symbols of Church and Kingdom: A Study in Early Syriac Tradition.* Cambridge: Cambridge University Press.

Neusner, Jacob. 1987a. *The Death and Birth of Judaism: The Impact of Christianity, Secularism, and the Holocaust on Jewish Faith.* New York: Basic Books.

————. 1987b. *Self-Fulfilling Prophecy: Exile and Return in the History of Judaism*. Boston: Beacon Press.

————. 1986a. *Judaism in the Matrix of Christianity*. Philadelphia: Fortress Press.

————. 1986b. *Sifré to Numbers*. An American Translation, vol. 1. Atlanta: Scholars Press.

————. 1985a. *Genesis Rabbah. The Judaic Commentary on the Book of Genesis*. A New American Translation. Vol. 1, *Parashiyyot One through Thirty-Three. Genesis 1–8:14.* Vol. 2, *Parashiyyot Thirty-Four through Sixty-Seven. Genesis 8:15–28:9.* Vol. 3, *Parashiyyot Sixty-Eight through One Hundred. Genesis 28:10–50:26.* Atlanta: Scholars Press, for Brown Judaic Studies.

————. 1985b. *Judaism and Scripture: The Evidence of Leviticus Rabbah*. Chicago: University of Chicago Press.

————. 1985c. *Genesis and Judaism: The Perspectives of Genesis Rabbah. An Analytical Anthology*. Atlanta: Scholars Press, for Brown Judaic Studies.

————. 1984a. *Messiah in Context: Israel's History and Destiny in Formative Judaism*. Vol. 1 of Foundations of Judaism. Philadelphia: Fortress Press.

————. 1984b. *Torah: From Scroll to Symbol in Formative Judaism*. Vol. 2 of Foundations of Judaism. Philadelphia: Fortress Press.

————. 1983a. *Midrash in Context: Exegesis in Formative Judaism*. Vol. 3 of Foundations of Judaism. Philadelphia: Fortress Press.

————. 1983b. *Judaism in Society: The Evidence of the Yerushalmi*. Chicago: University of Chicago Press. I have made use of materials from pp. 117–21, 196–97, 247–53.

————. 1982–. *The Talmud of the Land of Israel. A Preliminary Translation and Explanation*. Vols. 9–12, 14–15, 17–35. Chicago: University of Chicago Press.

————. 1976. *Negaim. Sifra*. Pt. 7, *History of the Mishnaic Law of Purities*. Leiden: E. J. Brill.

————. 1971. *Aphrahat and Judaism: The Christian-Jewish Argument in Fourth-Century Iran*. Leiden: E. J. Brill.

Palanque, J. R.; Bardy, G.; Labriolle, P. de; Plinval, G. de; Brehier, Louis. 1953. *The Church in The Christian Roman Empire*. Vol. 1, *The Church and the Arian Crisis*. New York: Macmillan.

Parkes, James. 1964. "Jews and Christians in the Constantinian Empire." In *Studies in Church History*. Oxford: Basil Blackwell and Mott. 1:69–79.

Payne, Robert. 1958. *The Holy Fire: The Story of the Fathers of the Eastern Church*. London: Skeffington.

Pelikan, Jaroslav. 1971. *The Emergence of the Catholic Tradition (100–600)*. Vol. 1 of *The Christian Tradition. A History of the Development of Doctrine*. Chicago: University of Chicago Press.

Ramsey, Boniface. 1985. *Beginning to Read the Church Fathers*. New York: Paulist.

Rankin, Oliver Shaw. 1956. *Jewish Religious Polemic of Early and Later Centuries*. Edinburgh: Edinburgh University Press.

Ruether, Rosemary Radford. 1979. *Faith and Fratricide: The Theological Roots of Anti-Semitism*. New York: Seabury Press.

————. 1972. "Judaism and Christianity: Two Fourth-Century Religions." *Sciences Religeuses/Studies in Religion* 2:1–10.

Simon, Marcel. 1964. *Verus Israel. Etude sur les relations entre chrétiens et juifs dans l'empire romain (135–425)*. Paris: Editions E. de Boccard, pp. 111–18, on the Mishnah as a second Torah; on Christians as a third type of people, pp. 135–39; on Julian, pp. 139–43; on the *Adversus Judaeos* literature in general, pp. 166–76; on anti-Jewish polemic in Christian biblical exegesis, pp. 177–88; pp. 239–276.

Steinmann, Jean. 1959. *Saint Jerome and His Times*. Translated by Ronald Matthews. Notre Dame: Fides.

Talmage, Frank Ephraim, ed. 1975. *Disputation and Dialogue: Readings in the Jewish-Christian Encounter*. New York: Ktav Publishing House and Anti-Defamation League of B'nai B'rith.

Von Campenhausen, Hans. 1972. *The Formation of the Christian Bible*. Translated by J. A. Baker. Philadelphia: Fortress.

————. 1959. *The Fathers of the Greek Church*. Translated by Stanley Goodman. New York: Pantheon.

Wallace-Hadrill, D. S. 1960. *Eusebius of Caesarea*. London: A. R. Mowbray.

Williams, A. L. 1935. *Adversus Judaeos*. Cambridge: Cambridge University Press.

Wilken, Robert L. 1984. *The Christians as the Romans Saw Them*. New Haven: Yale University Press.

————. 1983. *John Chrysostom and the Jews: Rhetoric and Reality in the Late Fourth Century*. The Transformation of the Classical Heritage, ed. Peter Brown, vol. 6. Berkeley: University of California Press, on Julian, pp. 138–48.

Index of Biblical and Talmudic References

General Index

Abba bar Kahana: history of Israel, 155; identification of Israel, 204–5
Abba bar R. Pappi, history of Israel, 50, 172
Abba bar Zabeda, identification of Israel, 214
Abbahu: identification of Israel, 92, 212, 226; messianic crisis and history of Israel, 79
Abin: history of Israel, 164, 186; identification of Israel, 89, 206
Aha: history of Israel, 157, 176, 180–81, 186; identification of Israel, 96, 210, 215; messianic crisis and history of Israel, 73
Aibu, history of Israel, 187
Aland, Kurt, 16–17
Ami, identification of Israel, 208
Ammi, genealogy of Israel, 111, 229
Aphrahat, 123, 151; Christianity and Roman Empire in the Age of Constantine, 13, 24; God and reconciliation with Israel, 198–99, and history of Israel, 34; identification of Israel, 85–103; Israel and the nations, 195–97; redemption of Israel, 197–98, 201–2; rejection of Israel, 192–95, 199–201; vocation of gentiles, 191–92
Aqiba: identification of Israel, 98–99, 222; messianic crisis and history of Israel, 69–70
Arcadius, 22
Arius (Arianism), 15–16
Augustine, 26
Avi-Yonah, Michael, 19–20, 22–23
Azariah, identification of Israel, 224

Ba, messianic crisis and history of Israel, 74
Baron, Salo Wittmayer, 20
Benaiah: history of Israel, 51, 173, 185; identification of Israel, 92, 212

Benjamin bar Levi, history of Israel, 183
Berekhiah: history of Israel, 157, 159, 169, 178, 180; identification of Israel, 95, 206, 208, 212–15, 217, 221, 224–25
Berger, David, 150
Bickerman, 17, 19
Bowersock, G. W., 21
Brown, Peter, 13
Bun, messianic crisis and history of Israel, 69
Burckhardt, Jacob, 16

Celsus, 7
Chesnut, Glenn F., 31, 35
Childs, Brevard S., 130–31
Christian historiography, Israel's history and meaning of, 29–58
Christianity: canonical character of, 118–19, 128–32; confrontation with Judaism, 1–6; control of institutions of state and government, 1–28; exegetical traditions, 118–23; messianic hope and Christian identity, 81–113
Chrysostom, John, 152; Christianity and Roman Empire in Age of Constantine, 13, 17, 22, 24–25; identification of Israel, 85; messianic crisis, 59–66, 76, 78–80
Constantine: in Christian historiography, 29–58; messianic crisis, 59; tolerance of Christianity, 1
Constantius, 146
Council of Nicaea, 15–16, 142–44
Cross, F. L., 131

Daniel, vision of, 98–99
Diocletian, 14–15, 17
Donatus, 15